Jews in Australian Society

Jews
in Australian Society

EDITED BY
Peter Y. Medding
Reader in Politics, Monash University

MACMILLAN
MONASH UNIVERSITY

This book was published
with financial aid from the
Memorial Foundation for Jewish Culture, New York

First published 1973 by
THE MACMILLAN COMPANY OF AUSTRALIA PTY LTD
107 Moray Street, South Melbourne 3205
12 Berry Street, North Sydney 2060 and
MONASH UNIVERSITY
Wellington Road, Clayton, Victoria 3168

Associated companies in
London and Basingstoke, England
New York Toronto Dublin
Johannesburg Madras

National Library of Australia card number and
ISBN 0 333 13903 8

Set in Monotype Times by
The Universities Press Pty Ltd, North Melbourne 3051
Printed in Hong Kong

Contents

v

Part 4

On Being Jewish in Australian Society

Appendices

Preface and Acknowledgments

This book is broadly divided into four parts. The first sets the stage for later analysis, dealing broadly and briefly with the history and life patterns of Jews in Australian society, particularly their demographic, socio-economic, occupational and educational aspects. Part two looks closely into the internal religious, national and cultural life of the Jewish community, but still within the context of the influences which the broader society has upon these internal Jewish concerns. Part three focuses outward again, dealing with the social acceptance and political integration of Jews in Australian society. Part four looks to the future by examining the question of perpetuating the Jewish heritage and tradition in Australia. It also moves out of the world of sociological research and analysis into the realm of the personal experiences and outlooks of a number of younger intellectuals.

The material in this book is drawn mainly from two sources – from the 1966/7 Jewish Community Survey (referred to as the 1967 Survey) sponsored by the Jewish Social Service Council of Victoria, and from the related findings of a number of individual researchers. Chapters 2, 4, 5, 8, 9 and 11, report directly upon the 1967 Survey findings, and chapters 7 and 13 are follow-up studies based upon samples selected from the 1967 Survey sample. Chapters 3, 6, 10 and 12 are mainly the result of the individual research of the writers; whilst the Introduction and Conclusion were specially written for this volume.

Chapter 14 which incorporates the views of younger intellectuals was commissioned for this book. The writers were chosen because it was believed that they had something of interest to contribute, and, in fact, collectively their views cover a wide spectrum. It was thought that their personal experiences, presented outside the structured context of an interview situation, would add depth and colour to many of the problems dealt with statistically in other chapters. While many young Jews in the community might agree with some or all of their views, they were not intended to be representative or characteristic of the majority opinions of young Jews, and there is no way of knowing to what extent they are such.

The 1967 Survey was conceived of, and instigated by Mr Walter Lippmann, as Chairman of the Jewish Social Service Council of Victoria. Without his initiative, sense of purpose, and organising abilities that Survey would not have taken place, and this book not been written. He obtained the funds for the Survey, and brought together a Steering Committee whose members were Mr Arnold Bloch, Professor Zelman Cowen, Professor Joseph Isaac, Mr Walter Lippmann (Chairman), Dr Leon Mann, Professor Max Marwick, Dr Peter Medding, Mr Lionel Sharpe, Professor Ronald Taft and Dr Colin Tatz. Mrs Geulah Solomon joined the Committee in 1969. Professors Cowen, Isaac and Marwick, and Dr Mann resigned at various times between the middle of 1966 and the end of 1968 due to other commitments.

The members of the Steering Committee were responsible for questionnaire design, sampling, selection and training of interviewers, conduct of the interviews, coding and data processing. Special tribute must be paid to Professor Taft, whose invaluable contribution to the professional and technical aspects of questionnaire design, sampling, interviewing, and index construction was instrumental in bringing the whole project to fruition. Interviewer training was conducted by Dr Mann. Technical direction of the project was undertaken first by Mrs Ruth Beebe and subsequently by Mrs Leah Mann. After the data had been coded and punched, complete sets of these computer cards were made available to members of the Committee for analysis and interpretation. They were also made available to Mrs Solomon who was asked to analyse the topic of Jewish education, and to Mr Michael Liffman who was requested to analyse data relating to discrimination. (Sampling procedures, the questionnaire, and the scoring of indices devised for analysing the data are reported in Appendices I–III.)

Some of the material in this volume was first presented publicly at a Conference on Sociological Studies of Jews in Australia, held at Monash University, Clayton, Victoria, on 24 and 25 August 1969, which was sponsored by the Jewish Social Service Council of Victoria, in conjunction with the Jewish Community Survey Steering Committee. About seventy scholars and Jewish communal leaders from all over Australia attended.

In March 1970 the Steering Committee requested the editor to produce a book based on the Survey and other Conference papers and the following volume is the result.

*

It is appropriate at this stage to record with thanks the financial support of the Memorial Foundation for Jewish Culture, the Australian Jewish Welfare Society, the Jewish Social Service Council of

Victoria, the State Zionist Council of Victoria, the United Jewish Education Board, Mt Scopus College and the District Grand Lodge of Bnai Brith whose contributions supported the conduct of the Survey.

The financial assistance of the Memorial Foundation for Jewish Culture and the Publications Committee of Monash University towards the publication of this book is noted with gratitude. I also wish to thank Mr Michael Liffman for his perceptive editorial assistance, Mrs Joy Smith who bore the burden of typing, Mrs Judy Irvine, who undertook most of the computation, data analysis, and proof-reading, Dr Tran Van Hoa for assistance with computer programming, and Mrs Jenny Sprague and Mrs Leah Andrew for helping to prepare the manuscript for publication. I have already noted the special contributions of Mr Lippmann to the Survey; let me record my personal gratitude for his assistance and wise counsel at all times during the preparation of this book.

*

'The Impact of the Middle East Crisis in June 1967 on Jews in Melbourne,' first appeared in *The Jewish Journal of Sociology*, Vol. 9, No. 2 (December 1967), pp. 243–62; 'Yiddish in Melbourne' first appeared in *ibid.*, Vol. 12, No. 1 (June 1970), pp. 59–76, and 'The Persistence of Ethnic Political Preferences: Factors Influencing the Voting Behaviour of Jews in Australia', Chapter 9, first appeared in *ibid.*, Vol. 13, No. 1 (June 1971). The permission of the editor of this journal to republish these articles is gratefully acknowledged.

P.Y.M.
Melbourne, March 1972

Notes on Contributors

DENNIS ALTMAN, graduated B.A.(Hons) from the University of Tasmania, and an M.A. from Cornell University, and is a Lecturer in Government at Sydney University. He is the author of *Homosexual: Oppression and Liberation* (N.Y., 1971, Sydney and London, 1972) and has contributed to H. Mayer (ed.), *Australian Politics* (1969 and 1973); R. Gordon (ed.), *The Australian New Left* (Melbourne, 1970) and published numerous articles in *Australian Outlook; Australian Quarterly; Politics; Dissent; Meanjin; Arena;* etc.

LEON GLEZER is a Lecturer in Politics at La Trobe University. He was co-editor of *Dissent* from 1962 to 1969.

JOHN GOLDLUST, graduated B.A.(Hons) in Psychology and M.A. in Political Science, both from the University of Melbourne. After occupying teaching and research positions at the University of Melbourne, Monash University, the Hebrew University, and York University, Ontario, he is currently a Ph.D. candidate in Sociology at York University, Ontario, Canada.

JACK GRINBERG is at present completing a combined Law/Arts (Hons) course at the University of Melbourne, majoring in English and Politics. He is active in political and literary circles both at the University and within the Melbourne Jewish community.

SUE HEARST graduated B.A.(Hons) in History and Politics from the University of Melbourne in 1968. She tutored in History at the University of Melbourne and at La Trobe University and commenced research for a Master's degree at the University of Melbourne. At present she is engaged in social work in England.

MANFRED KLARBERG, B.A.(Hons), M.A.C.E., is Director of Education, United Jewish Education Board, Melbourne. He is currently engaged in linguistic research on spoken Hebrew, and has published 'Yiddish in Melbourne', *Jewish Journal of Sociology*, London, June 1970; 'Stress Patterns in Modern Israeli Hebrew', *Abr Nahrain*, Melbourne, 1970.

MICHAEL LIFFMAN, graduated B.A.(Hons) in Political Science from the University of Melbourne in 1968, where he tutored in Politics from 1969 to 1970, and was editor of *Melbourne University Magazine*, 1969. He graduated M.Sc. in Social Policy and Social Administration at London School of Economics 1971, and has since been active in the field of community work in Britain.

WALTER M. LIPPMANN, actively involved in Jewish communal affairs since 1939, has been a member of the Commonwealth Immigration Advisory Council since 1967 and is Chairman of the Migrant Welfare Committee of the Australian Council of Social Service. He is the author of numerous articles on demographic and sociological aspects of Jewish life, and on welfare services in Australia.

PETER Y. MEDDING, Reader in Politics at Monash University, received his M.A. from the University of Melbourne and his Ph.D. from Harvard University. He is the author of *From Assimilation to Group Survival* (Melbourne, 1968), and *Mapai in Israel: Political Organisation and Government in a New Society* (Cambridge, 1972), and is currently engaged in research on social class and political attitudes in Australia, and on empirical democratic theory.

CHAIM MEHLMAN, received his B.A. from the University of Melbourne in 1971, having majored in English, and History and Philosophy of Science. He was a reporter for the *Australian Jewish News* from 1969 to 1971 and is currently teaching English at Frankston Technical College.

DAVID MITTELBERG, graduated in 1970, B.A.(Hons) in Sociology and Politics at Monash University. He was a Teaching Fellow in the Department of Politics at Monash in 1971, and a Tutor in Sociology at RMIT, 1970–71. A former Zionist Youth leader, he recently settled in Israel with his wife on Kibbutz Yizreel.

HENRY ROSENBLOOM, graduated B.A.(Hons) University of Melbourne, 1968. He was part editor of *Melbourne University Magazine* and *Farrago*, and is an undercover freelance journalist.

LIONEL SHARPE, B.A., Dip.Soc.Stud., M.A.Ps.S., is a social worker and psychologist who joined the Australian Jewish Welfare & Relief Society in Melbourne in 1963. He recently resigned from the society as Director of Social Work Services to take up an appointment at a private clinic for the treatment of alcoholics and drug addicts. He has carried out a number of research studies into the welfare needs of the Melbourne Jewish community and is at present Treasurer of the Federal Council of the Australian Association of Social Workers.

Mrs GEULAH SOLOMON, B.A.(Hons), B.Ed.(Hons), is Lecturer in Education at Monash University. She has contributed to a number of journals, and is currently completing her doctoral dissertation on a history of Jewish education in Australia.

RONALD TAFT is Professor of Social Psychology in the Faculty of Education at Monash University, a graduate of the University of Melbourne and holds an M.A. from Columbia University and a Ph.D. from the University of California, Berkeley. He has been conducting a programme of research into aspects of immigrant assimilation and ethnic identification in Australia for many years, and is the author of *From Stranger to Citizen* and numerous publications on the Australian way of life. He was the author, with T. R. Sarbin and D. E. Bailey, of *Clinical Inference and Cognitive Theory*.

1

Introduction: *Ethnic Minorities and Australian Society*

Peter Y. Medding

Studying a particular ethnic group – the Jews – in a society such as Australia can involve many different foci of interest. The range of enquiry remains vast even after the question is narrowed down to the effects that the society has upon the group's concerns, commitments, loyalties, values, goals, aspirations, and patterns of behaviour. In order to introduce some order into this potentially endless set of questions, we shall, in the main, be concerned with two basic problems: the nature of ethnic commitments and identity; and the consequences for these of their existence in the free society. We shall not be concerned at all with the other side of the coin, with the effects of the particular ethnic group upon the larger society. Not only is this beyond the scope of this book, but factually the Jews as a group have left only a minor and peripheral imprint, if any, upon Australian society. In this, the situation of Jewry in Australia, comprising some 70,000 persons, little more than half of 1 per cent of the total population, differs markedly from both Australian Catholics who comprise nearly 30 per cent of the population, and from the five million American Jews who, although less than 3 per cent of the population, possess political, religious, cultural and symbolic significance far greater than their numerical proportions would suggest.

By ethnic group we mean any group which is distinguished from others by characteristics of national origins, religion or race, or by a combination of them.[1] These characteristics create a feeling of belonging together and of unity, or what Kurt Lewin called 'a community of fate'. They may be, and often are, reinforced by history, culture, values, or by current and immediate political, economic or social situations, and may be perpetuated by group institutions specifically established for these purposes. Above all they express a belief in a common destiny of all members of the group as distinct from the destiny of other groups. For the individual there are also important socio-psychological concomitants and consequences of ethnic membership: ethnic membership constitutes part of the individual's sense of identity, part of his self-image, and engages an important

1

segment of his loyalties and commitments. This is not to argue that it is his sole or even his basic identity – modern man is blessed with many roles (and therefore loyalties and identities) – but it is one that lies close to the core of personality and self-image. Thus Jews, Catholics, Protestants, Italians, Chinese, Greeks, and Negroes are all ethnic groups.

What is important and relevant in a discussion of ethnic identity and commitment and the effects of a wider society upon them, always depends upon the circumstances. Thus for purposes of definition it is useful to exclude national origins as a factor of ethnicity in the actual country of national origin. In this respect, it is convenient to distinguish between national origins, as in the definition of ethnic group above, and nationality, in the sense of citizenship which is a legal concept and definition, although it is often closely tied to ethnicity. To make the point briefly, not all American citizens belong to the same ethnic group, despite the fact that they travel under the same passport. One can quite easily identify a few dozen different ethnic groups in America beginning with the (presumably) dominant WASPS, White Anglo-Saxon Protestants.

The notion of dominance raises the important question of relations between ethnic groups. The effects that a society has upon a particular ethnic group may, in fact, amount to the effects of a dominant (usually a majority) ethnic group, upon one or various ethnic minorities. (The case of South Africa is an example of a dominant group that is far from a majority.) Being a minority usually implies being in a subordinate position and subjected to various pressures from the majority, which affect all aspects of the minority ethnic group's existence. We shall examine these in greater detail below, but at this juncture it is sufficient to mention that these pressures may be cultural – to give up the group's norms and values and to replace them with those of the majority; psychological – prejudice, and the low esteem and prestige ranking, often culminating in occupational, residential, and recreational discrimination; and political – the use of political authority to ensure the majority's continued dominance and control of key resources. It is the combination of such pressures that comes to constitute and define the minority's subordinate position.

The pressures affecting ethnic minorities vary from society to society, and from epoch to epoch. But before proceeding further to analyse the effects that societies have upon ethnic groups, it is first necessary to examine some key aspects of ethnic commitments more closely.

We have referred above to one of these, that ethnic loyalty represents an important aspect of self-identity for many ethnic individuals, part of their self-image. It provides them with a sense of belonging in the wider world, and as such relates both to their own personal ancestry and to their group's history. Ethnic loyalty and pride lead to the transmission of ethnic identity and belonging to the next generation. This, of course, does not apply to individuals who reject or are unaware of their ethnic identity. The society, too, may react positively or negatively to the individual's choice. It may simply accept the individual's own choice and self-definition, and permit him either to further ethnic identity, or 'pass'. On the other hand, it may not permit the latter, and for various reasons pin an ethnic label upon him. In addition, other individuals may actively seek to engage his ethnic loyalty and to strengthen it.

The ethnic cultural value system constitutes the second key aspect of ethnic commitment. The range of values and areas of life that ethnicity affects varies with the different groups. Clearly, the values of religious groups have far-reaching effects upon major aspects of the behaviour of their adherents, whilst those of national groups are usually more limited in effect and scope. These cultural values gain continuity through being supported and promoted by individuals and institutions within the ethnic group which seek to transmit them to succeeding generations. This may occur for at least two main reasons: belief in the inner worth of the group and its values have something to contribute to the wider society.

The third key aspect is sociological. Ethnic groups consist of networks of primary and secondary group affiliations that provide important social support and reinforcement for their members. Family, peer groups, intimate friendship circles, together with a whole range of associational activities encircle ethnic individuals in the concerns and commitments of the ethnic group, and while fulfilling the general purposes of sociability simultaneously reinforce ethnic values and goals.

These three key aspects of ethnic group membership and commitment in free societies do not represent an exclusive list, but highlight only those that seem to be most significant for our present purposes. In other societies different variables, notably socio-economic class, may constitute a key element of the ethnic situation, and may become coupled with direct political action.

Ethnic groups in free societies, both recently arrived and long-established, must cope with the pressure of economic survival. Whilst true of all members of society, it affects minority ethnic groups and immigrant newcomers somewhat differently. For them it involves the process of economic integration, which can be broken down into at least two main aspects. There is firstly the extent to which they can adapt to the economic practices of the new society, gain needed skills and facilities, and adopt attitudes and outlooks that enable them to function successfully in the economic sphere.

This may not be an easy task. The changes needed to be made by the foreign peasant coming for the first time into an industrialised urban or metropolitan environment illustrate this point. Similarly for the Orthodox Jew, intrinsic religious values may be put under pressure; for example, the prohibition of work on the Sabbath and Festivals, and strict observance of the dietary laws. Second, even in a free society, economic values may be directly or indirectly allocated on the basis of ethnic membership. Occupational discrimination, policies of educational exclusion, and residential closure on ethnic grounds are all examples of direct economic pressure that prevent full economic integration. Non-admission to trade unions, and social and recreational clubs, which are regarded as informal entrance requirements for specific occupational opportunities, are indirect economic pressures with similar consequences. In such cases disadvantaged groups often call on the political, administrative and legal institutions of the society to remove the ethnic criteria of disqualification and exclusion, and to enforce equal opportunity for all.

Nationality, national identity and dominant cultural values also place considerable pressure upon the ethnic group. In all areas of social life, in primary groups and secondary associations, and in the educational system, the question will continually arise as to the relationships between the particular values of the ethnic group and those of the dominant group or groups in society. Are they in conflict? Are they mutually exclusive? Are they complementary? Can they be synthesised? Can they be maintained simultaneously and independently? are the kinds of questions that continually arise in this connection. Whatever the answers, the society places the ethnic groups under pressure to adapt. In response to these questions and pressures different answers to the same questions will be given, both within the ethnic groups, and within the society at large. Yet some common agreement on values must be achieved if the society is to continue to function peacefully.

The society further puts the ethnic group under pressure at the level of primary and secondary social relations. Classic manifestations are the generational conflict between uneducated immigrant parents and educated native-born children; marriage between members of the dominant groups and ethnic minorities; the establishment of intimate friendship circles across ethnic lines facilitated by common educational, occupational or recreational pursuits; and participation in the broad range of the society's instrumental associational activities. Various forms of pressure upon the ethnic group develop from these and other similar interactions. Ethnic values may appear to be in conflict with those of the wider society, or may seem to be less important or less satisfying than others; or to stand in the way of valued association with those outside the ethnic group. In all these instances ethnic values will tend to be ignored or rejected, and often replaced by those of the dominant groups in the society.

Finally the ethnic group is put under pressure by the attitude taken towards it by individuals, groups and institutions in the society. One of the themes running through the previous discussion is the importance to minority ethnic existence of prejudice and discrimination. The effects of such negative treatment vary: members of ethnic groups may seek to avoid prejudice and discrimination by attempting to separate themselves from the ethnic group. This will tend to weaken ethnic identification and participation, and erode the cohesion of the ethnic group. Alternatively, ethnic individuals subject to prejudice and discrimination may react by removing themselves from such tension-creating situations and gain security by remaining within, and strengthening the ethnic group. In this way prejudice and discrimination contribute to ethnic strength and continuity.

At the cultural level, too, societies develop attitudes and even ideologies specifying the expected or desired behaviour of ethnic and immigrant minorities. Broadly speaking there are three basic approaches. Firstly, conformity to a dominant culture and a set of values believed to be superior. This seeks displacement of the ethnic values and their replacement by the dominant ones. Second is the notion that all groups, values and cultures alike have something to offer so that a new synthesis will emerge embodying the best of each of its constituents. This results in the retention of some ethnic values, the redirection of others and the disappearance of yet others. The third possibility is recognition of, and support for, the plurality and diversity of values and cultures of different groups, accompanied by agreement upon other common national goals, values, and understandings, and accepted procedures for settling differences. Under these conditions ethnic groups are free to go their own way and to develop their own particular values, institutions and social networks, while at the same time identifying with, and participating in, the greater whole. This permits the maintenance of ethnic values, although it also presupposes the addition of new values to them, which can only occur in the absence of a direct conflict between the national goals and values and those of the particular ethnic group. It assumes also the value and richness of cultural diversity, as opposed to cultural uniformity and conformity.

The interaction of ethnic groups with society at large, or more narrowly put, with dominant groups and values, is, as we have seen, an extremely complex process. It differs from place to place, and from period to period, as attitudes change, and historical events cast new light on old verities and accepted goals. It may involve economic, educational, value; cultural, social, political and attitude conflicts of varying scope and intensity. Then again it may not, and these areas of interaction may be characterised more by the absence of conflict, or by the prevalence of amity, co-operation and consensus.

*

Prior to 1940, and particularly during the period between the wars, Australia was predominantly British in its outlook. Whilst this was most true of the patriotic outlook of the middle classes it influenced the radical working classes as well. The patriotic British outlook was manifested in many ways; in the educational system,[2] in constant public reference to the British way of life, or the Anglo-Saxon way of life as the standard to be observed, in the semi-colonial dependence in finance and external affairs, and in Australia's immediate rallying to Britain in World War I. At that point Australian nationalism became submerged in British imperial loyalty. Whilst the radical, egalitarian, democratic traditions of mateship continued, the patriotic, imperial sentiment gathered strength, and for the first time affected all classes in Australian society. They merged in the attitude to the outside world, especially to immigration and to migrants.[3]

There are at least two strands of thought entwined in egalitarianism, only one of which Australia inherited. The first strand is that of levelling, of uniformity and conformity, of cutting every one down to size, and the same size. As Hannah Arendt has put it: 'The more equal conditions are, the less explanation there is for the differences that actually exist between people; and thus all the more unequal do individuals and groups become'.[4] In short, equality of the levelling kind makes differences more conspicuous and less tolerable. The other strand of equality can be termed the equality of diversity: recognition of, and the search for, individual and group creativity and distinctiveness. This is the equality that gives rise to talent, intellect, creativity, in a word, to cultural brilliance. Needless to say, the first strand of equality, the levelling impulse of dull uniformity is the deadly enemy of individualistic and group creativity and diversity.

Australian egalitarianism, it appears, inherited much of the first strand and little of the second. Mateship, equality, a 'fair go', were predicated upon sameness and non-distinctiveness. In fact distinctiveness of class, of education, of accent, were often attributed to 'putting on airs' and subjected to marked antipathy. Moreover, it has been suggested that in the tradition of 'mateship' itself, supposedly the very core of Australian egalitarianism, there existed highly unequal impulses. Much of mateship was exclusive rather than inclusive, that is to say, based upon strong solidarity against outsiders, and antipathy and antagonism towards them.[5] In other words, not all were mates, and woe betide those who weren't. Similarly, Encel in a recent work[6] has suggested that the bureaucracy in Australia has become ascendant in the name of equality, but in point of fact has destroyed equality by its reliance upon bureaucratic authority, hidden from public scrutiny and above criticism.

These diverse strands in Australian values – nationalism, patriotism, egalitarianism of the levelling kind, and imperialism – were joined together before 1939 in attitudes to the immigration to Australia of non-British, including both Europeans and non-Europeans. Australia was conceived of by the patriotic and imperial-minded middle classes, and by the radical working classes alike, as an outpost of Anglo-Saxon society, civilisation and way of life. This was not only a white country, but a special brand of white country. Britain was thus regarded as the mother country, the centre and progenitor of the superior white Anglo-Saxon civilisation that was to be protected and emulated. Nevertheless, Australians were often ambivalent towards Britain on political grounds, particularly with regard to the fear that British action might one day lay Australia open to Asian invasion.

It was against this background that immigration policy operated until the end of World War II. British migration was sought and encouraged (except during the depression), some other northern European immigration was permitted, a trickle of southern European immigration was tolerated, and Asian migration banned in the name of White Australia. Thus before 1945 about 90 per cent of Australians were of British ethnic origin; the immigration figures between 1901–1921 maintained a rate of 89 per cent British migrants.[7] (This of course included Irish.) Not surprisingly, the few foreign-born were expected to conform to the dominant Anglo-Saxon way of life, culture, manners and mores, and subjected to considerable pressure to do so, and considerable prejudice if they did not (and even if they did). This immigration policy was justified in terms of the difficulties that southern and eastern Europeans, and Asians would have in adapting themselves to the British way of life.[8] It was therefore more convenient and better, simply to keep them out.

The position of Jews in Australian society between the wars was therefore not free of tension. They were the most visible non-British ethnic group, despite the protestations of their Australian-born and British-born members. This was so because in the two largest cities of Sydney and Melbourne in 1933 the 20,000 Jews were numerically the largest single non-British ethnic group (if we exclude Irish). They were also highly visible because like Jews elsewhere they were heavily concentrated in major metropolitan areas, and often in occupations which entailed large-scale public contact and awareness, and were often tension-creating as well, such as retail shopkeeping, or else in the legal and medical professions which also attracted public notice. Furthermore, a number of leading Jews with identifiable Jewish names (Benjamin, Solomon, Michaelis, Cohen etc.) were active in politics in a number of states, often to the extent of occupying ministerial positions, not to speak of nationally famous Jews such as Sir Isaac Isaacs and Sir John Monash. This combination of factors served to draw more attention to Jewry than mere numbers warranted.

Jews suffered from the Australian fear and rejection of foreigners at all levels. Sir Isaac Isaacs deeply felt what he regarded to be the anti-semitism of his legal colleagues and of politicians. More generally, elite and popular anti-semitism were quite common and open, without ever reaching serious proportions. Exclusive elite social, recreational and sporting clubs refused admittance to Jews including those who had achieved political, legal or economic eminence, and even to descendants of Jews who no longer regard themselves as Jewish. When Sir Isaac Isaacs was made Governor-General and automatically granted membership of the leading Melbourne Club, he refused the honour because of its anti-semitic exclusion policies.[9] Popular anti-semitism consisting mainly of verbal and written expressions of prejudice was quite common, especially around the time when Jewish refugees were first admitted in 1938. The racist, nationalist *Bulletin*, gave characteristically extreme expression to it, and it also appeared in more veiled form in sections of the Catholic press. Nor was the working class radical tradition in general free of anti-semitic prejudice either, as the poetry of Henry Lawson, the great exponent of mateship can attest to.[10] On the other hand, the leadership of the organised Trade Union movement in 1938 was genuinely well disposed to the Jewish refugees, though some individual unions expressed prejudice and practised discrimination in admission policies. The character of Jewry as foreign and non-British was further emphasised by the gradually divergent and conflicting roles of the British Government and the Jews in Palestine, which eventually reached the stage where Jews were regarded by many as the enemy of Britain. This certainly did not help Australian Jewry achieve greater and easier acceptance.

Events since 1945 have wrought changes in Australian society and cultural values. Since 1947 Australia has received some $2\frac{1}{2}$ million new settlers of whom 58 per cent were of non-British stock. With their children they represent about 20 per cent of the total population, and in the larger urban cities where they are concentrated, such as Melbourne, the figure is in the vicinity of 30 per cent. The official attitude to immigrants has changed (but to Asian immigrants only slightly, with small numbers in limited categories being granted permanent residence). Where previously only British immigrants were assisted now immigrant settlers are assiduously sought and assisted not only in Southern Europe but also in Mediterranean and Arab countries such as Turkey and Lebanon. The official ideology relating to immigrant groups is also slowly changing. Many manifestations of ethnic particularism and group life appear to be accepted by both the Immigration Department and the public, which now recognise that migrants need the social support of their ethnic community in the difficult task of integration, and that this promotes rather than hinders immigrant adaptation to Australian society. This seems to suggest the beginnings of an approach which is willing to live with cultural diversity and plural ethnic value systems and institutional networks.

The change in attitudes to immigration and immigrants has coincided with the loosening of ties with Britain. There is very little Empire sentiment left in Australia today, certainly none among the younger generations, and Australians are less stridently the defenders of white Anglo-Saxon civilisation and way of life. This is due to a combination of factors: the enormous influx of migrants from so many different countries; recognition that Britain cannot defend Australia; the recent defence and foreign policy reliance upon the United States and growing economic ties with it; and the natural consequence of independence. This has also had an important effect upon certain aspects of Australian national identity. It was argued above that Australian national identity prior to 1945 was intimately bound up with British and imperial sentiment. Having removed the latter, little of distinctively Australian content or substance seems to be left. Thus there are no clearly accepted specifically Australian cultural values to which the immigrant is expected to subscribe other than to be 'a good bloke', and give everybody 'a fair go'. What is more both native-born and immigrant are simultaneously heavily influenced by mass consumption of a mainly American brand of 'international' culture made possible by speedy international communication in many forms.

These changes have altered the position of all different, foreign immigrant and ethnic groups in Australian society. Jews, too, have benefited from them. Although they have increased in numbers, they have declined in public visibility, and are now only one of many ethnic and immigrant groups, and smaller in size than many others. Moreover, Jewish immigration has virtually ceased, with the result that as greater proportions of Jews become Australian-born, by way of contrast, more immigrants of other ethnic origins are arriving yearly to swell the ranks of the foreign-born. Whether anti-semitism has declined significantly is hard to estimate; it certainly still exists at the level of elite social club exclusion. On the other hand, generalised prejudice, especially among the better educated sections of the population (and Australians as a whole are becoming more educated) has clearly declined, probably as a result of recognition of the terrible effects of the racial anti-semitism of World War II. The press and media of communication are free of it, although mass attitudes are hard to gauge. If support for Israel is any indication then Gallup Poll findings in 1969 suggest that popular prejudice has become almost completely submerged.[11] Israel, in general, has had an important effect on both Jewish and non-Jewish attitudes. The then Prime Minister, Mr Gorton, often spoke of the need for Australia to develop 'an Israeli-type defence posture'. Similarly, he told a Jewish gathering when opening a Jewish day school in Melbourne in 1968 that

The school teaches what is in fact the great strength in Australia; whether one is of Scottish descent and the Presbyterian faith, or of Irish descent and the Catholic faith, or of English descent and a member of the Church of England, or of Jewish descent and the Jewish faith – we are members of the one community working for the same objective – that all may practise their faith without fear, that there is a place for the individual human spirit, and that the individual man is the cornerstone on which a nation can be built.

He then went on to speak in glowing terms of the historic attachment of Jews to their country, and assured the audience of his government's support for Israel. 'You have a country', he concluded, 'which you can look upon with pride and say that your traditions sprang from there.'[12] This was a far cry from the attitudes of the 1930s. Moreover, being bracketed with high-status Presbyterians and Anglicans must have indicated to many Jews that they 'had made it'.

The acceptance of cultural and religious differences suggests that in Australia today groups can behave as they are moved to by their own internal goals and aspirations. The tension between two forms of identity – Australian national identity and ethnic identity – while not completely removed has been reduced, and the pressures of the society upon different ethnic groups and cultures considerably minimised, as seen in the absence of value conflict between the dominant groups and ethnic minorities. It seems both possible and legitimate for ethnic minorities to wear both identities simultaneously and to share both commitments without any internal tension or conflict. The two mesh rather than seem mutually exclusive.

For Jews, then, the result of this is that they, too, can follow their own internal cultural, religious, institutional, and social goals, aspirations and drives, without feeling that they thereby detract from their contribution to the society at large or their participation in it. There is little direct and formal pressure from the wider society upon Jews to conform to a particular pattern of values and behaviour. There is however the considerable indirect and informal sociological pressure that, as was argued above, exists whenever there is inter-action between an ethnic minority and dominant groups in a larger society. Living in Australian society must leave its imprint upon the way in which Jews behave and think, and on what they believe. It cannot but affect the way in which they see themselves, particularly in the interaction between their internal cultural self-image and the one which society imposes upon them, or which they believe society imposes upon them. These may or may not be identical, but how they see themselves and how others see them, how they believe others see them, whether their own self-image comes to mirror the image which they believe others hold of them, how far their behaviour comes to conform to the external society's expectations of them, and how far it reflects their internal goals, norms, and traditions are what this book is about.

REFERENCES

1. On the definition of ethnicity see M. M. Gordon, *Assimilation in American Life: The Role of Race, Religion and National Origins* (New York, 1964), pp. 3–84.
2. See S. G. Firth, 'Social Values in the New South Wales Primary School 1880–1914: An Analysis of School Texts', in *Melbourne Studies in Education 1970* (Melbourne, 1970), pp. 123–59.
3. This whole section has been heavily influenced by the following: K. S. Inglis, 'The Anzac Tradition', *Meanjin Quarterly* 24 (March 1965), pp. 25–44; and 'Australia Day', *Historical Studies* 13 (April 1969), pp. 20–41; Geoffrey Serle, 'The Digger Tradition and Australian Nationalism', *Meanjin Quarterly*, 24 (June 1965), pp. 149–58, and 'Austerica Unlimited?', *Meanjin Quarterly*, 26 (September 1967), pp. 237–48; H. McQueen, *A New Britannia: An Argument Concerning the Social Origins of Australian Radicalism and Nationalism* (Melbourne, 1970).
4. H. Arendt, *The Origins of Totalitarianism* (New York, 1958), p. 54.
5. T. Inglis Moore, 'The Meanings of Mateship', *Meanjin Quarterly* 24 (March 1965), pp. 45–54.
6. S. Encel, *Equality and Authority: A Study of Class, Status and Power in Australia* (Melbourne, 1970).
7. See R. T. Appleyard, 'The Population', and Charles Price, 'Immigrants', in S. Encel and A. F. Davies (eds.), *Australian Society: A Sociological Introduction*, 2nd edition (Melbourne, 1970), pp. 3–15, and 180–99, respectively.
8. See the analysis of these attitudes and behaviour in Charles A. Price, *Southern Europeans in Australia* (Melbourne, 1963), pp. 200–22.
9. On club discrimination and the specific case of Sir Isaac Isaacs see Encel, *Equality and Authority*, pp. 131–3.
10. McQueen, pp. 107–8, 197.
11. Australian Public Opinion Polls – Gallup Poll 203, 18 April 1969, found that when asked 'On the fighting around Israel, are your sympathies with the Israelis or with the Arabs?' that 45·8 per cent of the respondents said Israelis, 3·2 per cent said Arabs, 5·4 per cent were sympathetic to both, 15·1 per cent were sympathetic to neither, and 30·4 per cent were undecided.
12. *Australian Jewish News*, 17 May 1968.

Part 1

The Jew in Australian Society: Economic Integration and Life Patterns

2

Melbourne Jewry: A Profile

Walter Lippmann*

The Melbourne Jewish Community: A Brief History

Melbourne Jewry first began as a miniscule community in the 1830s but grew rapidly after the Gold Rushes of the 1850s. By 1871 it numbered over 3,500, and 6,500 by 1891. After that its growth slowed, reaching 7,600 by 1921, and 9,500 by 1933. The Nazi persecutions caused it again to grow at a dramatic rate; by 1947 it had doubled to over 14,000, and by 1961 it had doubled again to approximately 30,000.

Demographically, there were three main sources of migration. The first major source were British Jews who made up about 90 per cent of the Jewish Community till 1851. By 1860 they constituted only half the population (having been joined by large numbers of European immigrants during the Gold Rushes) and by 1911 they constituted only 17 per cent of the community. The second major source were German Jews who made up 75 per cent of the non-British Jewish immigrants between 1830–80. As the immigration dried up around the turn of the century, these two sources gave way to their Australian-born offspring. In 1911, for example, over 63 per cent of the Jewish community was born in Australia and New Zealand, nearly 17 per cent in Britain, 10 per cent in Eastern Europe and only 4 per cent in Germany. (See Table 2.1.)

The third main source were Eastern European Jews who began to arrive in sizeable numbers about 1920. After 1945 they became both the largest source of immigrants, and the largest group in the Jewish community. (See Table 2.1.)

Jewish institutions were set up from the outset. In the nineteenth century these consisted mainly of synagogues and other religious facilities, welfare and philanthropic institutions, cemeteries and educational institutions (including a day school which lasted from 1859 till 1893). Leadership was at first in the hands of Anglo-Jews and there was considerable conflict between them and the newly arrived 'foreigners' from Germany. But by the early part of the

---

* I wish to thank Michael Liffman for his assistance in writing part of this chapter.

14

twentieth century these two groups had coalesced into a fairly cohesive and united leadership group, representing the numerically and culturally dominant Australian-born second generation.[1]

After World War I Melbourne Jewry began to diversify its institutional and organisational life in many different directions, by building upon and adding to the foundations which its leadership groups had provided. Many new foci of communal endeavour developed. Young people's organisations were set up to cater for social and sporting needs and to stem the tide of increasing intermarriage. Zionism, Jewish culture in general, and Yiddish culture, in particular, made their appearance. Synagogues multiplied, and a new religious movement, Liberal Judaism (Reform) was established. Jewish educational institutions began to spread, culminating in the growth of a day school movement after 1945. Welfare and philanthropic societies were expanded, and as time passed became increasingly professionalised. Of particular significance was the growth of what is today known as the Victorian Jewish Board of Deputies – the official roof body of the Jewish community, which co-ordinates its internal activities, and officially represents Jewry to the outside world, promoting and defending Jewish interests.

After the 1920s leadership passed out of, or to be more exact, was wrested out of the hands of the Anglo-Jewish elite by the new generation of East European immigrants and their second-generation offspring, who supported and led most of the new and diversified activities in the community (except for Liberal Judaism which was primarily founded by long-established Australian Jews and supported by the influx of German Jews after 1933).

In the 1930s and 1940s there was bitter conflict between these rival Australian-born and Eastern European leadership groups. In contrast the Jewish leadership group of the 1970s displays a greater sense of unity and common purpose. The impact of the Nazi holocaust, and of Israel have deprived many of the old differences of their meaning. In general national origins and cultural outlook have lessened considerably as sources of conflict, if not disappeared completely. This process has been further reinforced by the growth of an Australian-born and -educated second generation sharing common commitments to both Jewish and Australian values, irrespective of their parents' countries of origin. Thus today the communal leadership is not dominated by a single national group, but includes within its ranks Jews from every country of origin.

Melbourne Jewry is then a highly organised community with a network of institutions serving almost every conceivable communal need. At the same time it is demographically and culturally differentiated, incorporating within its boundaries many diverse groups, attitudes and patterns of behaviour.[2]

The Survey

In an attempt to study what united this Australian-Jewish community, and at the same time what differentiated its members from each other, and from their non-Jewish fellow-Australians, and also in order to analyse and assess the impact of some of the community's major institutions, a random sample survey of 504 Jewish families was conducted between November 1966 and May 1967. (How the sample was constructed and the questionnaire used can be found in the Appendix.) Information was also gathered about other members of the family of the respondent, which led to data about a total of 1625 members of these 504 households.

This chapter will provide a brief introductory overview of the structure of the Melbourne Jewish community. Much of the material contained here is further analysed in detail elsewhere in the book; the following is merely a brief description of its subject.

Household Structure

In 1966, the Jewish population of Victoria totalled just over 34,000, of whom less than 500 lived outside the metropolitan area of Melbourne. Our study sample (N = 504) embraced about 5 per cent of its approximately 11,000 households.[4] The sample households consisted of 49 per cent males and 51 per cent females which differs slightly from the 1966 Commonwealth Census which found 49·7 per cent Jewish males, and 50·3 per cent females.

In our sample households there were 913 children (average 1·81 per home) of whom 641 were still living at home whilst 272 or nearly 30 per cent of our householders' offspring lived apart from their parents. 85·7 per cent of the latter were married (28 of them, 11·5 per cent, to non-Jewish partners), 2·9 per cent were divorced, separated or widowed, and the remaining 11·4 per cent were still single. Of the children living away from their parents, 15·5 per cent lived overseas and another 7·0 per cent in another Australian city. If this trend is maintained it will have direct implications for the future size of the Melbourne Jewish community, given present low immigration figures.

National Origins and Age

Although it has always included within it a substantial proportion of Australian-born Jews, Melbourne's Jewish community, particularly since the beginning of the 1939 war, has in large part been an immigrant one as seen in Table 2.1. Thus even when all the Australian-born children of the adults are included fewer than half of Melbourne's Jews in 1966 were born in Australia. The bulk of our sample respondents (52 per cent) arrived in Australia between 1940 and 1959, 27 per cent of these before 1949. 17 per cent came to Australia between

Table 2.1   Birthplaces of Melbourne Jewry (in percentages)

	1967 Survey – Total living in households	1966 Census	1967 Survey – Adult Sample	1911 Census
Australasia	38·0	40·3	16·2	63·5
U.K.	5·6	6·9	6·9	16·7
Western & Central Europe	17·9	17·0	28·7	4·4
Eastern Europe	31·6	29·2	44·2	10·0
Israel	2·2	3·2	2·8	
Other	4·7	3·4	1·2	5·4
N	1,625	31,058	504	6,270

1930 and 1939, and a further 10 per cent arrived before that time. In the last decade, Jewish immigration to Australia has decreased dramatically, only 5 per cent of Melbourne's population having arrived between 1960 and 1966. A further significant aspect of the sample's immigrant status is that 15 per cent had been in a Nazi concentration camp, a further 25 per cent had been in Nazi-occupied Europe after 1940, and another 15 per cent had been in Nazi-occupied Europe prior to 1940.[5]

Examination of the age distribution of the sample confirms the disproportionately large number of older Jews, previously noted in other studies based upon Census figures.[6] 41·5 per cent of the persons living in our sample households were aged forty-five years and over, whilst only 29·6 per cent were under nineteen years of age. In the Australian population generally, the corresponding figures are 28·5 per cent and 38·5 per cent, respectively.

Looking at the combined effects of age and national origin, we find that among the adults surveyed, Eastern Europe was the predominant place of origin, whilst 85·6 per cent of those under nineteen were born in Australia. In the age group 19–34, Australia is the country of birth of the largest number with 42·9 per cent. In all age groups over thirty-five, Poland is the predominant country of birth, with Australia representing only 10 per cent of those in the largest age group (45–64). Clearly, without further immigration, Melbourne Jewry will change into a predominantly Australian-born community during the next generation.

Integration and Language Usage

Identification with Australia, nevertheless, appears to be strong. Only 3·3 per cent of the total sample were not naturalised. Identification with Australia, however, is not synonymous with speaking English. 43·4 per cent of the non-British born Jews in Melbourne (N = 389) spoke no English in their homes, made up of 21 per cent Yiddish, 6·7 per cent German, 1·2 per cent Hebrew and nearly 15 per cent other European languages such as Hungarian, Polish, French or Dutch. In only 40 per cent of these homes was English the sole language, and in the rest English was used in conjunction with other foreign languages. Nevertheless about two-thirds of the sample had 'strong' or 'very strong positive feelings about being Australian' which is indicative of a high degree of identification with Australia.

Socio-Economic, Educational and Occupational Structures

Examination of the educational background of Melbourne Jewry showed that of the adults surveyed, only one-quarter had received thirteen or more years of education. Among Jews in Melbourne, aged sixteen to twenty-five, by way of contrast, approx. 55 per cent were full-time students, and only 26·9 per cent were in the workforce. This is sharply differentiated from the general Australian figures of the 1966 Commonwealth Census, which showed only 25·7 per cent of those aged fifteen to twenty-four still studying, and 74·3 per cent in the workforce. The discrepancy is further amplified if one separates the sexes; according to the 1966 Census 59·1 per cent of Jewish males aged fifteen to twenty-four and 47·7 per cent of Jewish females of that age were still at school or studying, compared with 23·1 per cent for males and 28·2 per cent for females of the same age among the general population.

Areas of Residence

Table 2.2 shows the areas of residence of Melbourne Jewry in five different phases.

It reflects the continuous move of Melbourne Jewry from the suburbs of their first settlement in Melbourne, the industrial inner suburbs, to the middle and upper middle class suburbs in the south eastern and eastern parts of the city. This movement is underlined by the fact that 43 per cent of the sample had lived in their present homes for five years or less, and 30·8 per cent for less than ten years.

An examination of the socio-economic aspects of the life of Melbourne Jewry in Table 2.3 shows that 22 per cent of a sample of 200 males occupied high managerial and professional positions (and 41 per cent of a sub-sample of British-born males). A further 30 per cent belonged to lower managerial occupations, 24 per cent occupied skilled supervisory positions, and 12 per cent held positions described as 'skilled manual'. A subjective class identification resulted in 63·5 per cent identifying as middle class, another 7 per cent as lower middle class and 11 per cent as upper middle class. Only 10 per cent identified as working class, while at the other end of the scale a mere 1·6 per cent identified as upper class. These 1·6 per cent were all Australian-born Jews or Jews born in Russia or Palestine who have lived in Australia since early childhood. On the other hand, the 10 per cent working-class Jews represent 12 per cent of the immigrants and only 2 per cent of those Jews who have lived in Australia at least since the age of ten.

Table 2.2   Areas of Residence of Melbourne Jewry 1891–1967[7] (in percentages)

	1967 Study (N = 504)	Previous residence	1966 Census	1954 Census	1921 Census	1891 Census
Melbourne	1·6	11·1	3·0	11·2	28·2	61·9
Inner Eastern	0·8	2·0	0·5	2·4	12·5	19·9
Northern	1·8	6·3	4·4	11·0	7·3	0·5
Western	0·8	1·0	0·6	1·1	2·0	0·2
Southern	0·2	0·8	0·5	1·3	5·5	4·6
South Eastern	67·7	58·1	64·2	55·6	4·07	12·5
Outer South Eastern	8·5	4·8	9·4	5·9	0·6	0·1
Eastern	14·2	11·9	13·2	10·5	3·0	0·3
Outer Eastern	4·4	1·4	4·2	1·0	0·2	0·0
Not answered		2·6				
	100·0	100·0	100·0	100·0	100·0	100·0

The predominantly middle class character of Melbourne Jewry is confirmed by an examination of their occupational status. This shows 68·1 per cent as either employers or self-employed as compared to only 9·6 per cent of the Australian male population in these categories. This figure, however, represents the only major discrepancy between the results of our study and similar characteristics extracted from Government Census figures. The 1966 Census lists only 38·9 per cent of Jewish males as employers or self-employed. It should, however, be pointed out that many Jews conduct their businesses as limited proprietary companies, in which legally they are 'employed' as working directors. In the Census they presumably followed their correct legal identification as 'employees' of their own companies, whilst in the personal interview conducted during our survey they identified their 'de facto' status as 'employer'. Table 2.3 which records details of the occupations of Melbourne Jewish males, confirms this assumption.

Table 2.3 with its breakdown of occupations and industries, clearly presents the range of occupations followed by Jews. Their absence from banking and heavy industry is noteworthy, as is the fact that, although the clothing industry offers livelihood to 21 per cent of them, this is by no means as pronounced an area of employment for Jews as it was in the countries of their origin. It is also interesting to note that, whilst law and medicine provide professional employment for 0·5 per cent of the Australian workforce, they

Table 2.3 Occupations of Sample of 200 Jewish Males, 1967 (in percentages)

	British-born N = 54	Non-British-born N = 146	Total N = 200
1. *High Managerial & Professional*			
1. Medicine	11·10	1·38	4·00
2. Law	3·70	·69	1·50
3. Business (type unspec.)	14·80	5.52	8·0
4. Business (clothing)	3·7	2·76	3·0
5. Engineers	0·00	4·83	3·50
6. Building	0·00	0·69	0·50
7. Miscellaneous	7·4	0·00	2·0
Total	40·7	15·87	22·5
2. *Lower Managerial*			
8. Manufacturer (unspec. or not clothing)	5·52	8·28	7·5
9. Retailer (clothing)	7·4	4·83	5·5
10. Building	0·00	6·90	5·0
11. Clothing	3·7	4·83	4·5
12. Accountant	11·1	0·69	3·5
13. Pharmacist	5·52	0·00	1·5
14. Engineer	0·00	1·38	1·0
15. Miscellaneous	1·85	2·07	2·0
Total	35·09	28·98	30·5
3. *Skilled/Supervisory*			
16. Retailer (unspec. or not clothing)	3·7	6·21	5·5
17. Clothing	0·00	6·21	4·5
18. Milk bar/cafe	3·7	4·14	4·0
19. Estate Agent	1·85	3·45	3·0
20. Sales Representative	0·00	3·45	2·5
21. Office Clerk	0·00	2·76	2·0
22. Miscellaneous	0·00	2·76	3·0
Total	9·25	28·98	24·5
4. *Lower Non-Manual*			
23. Salesman	0·00	1·38	1·0
24. Market Stall	0·00	1·38	1·0
Total	0·00	2·76	2·0
5. *Skilled Manual*			
25. Tailor	0·00	4·83	3·5
26. Motor Mechanic	0·00	2·76	2·0
27. Hairdresser	0·00	1·38	1·0
28. Miscellaneous	7·4	5·52	6·0
Total	7·4	14·49	12·5
6. *Unskilled & Semi-skilled*			
29. Clothing	3·7	6·21	5·5
30. Storeman	3·7	0·00	1·0
31. Miscellaneous	0·00	2·07	1·5
Total	7·4	8·28	8·0
Grand Total	99·84	99·36	100·0

Table 2.3   (continued)

	British-born N = 54	Non-British-born N = 146	Total N = 200
GENERAL			
Clothing (4, 11, 17, 25, 29)	11·1	24·84	21·0
Manufacturer (not clothing or unspec.) (3, 8)	20·32	13·8	15·5
Retail storeowner (not clothing or unspec.) (9, 16, 18)	14·8	15·18	15·0
Other sales/retail (19, 20, 23, 24)	1·85	9·66	7·5
Medicine, Law (1, 2)	14·8	2·07	5·5
Building (professional) (6, 10)	0·00	7·59	5·5
Engineering (professional) (5, 14)	0·00	6·21	4·5
Total			74·5
Not included in above General Accountant, Pharmacist, Clerk, Motor Mechanic, Hairdresser, Storeman, Miscellaneous			25·5
			100·0

attract 14·8 per cent of the Australian- and/or British-born Jews. They provide, on the other hand, the source of livelihood for only 2·1 per cent of foreign-born Jews. This is understandable in terms of the educational background previously examined. It is also of significance as a pointer to the future when Australian-born Jews will constitute the major element in Australian Jewish life. Similar observations apply to other professional groups such as pharmacists, accountants and engineers.

Although many Jews are listed as employers, the size of their undertakings appears to be relatively small. The vast majority of Jewish employers employ less than ten people. Only 17 per cent employ more than twenty-five, and only 5 per cent employ one hundred or more people. At the other end of the economic ladder, 9 per cent of our sample drew pensions. This is dealt with in detail in the next chapter.

Marriage and Fertility Patterns

Trends in marriage patterns and fertility, which are a crucial aspect of the future profile of a community, have been examined in two other studies.[8] Marriages in 1968 in which both partners were Jewish were at the rate of 6·6 per thousand of Jewish population (general Victorian marriage rate 8·9) and in 1969 at 7·6 per thousand (general rate 9·1). At this stage, we are primarily concerned with the marriages celebrated within the Jewish community. Lippmann's study found that approximately 79 per cent of these marriages were celebrated at various Orthodox synagogues, 21 per cent at Liberal congregations. When second marriages are excluded from the figures, the share of marriages at Liberal Temples drops, as their more flexible interpretation of Jewish marriage and divorce laws attracts nearly 50 per cent of all Jewish marriages involving at least one partner contracting a second marriage.

When we turn, however, to an examination of the birthrate, we are immediately confronted with a startling situation. The 1966 Australian birthrate was 19·1 births per 1000 of population. The Jewish rate on the other hand showed only 10·7 per 1000. Transferring these figures into a table of fertility ratios reveals that the Jewish reproduction rate is considerably below that of the general community.

Table 2.4   Fertility ratios: Australian and Jewish Populations 1933–66

	1933	1947	1954	1961	1966
Victorian Jewish	25·8	35·0	41·8	36·3	28·4
General Australian	36·7	44·4	51·5	52·8	48·3

(Fertility ratios calculated as number of children aged 0–4 as a proportion of females aged 15–44.)

This factor is further underlined by an examination of the average issue of Jewish wives in Australia which is 1·76 (Jewish mothers 2·11), whilst the corresponding rates for all wives in Australia is 2·40 (mothers 2·83). Most Jewish marriages result in two children (39 per cent); another 22·5 per cent have one child; childless marriages and marriages resulting in three children, each accounting for a further 16 per cent of Jewish marriages; another 5 per cent have four children, and only 1·5 per cent of Jewish marriages have five or more children. One ray of hope for increased fecundity during the next decade arises from the fact that in the Jewish group of females aged fifteen to forty-four in 1966, the younger ones outnumbered those of the older age groups (1565 aged fifteen to nineteen, 914 aged twenty to twenty-four, 681 aged twenty-five to twenty-nine, 639 aged thirty to thirty-four, 1003 aged thirty-five to thirty-nine and 1436 aged forty to forty-four).

Any impact which this group of young women will make upon the Jewish fertility rate will, however, depend upon their choice of marriage partners. The extent to which young Jews seek these from outside the Jewish community therefore represents an important question for the future of Melbourne Jewry. Historically, Jewish communities have attached great importance to the preservation of their religious homogeneity, and have strenuously opposed marriage to non-Jews. This is dependent not only upon religious and cultural values and their degree of acceptance by both parents and children but also upon the availability of suitable marriage partners from within the Jewish community. Studies of Jewish out-marriage patterns show that out-marriages increase as the proportion of Jews in the population decreases. In Victoria in 1961, for instance, about

7·8 per cent of Jewish males and 3·6 per cent of Jewish females were married to non-Jews; yet the corresponding rates for Victorian country towns where few Jews live were 34·6 per cent and 23·4 per cent, respectively.

Coupled with this must be the recognition that out-marriage is a predictable by-product of the assimilatory process operating in an open society. In Australia, the environment has been conducive to out-marriages since the earliest days of Jewish settlement. Official statistics, however, are only available in more recent days. The 1921 Census, for instance, disclosed that 29 per cent of Jewish males and 16 per cent of Jewish females were married to non-Jewish partners. In the intervening years, the influx of large numbers of Jewish immigrants and the development of closer community ties among this new first generation of immigrants resulted in a significant drop in these rates. The 1966 Census for Victoria showed 91·9 per cent of Jewish males and 92·2 per cent of Jewish females married to Jewish spouses, 7·8 per cent of Jewish males and 3·8 per cent of Jewish females married to non-Jewish spouses, and 1·0 per cent of Jewish males and 4·0 per cent of Jewish females married to spouses classified as 'other' which included no reply, indefinite, spouse absent. (The disproportion of males to females in the 'other' category is almost entirely made up of the last category – husbands not home on Census night, either away on business or overseas.)

The 1967 Survey has now added more detailed data in respect of out-marriages. 19·7 per cent of the respondents had at least one relative who had married out. More significant even for the assessment of future trends is the fact that 11·5 per cent of Jewish parents have at least one child who has married out. In one-tenth of these cases, the non-Jewish partner had converted to Judaism. 65 per cent of those who had married out were British-born (Australia, New Zealand or U.K.) whilst 26 per cent were born in Central or Western Europe. 77 per cent of them had some tertiary education (35 per cent were doctors) and only 4 per cent had less than eleven years' education. In view of the current high rate of tertiary education the likelihood is for this trend to continue.

In so far as an analysis of the characteristics of parents can offer any guide as to the likely behaviour of their children in the choice of marriage partners, the study indicated that high Jewish identification either religiously or through Yiddish or Israel, provided some hedge against the likelihood of children marrying out. Overall, 41 per cent of our sample indicated complete opposition to out-marriages, another 39 per cent opposed it, but would accept conversion by the non-Jewish partner, whilst only 20 per cent indicated that they would not oppose out-marriages. Most of those opposing out-marriages do so for personal rather than religious reasons, such as anticipated unhappiness because of different backgrounds (61 per cent), the fear of problems for the children of such marriages (22 per cent), with another 10 per cent mentioning other personality-centred problems as reasons for opposition. Only 7 per cent opposed out-marriages because of the effects on Judaism. In these matters, no significant difference was disclosed between Australian-born and immigrant Jewish parents.

Important, however, as the attitude of parents may be towards these matters, ultimately it is the choice of the younger generation which will determine their choice of marriage partners. A number of studies have examined these,[9] and suggest that the rate of out-marriages is likely to increase, which will bring with it serious losses to the community. Mol, in a study of religion in Australia,[10] found that among Jewish fathers with non-Jewish wives, 27 per cent of the children followed the father's Jewish religion, and among Jewish mothers with non-Jewish husbands 36·4 per cent of the children would follow her religion.

While the prognosis for the continuation of Jewish life in Melbourne in numerical terms is somewhat discouraging, this may be partially counteracted by the strength of its institutional development.

Communal Involvements

The establishment of new synagogues, community centres, Jewish schools, coupled with the extension of communal welfare services, sports centres, youth groups and the very active social life and fund-raising programmes during the 1950s and 1960s are evidence of great vitality in Melbourne's Jewish community life.

The extent of the involvement of individual Jews in these organisations was one of the aspects probed by our study. 44 per cent of Melbourne's adult Jews are members of Orthodox congregations, 15 per cent belong to Liberal congregations, whilst 41 per cent belong to no congregation. Only 4 per cent of the sample rated themselves as very religious, 43 per cent were moderately religious, 30 per cent somewhat religious, 19 per cent declared themselves not religious at all, and 2·5 per cent were opposed to religion. Attendance at religious services is comparatively infrequent. 30 per cent attend at major festivals, and another 35 per cent attend only on High Holidays. More regular attendance accounts for another 15 per cent, as does total non-attendance, with occasional attendance comprising the rest.

70·2 per cent of the respondents belonged to at least one Jewish organisation. On the other hand, only 22·2 per cent were members of non-Jewish organisations. The immigrant characteristic of the present generation of Australian Jewish householders is reflected in this discrepancy. Of those born in Australia (including those migrating here under age ten), 35·4 per cent belonged to general community organisations, whilst of the immigrants, only 15·5 per cent did so. Unfortunately, the questionnaire did not draw a distinction between service clubs (Lions, Rotary, etc.), lodges, trade organisations, sporting clubs, political organisations, art societies, etc., which precludes further examination of these affiliations.

In respect of Jewish affiliations, however, a little more information was extracted. Of members of Jewish organisations, 43 per cent belonged to one organisation only; 26 per cent belonged to two, 22 per cent to three or four, whilst 9 per cent belonged to five or more. About 48 per cent described their participation in these organisations as 'active'. Over 90 per cent of the adult community read at least one Jewish newspaper, two-thirds of the readership being in English rather than Yiddish.

The respondents regarded the arrest of assimilation and the need for internal harmony as the most important problems confronting Melbourne Jewry. This, coupled with the next highest priorities, more Jewish education and youth work, indicates a clear desire among Melbourne Jews for the strengthening of Jewish group identification in the Australian environment. It is interesting to note that this conclusion coincides with the ranking of priorities of important problems by Australian- and English-born Jews. Amongst the immigrants, youth work and anti-semitism are more likely to be seen as major priorities.

In this light, lack of knowledge of the work of the Victorian Jewish Board of Deputies – the representative organ of Victorian Jewry – appears somewhat surprising. 30·4 per cent of the respondents had never heard of the Board, and 31·3 per cent had heard of it but knew little or nothing of its activities. 45·9 per cent of the men knew something of the work of the Board, compared with only 31·6 per cent of the women. There appears to be little difference between the respondents from different countries of origin although more of the Australian- and U.K.-born Jews had heard of it than European immigrants.

Of those who know about the work of the Board of Deputies, most (54·3 per cent) identified it with 'community co-ordination'. Only 4·7 per cent regarded its conduct of Mount Scopus College as its prime function, while the remaining 41 per cent listed 'external representation and fighting anti-semitism' as its main purpose. 88·3 per cent of those who claimed to know about the Board of Deputies thought that it was doing a good or very good job, whilst 11·7 per cent were critical.

The Survey also analysed our subjects' responses to their Jewishness. While 45 per cent of the sample claimed that being Jewish played a 'very important part in their life', and another 40 per cent described it as playing an 'important part', very few saw it in terms of religion. Thus answers to the question 'What does your being Jewish mean to you personally?' revealed an overwhelming 78 per cent being conscious of their Jewishness in ethnic terms as seen in the following categories:

'ancestry, born Jewish, upbringing, "cold fact" ' (27 per cent); 'share fate of Jews (belonging), pride' (25 per cent); 'way of life, culture, tradition; yiddish' (14 per cent); combination of above (12 per cent); 'nothing, never thought of it'; indifferent or unfavourable reply (8 per cent); religion (6 per cent); ethical behaviour (3 per cent); Jewish nation, Israel (2 per cent).

In response to another question, 41 per cent of the sample claimed 'a very strong positive feeling about being Jewish', and another 40 per cent had 'strong positive feelings'. About 5 per cent expressed indifference, and 2 per cent admitted to some negative feeling. This provides an interesting comparison with a similar question about 'being Australian'. Here 24 per cent expressed 'a very strong positive feeling' about being Australian, and another 39 per cent expressed 'strong positive feelings', while 'slightly positive feelings' were claimed by 23 per cent, and 11 per cent were indifferent. Only 0·39 per cent expressed slightly negative reactions; no one admitted any strong resentment. Appropriately then, 40 per cent felt 'completely satisfied with life in Australia', and another 25 per cent 'very satisfied'. A further 29 per cent were 'fairly satisfied', while 4 per cent were 'a little dissatisfied' and 1 per cent 'very dissatisfied'. Thus there was clear commitment to both aspects, the diffreence being a greater intensity of commitment to Jewish identity.

Charity

Fund-raising plays an important role in the life of the Melbourne Jewish community. 95·2 per cent of the respondents indicated that they supported Jewish appeals, whilst non-Jewish appeals attracted the support of 66 per cent. Among Jewish appeals, there was overwhelming support for Israel, as reflected in responses to the question to which only 5 per cent would contribute nothing at all. Overall, the respondents' distribution of a hypothetical $100 would result in $70 being given to Israel and $30 to local Jewish causes. In the distribution of support for non-Jewish appeals, hospitals and auxiliaries would benefit most, followed by charities for the disabled, and emergency and special appeals such as Cancer, Heart, Asthma. Red Cross and charitable fraternities such as Freemasons, Rotary, etc. were also mentioned as non-Jewish causes supported by Jewish donors.

When asked to make a hypothetical choice between either Jewish and/or non-Jewish charities, 79 per cent would give to Jewish causes,

19 per cent replied that it would depend on the particular cause and only 1 per cent indicated a clear preference for non-Jewish causes.

Israel

The attitude of Jews to the State of Israel is a subject of special interest. It was probed in our study by a number of questions such as 'What does the State of Israel mean to you personally?' Only 5·8 per cent replied 'Nothing' or gave a similar negative reply. 37·7 per cent saw Israel as the national home of Jews, 12·3 per cent described it as a 'place of refuge', whilst 24·8 per cent referred to Israel as normalising Jewish life, a source of pride, prestige, respect and as the focus for Jewish life. 2·4 per cent saw Israel as the representative of Jewry, whilst there were similar positive responses from another 16·4 per cent.

The extent of Melbourne Jewry's feeling for Israel was further probed by a question 'What personal obligations, if any, should Jews in Australia feel towards Israel?' Table 2.5 records the answers which indicate that the overwhelming majority (62·7 per cent) of the community saw their obligation in terms of financial support.

Table 2.5 Obligation to Israel (N = 504)   (in pecentages)

Response to question:	'What personal obligations, if any, should Jews in Australia feel towards Israel ?'
Financial	62·7
Immigration – self	1·3
Immigration – not self, but children	1·2
Work for Zionist causes	1·0
Support Israel in politics	0·4
Educational and cultural support	1·6
Several of the above	22·4
Other – not specified	3·6
No obligations at all	3·0
Don't know – not answered	2·8
	100·0

Nevertheless, personal identification with Israel must also be strong, for in reply to the question 'If you did not live in Australia, in which country would you most like to live?', 53 per cent chose Israel. Only 29 per cent indicated that they would not like to live in Israel, whilst the remainder had other first preferences (including 5·6 per cent their former country).

The extent of personal identification with Israel was further probed by the question 'Would you like your children to settle in Israel?' 22·8 per cent responded in the affirmative (25·6 per cent of the female respondents, 19·5 per cent of the male). 33·3 per cent replied firmly 'No' (37·2 per cent of the female respondents, 28·9 per cent of the male). 6·2 per cent had no children, but the remainder of our sample was evasive, or replied that the children must decide for themselves. Whilst on the previous questions relating to Israel, the response from Australian-born and/or educated and immigrant Jews did not vary greatly; the answer to this last question disclosed a strong difference. Only 6 per cent of the respondents living in Australia since the age of ten would like their children to settle in Israel, and 53 per cent would not like it. On the other hand, of the immigrant parents 27 per cent would like it and another 27 per cent would not.

Social Relations

These attitudes to the general community should be seen in the context of the extent of the direct contact between Jews and that community. 38 per cent of the total sample had no non-Jewish personal friends, 40 per cent had between 1–20 per cent, and 16 per cent had between 20–50 per cent non-Jewish personal friends.

Greater length of education and higher status occupations were strongly associated with more extensive social relations with non-Jews. Conversely, there was an inverse relationship between general commitment to Jewishness (as measured by 'Defence of Jewish Identity', 'Positive Identification with Judaism' and 'Religious Involvement and Observance' scales – see Appendix III) and social relations with non-Jews. Australian and British Jews had the most extensive social relations with non-Jews, followed by German/Austrian Jews, Hungarians and Czechs, and then Poles.

Conclusion

This chapter has examined characteristics of Melbourne Jewry, emphasising that we are dealing with a predominantly immigrant group, with a high degree of social and economic upward mobility. It has revealed the changing character of the community, with an emerging Australian-born generation of a high educational level, confronted with a diminution of its numbers through low birthrates and rising rates of out-marriages.

At the same time, however, we have also found that the community is still enjoying great vitality derived from a generation of immigrants highly motivated in terms of their own advancement, as well as of Jewish involvements. Yet demographic factors indicate that Australian Jewry may have passed the peak of its development.

In assessing its future, perhaps the most crucial factor will be the effects which the intensive Jewish activities of the past two decades will have upon the ultimate attitudes of the rising generation of Australian Jews in respect of their Jewish affiliations and involvements. The day school movement, in particular, as well as the activities of many of our youth groups would undoubtedly have a vital bearing upon the future of Australian Jewry. Only a study carried out when the present generation of young and adolescent Jews has grown to full adulthood and assumed their communal responsibilities can indicate whether the numerically diminishing numbers will be able to maintain the network of Jewish communal organisations and services which have been established with so much devotion and hope during the past two decades.

REFERENCES

1. On Jewish life in the nineteenth century see L. M. Goldman, *The History of the Jews in Victoria in the Nineteenth Century* (Melbourne, 1954); C. A. Price, *Jewish Settlers in Australia* (Canberra, 1964); and I. Getzler, *Neither Toleration nor Favour* (Melbourne, 1970).

2. On the history and development of the Melbourne Jewish Community since 1920 see P. Y. Medding, *From Assimilation to Group Survival: A Political and Sociological Study of an Australian Jewish Community* (Melbourne, 1968).

3. This number is comprised of 31,058 who replied Jewish on the Census, and an additional 10·3 per cent to cover those who did not reply to this Census question. Our 1967 Survey found that about 10 per cent of our respondents did not fill in the Census question.

4. See Appendix I for further details on the sample and the household structure.

5. A special study of these Jewish refugees and concentration camp survivors based on our sample has been reported elsewhere. See R. Taft and J. Goldlust, 'The Current Status of Former Jewish Refugees in Melbourne', *Australian and New Zealand Journal of Sociology*, 6 (1970), pp. 28–48.

6. W. M. Lippmann 'The Demography of Australian Jewry', *Jewish Journal of Sociology*, Vol. 8, No. 2 (December 1966).

7. The 1871 figures are from C. A. Price, *Jewish Settlers in Australia*. The municipalities or suburbs included in these general categories are: *Melbourne:* City of Melbourne, Carlton and East and North Melbourne; *Inner Eastern:* Richmond, Collingwood and Fitzroy; *Northern:* Northcote, Brunswick, Preston, Heidelberg, and Coburg; *Western:* Essendon, Footscray, Williamstown; *Southern:* Port Melbourne, South Melbourne; *South Eastern:* Prahran, St Kilda, Caulfield, Malvern, Brighton; *Outer South Eastern:* Sandringham, Mordialloc, Chelsea, Moorabbin, Oakleigh; *Eastern:* Kew, Hawthorn, Camberwell; *Outer Eastern:* Box Hill, Nunawading, Ringwood, Dandenong, Springvale, Waverley.

8. W. M. Lippmann 'Marriage Trends in the Melbourne Jewish Community', paper presented to 5th World Congress of Jewish Studies, Jerusalem 1969; and Rabbi John Levi 'Intermarriage in Melbourne', paper presented to Conference on Sociological Studies of Jews in Australia, Jewish Social Service Council of Victoria, 1969.

9. See Chapters 12 and 13 for an analysis of the responses to this question of those under twenty-five.

10. Hans Mol, Department of Demography, A.N.U., Canberra, personal communication 1968.

3

A Study of Poverty among Jews in Melbourne

Lionel S. Sharpe

Poverty is a relative concept. It refers to a state of being in need, the evaluation of which involves a subjective judgment on the part of the observer. What one might consider as poverty in Australia, might be regarded as affluence in many Asian countries. Nevertheless, by Australian standards, our identified poor are considered to be facing very real hardships in maintaining an adequate standard of living in relation to the rest of the population.

Any attempt to estimate the extent of poverty among Melbourne's 34,000 Jewish citizens is beset by the problem of determining a base below which a family or person might be considered to be living in poverty. As there is little class differentiation within the Jewish community it might be expected that the poor will have the same expectations for a comfortable standard of living as the majority of the Jewish group.

This chapter is based on the premise that any evaluation of poverty in such an ethnic enclave as the Jewish group must not only take into account economic yardsticks such as adequacy of housing, food, clothing, medical care, education and the means to obtain them, but also psycho-social and cultural dimensions arising from the socio-historical background of the Jewish population in Melbourne. In other words the criterion of poverty must include factors over and above the satisfaction of basic physical needs.

This is not to say that the social and psychological elements are not relevant when examining poverty among other sub-groups in society. These aspects have in fact been emphasised by Hayes[1] who points out that they are frequently neglected in studies of poverty. Their heightened importance in relation to the Jewish group results from the excellent resources available to help those in need, which make it unlikely that there are cases of poverty involving such extremes as malnutrition, bad housing and lack of educational opportunity. The poor in the Jewish community, therefore, is that group which is dependent on assistance from voluntary welfare services sponsored by the community itself.

In a survey of living conditions in Melbourne carried out by the Institute of Economic Research in 1966 it was found that about 7·5 per cent of Melbourne's population living in private dwellings had insufficient income to meet basic needs. In this study, the poverty line was judged to be the basic wage plus child endowment for a man, wife and two children.[2]

The 1967 Survey of 504 Jewish householders reported in this book made no deliberate attempt to assess or measure the standard of living prevailing in the Melbourne Jewish community. The data available however clearly places the Jewish population in what is commonly described as the middle-class sector of the general community. Data relating to areas of residence, home ownership, occupational status all lend evidence to this fact. 43 per cent of respondents claim to have their homes fully paid-off and 70 per cent of the 504 interviewees live in Prahran, St Kilda, Caulfield, Malvern and Brighton and significant numbers live in Kew and similar areas of middle-class residence. 68 per cent of males described themselves as self-employed or employers. Only 10 per cent of males held lower non-manual, unskilled or semi-skilled jobs and of these more than half were employed in the clothing industry.[3]

Furthermore, about 85 per cent of the population studied, rated themselves as middle class and upwards. It can be assumed that a Jewish person living and associating with other Jews in Melbourne will set his goals and expectation in relation to the prevailing middle-class norms – home ownership, self-employment, upward social mobility for himself and his children. The value placed on educational attainment is reflected in the fact that only 14 per cent of adolescents aged sixteen years to twenty years were in the workforce (N = 206). Even 50 per cent of males and females aged twenty-one years to twenty-five years were still full time students or trainees. This movement into professional and skilled occupations is indicative of the upward mobility of the Jewish community as a whole.[4]

If we accept a view of poverty as the discrepancy between recognised needs or desires and the opportunity for satisfying them,[5] then any discussion of poverty among Jews must take into account psychological factors bearing on those who are unable to attain the middle-class standards of living enjoyed by the majority of the community with whom they associate.

Taft and Goldlust in their study of Jewish refugees[6] estimate that of the 34,000 Jews living in Melbourne, 12,000 have been victims of Nazi persecution. Many arrived with little more than a suitcase of clothes, no knowledge of English and no relatives to welcome them. In more recent years many hundreds have arrived from Eastern Europe dispossessed of all assets and seeking a new start in life in Australia. The hardships faced by these refugees and their rapid integration into Australian society could be the subject of a separate study. Nevertheless, it should be noted here that three factors contributed to the economic success of the majority of Jewish migrants. These are:

1. Their resourcefulness, skill and motivation arising from historical factors which fitted them for business and the professions.[7]

2. Factors prevailing in Australia during the post-war reconstruction boom, coupled with large-scale immigration led to a demand for consumer goods, housing and public facilities. This gave an opportunity for Jewish settlers to rapidly integrate in the expanding sectors of the economic life of the country.

3. Collective self-help schemes provided by the Jewish community through the Australian Jewish Welfare & Relief Society (AJWRS) and *landsmanshaften* enabling newcomers to obtain loans and other assistance so that they may live in areas accessible to Jewish social and cultural facilities, to purchase tools of trade or raw materials, and to avoid large hire purchase commitments.[8]

Despite the economic success pattern of the majority of the Jewish community, one of the major tasks of the Australian Jewish Welfare & Relief Society is to deal with the existence of groups 'at risk' who face real economic hardship. To obtain a sample of families and persons living in poverty, it seemed most appropriate to undertake a study of the caseload of the agency, the only professionally staffed Jewish family casework agency in Melbourne.

The services of the AJWRS are well known throughout the Jewish community as a result of its activities in the field of migration: its administration of loans, cash relief and in more recent years its social casework services and projects for the aged and mentally ill.[9] The 1967 Community Survey revealed that 92 per cent of male respondents and 84 per cent of female respondents said that they knew something of the work of the Society. Its rapport with the community is indicated by the fact that of some 391 cases helped by the social workers between January and June 1969, 68 per cent were self-referred or referred by a relative, friend or a Jewish institution.

Every year the AJWRS serves over 1,000 cases in its various departments. All those requiring financial assistance or seeking help to resolve serious social or psychological problems are referred to one of the professionally trained social workers employed by the Society. The caseload of this section during the first six months of 1969 consisted of 391 families or individuals living alone. It is assumed that an analysis of this caseload together with an additional 21 cases receiving regular cash subsidy will identify the major groupings of people facing hardship in the Jewish community. Seven broad categories emerged:

1. The unemployable aged (males over sixty-five and females over sixty years) who are solely dependent on Commonwealth Government or other pensions and those receiving supplementary help from relatives, the AJWRS, sheltered workshop earnings, etc.

2. The unemployable incapacitated whose condition is the result of chronic illness, either physical and mental or both.

3. The chronically dependent multi-problem family whose problems range from excessive hire purchase debts and frequent illness to disturbed parent—child relationships and marital problems.

4. The lone male with no family who is unable to cope without supportive casework.

5. Those who apply for assistance because of some situational crises such as mental or physical illness of a breadwinner, temporary unemployment, business failure or death or desertion of a spouse.

6. The recent migrant whose economic circumstances are largely attributable to migration and who may also have problems similar to the above groups.

7. The marginally poor, who, although appearing to be coping well at a superficial level, feel excluded from the collective social life of the community as a result of their economic circumstances.

The breakdown of 300 cases classified as poor or marginally poor, assisted during six months ending 30 June 1969, was as follows:

Unemployable aged	49
Unemployable incapacitated	50
Multi-problem families	23
Lone persons without families	9
Situational crises	47
Newly arrived migrants	38
Marginally poor	84
	300

These figures reveal that those seeking help were for the most part in those categories usually referred to as 'primary poverty'. These persons are dependent on inadequate pensions and cannot meet the basic needs of clothing, food and shelter without help. Thus the aged, the incapacitated, the unemployed, the sick, and the migrant with no resources to fall back on, are very vulnerable. The loss of a breadwinner through death or marriage breakdown is a frequent cause of sudden reduced circumstances.

What is notably absent is the presence of what has been called inherited poverty, i.e. that people born into poverty hand it on to the next generation.[10] The few multi-problem families (N = 23), and these probably comprise the total extent of such families in the community, may produce some carryover in the next generation. Resources available to help them may ameliorate their condition especially if motivation for upward mobility is present.

Small family size (1·81 children per home in the 1967 Community Survey) is a factor minimising the extent of hardship. Only four families in the poverty sample had in excess of four dependent children. Desertion of a male breadwinner was practically non-existent, only two cases were known where alcoholism led to family breakdown and in only one of these was the standard of living of the spouse and children seriously affected.

Much .has been written about cohesiveness and child—parent relationships in the Jewish family. In brief, small family size is probably related to maximising the family's economic resources to ensure that the children have opportunity to finish their schooling and continue to higher education, to acquire a home and pay it off, and, to save for unforeseen contingencies. Large family size would obviously be seen to hinder socio-economic mobility.

Sobriety among Jews has been a subject of careful study by C. R. Snyder[11] of American Jewish drinking patterns. He analyses both cultural factors originating from religious rituals and factors deriving from the minority status of the Jewish group to explain why the rates of alcoholism and other drinking pathologies for Jews are very low. Findings in this poverty study concur with Snyder's observations in the American Jewish group.

Mental illness was found to be a major factor contributing to unemployment and financial hardship. 40 per cent of the caseload had current or recent contact with a psychiatric clinic or private psychiatrist. Many of these, especially post-war arrivals from Eastern Europe, had suffered in Nazi concentration camps and many had moved from one country to another before settling in Australia. High motivation to achieve rapid economic success, trauma resulting from their war-time experiences and loss of family members in Nazi Europe may have contributed to their mental ill-health. 56 per cent of all immigrants in the caseload analysis had suffered for a period of time in a concentration camp. 40 per cent had no surviving relatives living in Melbourne.

Although only 38 migrant families or single migrants were identified in the sample studied, 88 per cent of the 300 cases were born outside Australia and the majority of these had migrated here since 1950. If these follow the success pattern of many of the earlier migrants, it is unlikely that their children will grow up in deprived circumstances. Special loan schemes for students and community administered scholarship schemes give an opportunity for most migrant children to attend tertiary educational institutions even at the point of arrival in the country.

The unemployable aged consist largely of migrants coming to Australia since 1947 (74 per cent in this category were post-war migrants). An analysis of the demographic distribution of the Jewish community indicates that this vulnerable group is increasing as a result of the immigration of large numbers of middle-aged persons two decades ago. In fact, the Jewish community has a disproportionately higher number in this group than in the community at large.[12]

The caseload in the old age group is largely diminished by the fact that the community provides adequate resources to care for its elderly. Two old age homes provide accommodation for 260 persons,[13] flats for the aged built with assistance through the Commonwealth Government Aged Persons' Homes Act now provide flats for independent living to one hundred persons (males over sixty-five years, females over sixty years).[14] A sheltered workshop conducted by the AJWRS provides part-time occupational activity for eighty elderly and handicapped persons enabling them to earn a small amount to supplement their government pensions.

In a number of cases rent is subsidised where the pension is inadequate to meet the high rentals in inner urban areas where synagogues and Jewish cultural facilities are located.

A related group, the unemployable incapacitated, face greater psychological stress as a result of lower age and the lack of sheltered employment opportunities. 44 per cent of this group (N = 50) are under fifty years of age and nearly 50 per cent are suffering from mental illness. Only 12 per cent are living with a marital partner and half are living alone in rooms or in low rental flats. The sex ratio is 50 per cent male and female and 69 per cent are post-war migrants. This group requires fairly intensive casework because of low self-esteem and feelings of hopelessness.

Those facing situational crises (N = 47) comprise 16 per cent of the poverty sample. Of these 21 per cent had lost a spouse, 32 per cent suffered mental or physical illness in the family, while in 16 per cent of the cases, separation or desertion following marital conflict was the precipitating factor causing financial hardship.

The marginally poor (N = 84) are made up of a wide range of families, widows with children and lone persons. Their economic situation tends to exclude them from full participation in the religious and cultural life of the community. Many cannot afford synagogue membership dues and feel inhibited to participate in fund-raising activities for Israel and local projects. Heavy financial commitments in paying off a house and other debts generally place a strain which results in a breakdown of family cohesiveness and stability. Living in a milieu of a predominantly middle-class Jewish community gives rise to additional problems such as feelings of inadequacy and resentment about their situation. Wives frequently harass their husbands for not being able to improve their lot.

Only one-third of heads of households in this group are unskilled or semi-skilled workers while nearly one-third are self-employed in small manufacturing or in shopkeeping. The latter tend to lack both personal and financial resources to make a success of their enterprise.

Assistance in some cases from Restitution Pensions from Germany and help from AJWRS and other organisations[15] protect families from the harsh consequences of poverty.

Jewish day schools frequently permit children in this group to attend without fees. Nevertheless strain is often placed on family resources by the need to purchase uniforms, books and other educational requisites. Moreover, families often mask their poverty in order to integrate into the group life of the Jewish community and maintain their self-esteem.

This particularly relates to families living in areas where there is a concentration of Jewish population and in cases where children attend Jewish day schools. Demands from school parent associations, parents' groups assisting Jewish youth movements and other fund-raising groups obligate families to participate in the communal life around them. Failure to do so is interpreted as a disinterest in the welfare of one's children and a withdrawal of responsibility toward strengthening Jewish communal life. Families on low incomes frequently re-order their priorities in spending to protect themselves from loss of pride and self-esteem. Thus value is placed on suitable attire and other outward symbols which might prevent the observer from being aware of the family's real financial situation.

The social pressures to participate in some aspect of organised communal life which is largely supported by the more affluent members of the community, places considerable psychological stress on those who are excluded as a result of their inadequate income. Some migrants have remarked how, in their less affluent situations back in their country of origin, poverty was no barrier to active participation in the religious and broader social life of their Jewish community.

It seems evident that the maintenance of well-organised resources to help those in need will continue to alleviate the economic condition of the groups 'at risk' in the Jewish community of Melbourne. Collective responsibility to provide services has its origin in Biblical precepts and much of the organised social life in the community revolves around fund-raising activity for local and overseas causes (notably Israel).

The roots of the Jewish philosophy of social welfare are found in the basic tenets of the concepts of *Tzedekah* and of *Chesed*. The former relates to Social Justice while the latter represents 'acts of human kindness' – the true love and concern for one's fellow man. Chetkow[16] has adequately summarised the heritage as follows: 'The Jewish welfare traditions, in rigid summary, derive from G-d's commandments and from man's love of his deity. It then takes the form of a love of one's fellow being, feeling "charitably" towards others and judging their needs with leniency. It obligates the Jew to contributions of both money and personal effort. The tradition insists that assistance be given when it is needed, to the extent that help is needed, and in the manner which does not lessen the personal dignity of the recipient. It places the highest premium on prevention. The needy person has a G-d-given right to expect assistance, and it is the community's obligation to take care of such needs. Misfortune is ascribed to conditions over which the individual sufferer often has little personal control. The practice of charity is more important than prayers, but philanthropic activities should be undertaken with correct motives.'

This ancient tradition permeated the ghetto and *shtetl* life in Eastern Europe where Jewish communal organisation incorporated many of the rudiments of self-government. The provision of welfare services was an essential task in such communities and with the arrival of Jewish migrants in Australia analogous welfare structures and institutions developed to serve the needs of the community. One of these needs was the observance of Jewish dietary laws and other religious requirements. Thus the establishment of Jewish old age homes, Jewish children's homes and the like were considered priority projects when creating welfare services. Loan funds have also been an essential aspect of helping those in need.

Although the stresses of old age, death of the breadwinner, and sickness will continue to tax Jewish communal resources, unless more adequate steps are taken at governmental level to provide for these conditions, new developments will continue to take place in the orientation of Jewish welfare services. Already the AJWRS has entered the field of rehabilitation of the mentally ill and the Montefiore Homes for the Aged has developed a rehabilitation unit for the elderly sick. Other preventive services are envisaged such as marriage guidance, day care for the elderly, and services for the problem adolescent. Some decades will have to pass however before this predominantly migrant community is relieved of the task of supporting those who cannot provide for themselves the basic necessities under existing government welfare provisions.

REFERENCES

1. L. F. Hayes, 'Non-Economic Aspects of Poverty', *The Australian Journal of Social Issues*, Vol. 5, No. 1 (1970).
2. R. J. A. Harper, 'Survey of Living Conditions in Melbourne – 1966', *The Economic Record*, Vol. 43, No. 102 (June 1967).
3. The writer has observed that many employees in the clothing industry are in fact working for relatives or Jewish employers.
4. See Chapter 2 of this volume for further analysis of these factors.
5. F. L. Feldman, *The Family in the Money World*, Family Services Association of America (1957), p. 109.
6. R. Taft and J. Goldlust, 'The Current Status of Former Jewish Refugees in Melbourne', *Australian and New Zealand Journal of Sociology*, 6 (1970), pp. 28–48.

7. N. Glazer, 'The American Jew and the Attainment of Middle Class Rank', in M. Sklare (ed.), *The Jews: Social Patterns of an American Group* (Glencoe, 1958).

8. The Australian Jewish Welfare Society in Melbourne was formed following the amalgamation of the German Jewish Relief Committee and the Polish Jewish Relief Fund in 1937. In 1948 this Society merged with the United Jewish Overseas Relief Fund of Victoria to form the Australian Jewish Welfare & Relief Society.

A number of *landsmanshaften* (an association of Jews originating from one area or city in Europe) gave financial assistance, loans, and the larger ones actually established their own hostels to accommodate new immigrants. There are something over twenty such *landsmanshaften* in Melbourne.

9. During 1968, 1,116 unduplicated cases involving 2,218 individuals required services provided by the Society (1968 Annual Report). It also administers such loan funds as the Melbourne Jewish Aid Society's interest free loans (founded 1888) and bank interest loans provided by the Jewish Mutual Loan Co Pty Ltd, (registered 1955). Between 1947 and 1969, 5,804 families received such loans.

10. J. Paterson, 'The Causes and Relief of Poverty', in *Poverty in Australia*, Australian Institute of Political Science (Proceedings of the 35th Summer School), (Sydney, 1969).

11. C. R. Snyder, 'Culture and Jewish Sobriety: The Ingroup–Outgroup Factor', in M. Sklare (ed.), *op. cit.*

12. E. Martin and L. S. Sharpe, *Report on a Study of the Needs of the Jewish Aged in Melbourne* (Jewish Social Service Council of Victoria, 1965).

13. Montefiore Homes for the Aged and the Emmy Monash Home (Mutual Help Ltd).

14. AJWRS accommodates eighty elderly people in sixty-eight self-contained flats. The Bnai Brith Lodges have a similar project accommodating twenty.

15. In addition to the AJWRS, a number of other organisations provide direct financial and material assistance to those in need. The Melbourne Jewish Philanthropic Society (founded 1848) conducting the Montefiore Homes for the Aged, The Melbourne Hebrew Ladies' Benevolent Society (founded 1857), the Melbourne Jewish Women's Guild (founded 1896), The Jewish Orphan and Neglected Children's Society (founded 1882) and the Bnai Brith Lodges all play a role in this area.

The United Restitution Organisation was instrumental in obtaining compensation for large numbers of victims of Nazi persecution. The Melbourne office has processed 3000 applications since it opened in 1954.

16. B. H. Chetkow, 'Sectarian Social Work and the Changing Functions of Formal Religion', *Journal of Jewish Communal Service*, Vol. 39, No. 4 (Summer 1963), p. 362.

PART 2

*On Being Jewish: Religious, National
and Cultural Identification*

4

Orthodoxy, Liberalism and Secularism in Melbourne Jewry

Peter Y. Medding

Religious affiliation and practice remain a basic dimension of contemporary Jewish life. Despite increasing secularisation since the beginning of the nineteenth century and despite a decline in the intensity and hold of religious practice, most Jews in Western countries still retain some connection with their religious traditions and observances. Moreover, most Jews and non-Jews alike continue to regard religion as central to any definition of Jews or Jewishness.

The purpose of this article is to explore one of the major manifestations of Jewish religious life: the type of synagogue preference. Jews in Melbourne are divided into two main religious institutional networks: one Orthodox and one Liberal, to which they adhere in various degrees of strength. In addition, there is another group that has little connection at all with synagogues or religious practice, who might well be called Seculars. Our intention here is to examine the similarities and differences between these groups, to analyse their membership, and the consequences of the differing kinds and degrees of institutional loyalty. It will be argued that major differences in attitude exist between Orthodox and Liberal followers related to divergent approaches to the question of Jewish continuity and group distinctiveness in a pluralistic non-Jewish environment. First, we shall examine some of the basic sociological correlates of synagogue preference – who belongs to each of these groups; and then we shall consider the effects of these preferences upon the members.

I

In the 1967 Survey it was found that 62 per cent attended services at Orthodox synagogues, 18 per cent at Liberal (Reform) Temples, 16 per cent never attended, 3 per cent had no regular preference and 1 per cent gave no reply. (N = 504). The first three form our basic groups for investigation – and henceforth will be called Orthodox, Liberal and Secular.

There are some fundamental differences in the composition of these groups in terms of national origins and educational achievement, as will be seen below. On the other hand, their sex, age, and occupational distributions were similar.

Table 4.1 Country of Birth by Religious Preference

Country of Birth	Religious Preference (in percentages)			
	Orthodox	Liberal	Secular	Other
Australia/N.Z. (N = 81)	58	30	6	4
Poland (N = 199)	73	5	18	3
Germany/Austria (N = 75)	33	37	22	6
Hungary/Czechoslovakia (N = 52)	55	17	23	2

Significant at ·001 level using chi-square test.
Totals in this and subsequent tables may not add up to 100 per cent owing to the computer cutting off the decimal point.

Table 4.1 demonstrates the differing patterns of religious preference of each of these national groups. Jews from Poland carry on the religious tradition of Orthodox preference – Liberalism was unknown there – or else are Secular; thus nearly three-quarters attend Orthodox services, and about one-fifth never attend, whilst only one in twenty attend Liberal services. At the other extreme, those from Germany and Austria are clearly the least Orthodox – with only one-third attending Orthodox services, and are the most likely to be Liberal or Secular, with nearly four in ten in the first category and one in four in the second. This, too, follows the pattern established in their countries of origin, where the Liberal (Reform) movement began and flourished and where secularism, too, was strong. Jews from Hungary and Czechoslovakia present a somewhat different pattern based upon their particular historical antecedents; over half attend Orthodox services, while among the rest Seculars outnumber Liberals. For Australian-born Jews, yet another profile emerges. Whereas about six in ten attend Orthodox services, and three in ten Liberal, only one in sixteen never attend. Secularism does not seem to be a popular alternative among Australian-born Jews; put conversely, attendance at religious services is higher among them than among any other group.

It appears that for Jews born in Australia some degree of formal religious identity is part of being Jewish; for the immigrant Jews, on the other hand, Jewishness may well be part of immigrant minority status and needs no reinforcement from formal religious preference. Moreover, secular Jewish alternatives have generally been brought by the immigrants from the Jewish communities of Europe, and, till now, have never been initiated, flourished, or been given further development in Australia. Apart from the religious factor, the tendency has been for them to decline visibly and rapidly. Thus Secularism may mean very different things to the national groups: for the Australian Jew the absence of religious identity is less likely because the alternative is complete rejection of all aspects of Jewishness, in fact, leaving the faith of the people and becoming completely indistinguishable from the rest of society. What makes Australian Jews distinctive more than anything else is Jewish religious identity? The foreign-born Jew is often automatically identified with his Jewishness by virtue of his immigrant minority status – he cannot become indistinguishable however hard he tries. As a result, to identify as a Jew he does not have to adopt religious forms; he may either simply do nothing, or else on the basis of tradition, history and cultural experience, he may carry with him Secular forms of Jewish identification that already imply the rejection of the Jewish religion, but not of some other form of Jewish identity. If this theory is true we can expect many of the Australian-born children of parents of Jewish Secular identification to adopt a religious identification in the future. On the other hand the children of Seculars who do *not* have a Secular Jewish identification, that is, whose rejection of religion is accompanied by a rejection of all other aspects of Jewishness, will be less likely to adopt religious forms. As we proceed we will be able to examine these two different types of Secular – Secular with a high Jewish identification, and Secular with a low Jewish identification – more closely.

These religious patterns tend to maintain themselves, and to become further reinforced over succeeding generations. This becomes apparent when we compare those born in English-speaking countries of parents born there, with those of East European parents.

Table 4.2 Birth in English-speaking Country Holding Parents' Country of Birth Constant by Religious Preference (in percentages)

Respondent born in English-speaking Country, Parents born in	Religious Preference		
	Orthodox	Liberal	Secular
Eastern Europe (N = 59)	82	12	6
English-speaking Country (N = 44)	47	47	6
Significant at ·001 level using chi-square test			

Table 4.2 demonstrates that the Eastern European Orthodox tradition maintains itself into the second generation and even becomes strengthened at the expense of Secularism (as shown by the comparison with those born in Poland in Table 4.1). On the other hand, among the Australian-born children of English-speaking parents, while Secularism is low, the proportions of Orthodox and Liberals are equal.

While the data are capable of bearing such an interpretation, it should not be assumed that the phenomenon we are dealing with is a simple generational process of decreasing Orthodoxy and Secularism and increasing Liberalism, as we move from the East European migrants, to their children and then to their grandchildren. That is to say, it is by no means certain that the grandchildren of those born in Eastern Europe will move over in increasing numbers to Liberalism, as might appear to be indicated by the differences between the two groups in Table 4.2.

Table 4.2 reflects, rather, the very different cultural origins of the two groups. Liberal Judaism in Australia was founded in the early 1930s by already long-established Australian Jewish families mainly of British and German origin who sought a form of Jewish religious life more compatible and consistent with what they thought to be the exigencies of modern life, and less open to charges of hypocrisy, than the then prevalent non-observant Orthodoxy. They were soon joined by a greater number of German Jewish refugees. Orthodoxy in Melbourne was strengthened, reinforced and dominated by Eastern Europeans in the 1920s and 1930s and particularly after the War (although there was also a marked influx of strictly observant Jews born in Hungary and Czechoslovakia).[1] These findings seem to be more compatible with the conclusion that the children of the Australian-born, and German, Liberal families continue their tradition, whilst those of East European origin continue the Orthodox tradition.

The differential patterns of religious choice according to national origin produce very different membership profiles for the religious groups which must be constantly borne in mind as we compare them. The patterns are shown in Table 4.3. The Orthodox are

Table 4.3   Religious Preference by Country of Birth (in percentages)

Religious Preference	Country of Birth				
	Eastern Europe	Aust./N.Z.	Britain Other Eng. Speaking Country	Germ./ Austria	Hung./ Czech.
Orthodox (N = 312)	51	15	8	8	9
Liberal (N = 90)	15	27	8	31	10
Secular (N = 80)	52	6	0	21	15
Significant at the ·001 level using chi-square test.					

made up of one half from Eastern Europe, nearly a quarter from English-speaking countries, and somewhat less than a tenth each from Germany/Austria, and Hungary/Czechoslovakia. Among the Liberals, about a third come from English-speaking countries, and from Germany/Austria, less than a sixth from Eastern Europe and a tenth from Hungary/Czechoslovakia. Among the Seculars half are from Eastern Europe, a fifth from Germany/Austria, less than a sixth from Hungary/Czechoslovakia, and only a sixteenth from English-speaking countries.

There are also marked differences between the groups in terms of their educational achievements. As Table 4.4 shows quite clearly, Orthodox preference is highest where education is at its lowest, and declines as the amount of education increases. The pattern for the other groups is reversed: Liberal preference and Secularism increase with education.

Table 4.4 Education by Religious Preference (in percentages)

Education	Orthodox	Religious Preference Liberal	Secular	Other
0–8 years (N = 118)	75	8	12	5
9–12 years (N = 252)	59	21	15	5
13 + years (no degree) (N = 76)	62	12	19	7
University Degree (N = 55)	43	29	21	7

Significant at the ·001 level using chi-square test.

On the basis of these figures one might conclude that increasing education is prejudicial to Orthodoxy and favourable to Liberalism and Secularism. The two critical points appear to be the end of primary school, and the completion of a university degree. One might also assume that in the future Liberal and Secular support will increase at the expense of Orthodoxy as more Jews receive higher and university education in this country. But clearly, differing educational achievements are directly related to educational opportunities, and cultural attitudes to secular education in the respective countries of origin of our respondents. Thus in order to account for this factor the relationship between education and religious preference was examined holding country of origin constant.

Table 4.5 Education by Religious Preference Holding Country of Origin Constant (in percentages)

Education	Australia/N.Z. O L S			Poland O L S			Germ./Austria O L S			Hung./Czech. O L S		
						Religious Preference						
0–8 years	60	40	0 (N=10)	82	1	17 (66)	20	60	20 (5)	100	0	0 (8)
9–12 years	57	34	9 (N=44)	76	7	17 (88)	32	44	24 (41)	56	20	24 (25)
13 + years	88	12	0 (N= 8)	77	9	14 (22)	45	22	33 (18)	45	18	37 (11)
University	60	33	7 (N=15)	44	12	44 (16)	40	60	0 (5)	33	33	33 (6)

Table 4.5 demonstrates that the previous relationship between education and religious affiliation is not maintained when country

of origin is held constant. While it appears to hold for Jews from Poland, and for those from Hungary/Czechoslovakia, it does not hold for those born in Australia, or Germany/Austria. In neither of the latter cases is there a linear decrease in Orthodoxy, and a linear increase in Liberalism and Secularism as education rises. In the Australian case the figures, if anything, are reversed: Orthodox affiliation rises, and Liberal affiliation declines with increasing education. Amongst the German/Austrian born Secularism has increased with greater education, but Liberalism has not, nor has Orthodoxy declined; if anything, it has increased.

II

We now turn to the similarities and differences among these groups in an attempt to chart the effects of religious preferences upon attitudes and behaviour, and following that to an explanation of these differences.

In certain areas, notably religious observance and religious self-perception, the Orthodox and Liberals resemble each other quite closely, and stand clearly apart from the Seculars. For example, 88 per cent of Orthodox, 83 per cent of Liberals, but only 24 per cent of the Seculars regard themselves as being in some way religious. In some areas, Liberals even outscore Orthodox in their pattern of religious observance; for instance, 51 per cent of the Orthodox and 56 per cent of the Liberals attend synagogue more often than on the annual High Holydays. But in regard to other popular rituals the Orthodox tend to be more observant; 96 per cent of Orthodox, 86 per cent of Liberals and 52 per cent of Seculars had attended a *Seder* the previous Passover; 79 per cent of Orthodox, 56 per cent of Liberals and 13 per cent of Seculars had fasted on the previous Day of Atonement, whilst 17 per cent of Orthodox, 34 per cent of Liberals and 83 per cent of Seculars made no recognition at all of the Sabbath. It should also be noted that in each of these areas there exists within the Orthodox a core group of strictly observant – who attend Synagogue at least weekly if not daily, maintain all the Sabbath rituals, always fast on the Day of Atonement, etc. Taking strict Sabbath observance as one test, these ultra-Orthodox constitute about 7 per cent of the total sample and about 11 per cent of the Orthodox group.

When all these rituals were combined in an Index of Religious Involvement and Observance, the pattern of difference is quite clearly demonstrated as in Table 4.6.

In one important area, that of the perception of discrimination against Jews in Australia, there are no differences at all between these three groups, about 30 per cent of each group having a low

Table 4.6 Religious Preference by Religious Involvement and Observance (in percentages)

Religious Preference	Index of Religious Observance and Involvement		
	Low	Medium	High
Orthodox (N = 312)	23	47	28
Liberal (N = 90)	39	55	3
Secular (N = 80)	94	5	0
Significant at ·001 level using chi-square test.			

perception of discrimination, just over 50 per cent of each having a medium perception of discrimination, and between 12–16 per cent having a high perception.

Having examined some of the areas in which there are many similarities between the Orthodox and Liberals, in particular, we now turn to the main areas of difference.

Emotional Importance of Being Jewish

Our first major area of difference occurs in the emotional impact that Jewishness had for the subjects in our survey. This was investigated in a number of different questions, both open-ended and closed. In each, the same characteristic pattern of response was noted as shown in Table 4.7, where we find responses to the question 'Does being Jewish play an important part in your life?'

Table 4.7 Religious Preference by Importance in Life of Being Jewish (in percentages)

Religious Preference	Importance in Life of Being Jewish		
	Low	Medium	High
Orthodox (N = 312)	10	34	53
Liberal (N = 90)	15	56	25
Secular (N = 80)	27	32	36

Table 4.7 demonstrates that the emotional impact of Jewishness is considerably greater for the Orthodox than for the Liberals, with over half of the former attaching high importance to it. There is also an interesting contrast between Liberals and Seculars. Overall there are nearly twice as many Seculars as Liberals for whom being Jewish has little or no importance. But at the other end of the scale, 36 per cent of Seculars as compared with 25 per cent of the Liberals attach high importance to being Jewish. Clearly, the latter group, while not involved at all in the religious dimension of Jewish life, is deeply committed to other aspects of Jewish existence and derives deep personal meaning and emotional satisfaction from them. As this analysis proceeds we will be able to delineate those areas which engage the loyalties of Secular Jews.

When age, country of origin, education, and occupation were held constant the same basic pattern of response was maintained.

Cultural and National Distinctiveness

Identification with Zionism and Israel represents for Jews a distinctive ethnic, cultural and national commitment, although for some Jews, of course, it may not engage national loyalties, but serve merely as a secure haven of refuge for persecuted Jews. The questions in the Survey relating to Israel and Zionism were combined into an Index of Identification with Israel (see Appendix III).

Table 4.8 shows the degree of Identification with Israel of our different groups.

Table 4.8   Religious Preference by Identification with Israel (in percentages)

| Religious Preference | Identification with Israel | | |
	Low	Medium	High
Orthodox (N = 312)	12	26	60
Liberal (N = 90)	44	35	18
Secular (N = 80)	42	27	29

Significant at the ·001 level using chi-square test.

The Orthodox identify much more closely with Israel than do Liberals or Seculars. Orthodox are three times as likely as Liberals, and twice as likely as Seculars, to be highly identified with Israel. In contrast to our findings in Table 4.7, Seculars are overall more highly identified than Liberals. In general, Table 4.8 suggests that for the Orthodox, identification with Israel and traditional religious preference are concomitants, but for the Seculars, identification with Israel, and religious preference are alternatives. While the largest proportion of Seculars have very little identification with Israel, there is still a solid core of highly identified among them, contributing a significant proportion of the Seculars for whom being Jewish was personally very important.

The fact that nearly one-fifth of the Liberals identify highly with Israel suggests that there is nothing inherently contradictory in being Liberal and being Zionist. But the major pattern is one ranging from neutrality through to low and moderate identification. At the same time there is little negative feeling to Israel among them, as indeed there exists little among the other two groups. Here too, one can see the effects of historical and cultural changes; in the nineteenth century the Liberal and Reform Jewish movement was basically opposed to Zionism, and it was only in the twentieth century that this opposition lifted, and leading Liberal and Reform Jews took up key positions in the Zionist movement. Despite the political changes and increasing co-operation between the

Liberal and Zionist movements, Liberal theology did not alter appreciably. The basic Liberal religious teaching remained the missionary, non-nationalist (but not necessarily anti-nationalist) position that Jews serve as examples to the world wherever they live, as bearers of God's witness and message everywhere, rather than in any particular territory.[2]

The depth of this basic difference in approach is illustrated by the fact that when all other variables, such as age, education, occupation, national origins, religious involvement, the emotional importance of being Jewish and those dealt with later in this paper, were held constant, the same pattern of identification was repeated.[3]

Social Distinctiveness

Living in a pluralist society, Australian Jews are in a position to fashion their own pattern of social relations with non-Jews. In so doing they will be influenced by many factors – by their immigrant status, their own attitudes towards non-Jews, and to socialisation with them, the degree to which they believe non-Jews are receptive to such socialisation, or conversely are intolerant of it, and finally the feelings and emotions engendered by actual association with non-Jews. We have combined some of these various factors into an Index of Social Relations with non-Jews (see Appendix III) and here too, there exist major differences among Orthodox, Liberal and Seculars, as shown in Table 4.9.

Table 4.9 Religious Preference by Social Relations with Non-Jews (in percentage)

Religious Preference	Social Relations with Non-Jews		
	Low	Medium	High
Orthodox (N = 312)	46	29	20
Liberal (N = 90)	35	19	43
Secular (N = 80)	35	22	41
Significant at ·001 level using chi-square test.			

The pattern for Orthodox is clearly differentiated from those of Liberals and Seculars which are almost identical. Whereas only one in five among the Orthodox has a high degree of social relations with non-Jews, among Liberals and Seculars the proportion is over two in five. At the other end of the scale well over two in five among the Orthodox have a low degree of social relations with non-Jews as compared with just over one in three among the Liberals and Seculars. Interestingly, the Orthodox tend to be concentrated at the low and medium ends of the scale; Liberals and Seculars by way of contrast, are polarised between Low and High mixers.

When country of origin and residence in Australia at the age of 10 were held constant, the predicted differences were maintained, with the Orthodox consistently having a lower degree of social relations with non-Jews than Liberals or Seculars. Though overall, in each religious group the immigrants were more likely to restrict themselves to social relations with Jews, nevertheless, immigrant Liberals had higher social relations with non-Jews than did Australian Orthodox. This finding strongly underlines the strength of the association between religious preference and social relations with non-Jews. Similarly with education; at every level of educational achievement the Orthodox manifested a lower degree of social relations with non-Jews than did Liberals.

Ethnic Continuity

While one might logically assume from our previous findings that the Orthodox would be more concerned than the other groups about Jewish ethnic continuity, this is not necessarily so. Liberals, in particular, because of their religious ideology and institutional framework, might be expected to strongly favour Jewish ethnic continuity. Our next task then is to examine to what extent each of these groups is committed to Jewish ethnic continuity. This problem was touched upon in several survey questions, which were then combined in a total Index of Defence of Jewish Identity (see Appendix III). This was then cross-tabulated with religious preference and the results are shown in Table 4.10.

Table 4.10   Religious Preference by Defence of Jewish Identity (in percentages)

| | Defence of Jewish Identity | | |
Religious Preference	Low	Medium	High
Orthodox (N = 312)	8	37	50
Liberal (N = 90)	41	45	10
Secular (N = 80)	45	28	24
Significant at ·001 level using chi-square test.			

There are proportionately five times as many Orthodox in the High Defence category as Liberals, and twice as many Orthodox as Seculars. At the other end of the scale, less than one in ten Orthodox are low on defence compared with more than four in ten among Liberals and Seculars. The Liberals and Seculars are clearly less concerned about Defence of Jewish Identity than the Orthodox, yet there is a marked contrast between them. Within the Seculars there is a strong core – about one-quarter of the whole group – highly committed to Defence of Jewish Identity, which ties in directly with our earlier findings. Many Seculars who reject Jewish religious commitment compensate for it in other ways. Among

Liberals, on the other hand, religious identification is accompanied by consistently low identification with various aspects of Jewishness. Thus our earlier assumption that Liberal Judaism because of its values and institutional affiliation might engender a high commitment to preserving and defending Jewish Identity into the future is shown to be unfounded.

This pattern of Defence of Jewish Identity was tested by holding all other variables constant. When these were controlled, the Orthodox were consistently higher than Liberals in their Defence of Jewish Identity, whilst the Secular pattern was also maintained, thus showing the distinguishing power of this variable.

Religious Affiliation and Identification with Australia

Our evidence to date has suggested that Orthodox Jews maintain religious, ethnic and social distinctiveness more than Liberals. The question we now wish to ask is whether they maintain this instead of, or in conjunction with identification with Australian life. In other words, is high defence of Jewish identity and cultural and ethnic distinctiveness a bar to identification, or is it maintained side by side with identification? A partial answer to this question

Table 4.11 Religious Preference by Identification with Australia (in percentages)

Religious Preference	Identification with Australia		
	Low	Medium	High
Orthodox (N = 312)	14	49	32
Liberal (N = 90)	7	42	48
Secular (N = 80)	30	54	13
Significant at ·001 level using chi-square test.			

is found in Table 4.11 which cross tabulates the Index of Identification with Australia (see Appendix III) with religious preference. Table 4.11 confirms that the Liberals are more identified than the Orthodox. On the other hand it also finds, somewhat surprisingly, that Seculars are even less identified than Orthodox.

Further light is shed on this problem in Table 4.12 when we hold country of origin constant, which is necessary because Australian-born are clearly more likely to score high on the Identification Index. Table 4.12 in fact demonstrates that when country of origin is held constant, differences between Orthodox and Liberals disappear completely for those born in Poland and Germany/Austria. For those born in Australia the differences between Liberals and Orthodox have in the main been reduced, with Liberals only slightly more identified than Orthodox. At the same time Table 4.12 demonstrates that Seculars maintain two divergent patterns: among Australian-born they are the most identified, but amongst the European groups they are by far the least identified.

Table 4.12 Religious Preference by Identification with Australia Holding Country of Origin Constant (in percentages)

Religious Preference	Country of Origin								
	Australia/N.Z.			Poland			Germ./Austr.		
	Identification with Australia								
	Low	Med.	High	Low	Med.	High	Low	Med.	High
Orthodox	4	19	77(47)	24	58	18(146)	4	60	36(29)
Liberal	0	16	84(25)	18	64	18(11)	7	57	36(9)
Secular	0	0	100(5)	42	53	5(36)	35	53	12(12)

Our findings have demonstrated that compared with the Orthodox, Liberals have consistently been less committed to, and emotionally involved with Jewishness in its major facets. Seculars have generally followed the same pattern as Liberals, with the exception of a solid core of highly committed Jews, who scored higher than Liberals in most spheres. While some Liberals were highly committed, their proportion was far lower than among the Orthodox, or even the Seculars.

Explanations for lessened Jewish commitments must firstly be sought in their understanding of what it means to be Jewish and in their value system. Further explanation for the attenuated commitment among Liberals, however, might also be sought in their social situation, and in their understanding of the situation of Jews in a non-Jewish society.

Thus, as we saw, when national origin was held constant, differences between the Orthodox and Liberals regarding identification with Australia were greatly diminished. This suggests that the lessened Jewish commitment of Liberals was *not* accompanied by a significant heightening of commitment to Australian identity. Moreover, as we noted, more Liberals maintained closer social and personal relationships with non-Jews than did the Orthodox. This was found to be true even when we controlled for such a basic factor in the establishment of friendships as national origins and immigrant status. Not only did the Liberals mix more extensively than the Orthodox within each major national group, overall, immigrant Liberals even mixed slightly more extensively than Australian Orthodox.

These findings together suggest that the Liberals and Orthodox maintain different patterns of relations with the non-Jewish world, and that these have a different impact upon their Jewish identity. The Liberals clearly maintain a more integrationist approach towards the non-Jewish world. Not only in personal friendships but also in institutional commitments and activities, Liberal Jews seek greater formal and informal association with non-Jews. For example, they consistently undertake inter-faith activities to promote goodwill among non-Jews. This is consistent with a dominant theme in Liberal Judaism – of emphasising what Jews have in common with other groups, particularly shared social relations, citizenship and nationality.[4] While it does not logically follow that to do this Jewish commitments must of necessity be lessened, it is certainly easier in the absence of, or through the lessening of, Jewish distinctiveness.

While not caused or accompanied by a greatly heightened commitment to Australia and Australian identity, the lower Jewish commitment of Liberals does arise partly from the belief, engendered jointly by their values and social situation, that Jews ought not become, or appear, or act in too distinctively different ways from the rest of society.

Orthodox and Liberals tend to adopt two separate approaches to the general process of ethnic integration and assimilation into Australian society. Both maintain similar levels of Identification with Australia, and acculturation to it, once immigrant status is held constant. On the other hand, side by side with this Australian identification, the Orthodox adopt the path of emphasising and maintaining a high level of ethnic distinctiveness. The Liberal response, by way of contrast, maintains a much lower level of ethnic distinctiveness. It seeks greater conformity with the predominant patterns and trends in Australian society, yet without replacing Jewish identity with heightened Australian identity.

The relevance of the social situation and the pressure that it creates towards greater conformity and the lessening of ethnic distinctiveness can be seen from a comparison of two groups of Liberals – those who have extensive, and those who have limited, social relations with non-Jews. In every case, e.g. Identification with Israel, the emotional importance of Jewishness, the Defence of Jewish identity, Liberals who had extensive social relations with non-Jews were lower on Jewish ethnic distinctiveness than were those with limited social relations with non-Jews. The same trend, it should be noted, appeared in the case of the Orthodox – more social mixing with non-Jews was negatively correlated with concern to preserve and maintain Jewish ethnic distinctiveness. Nevertheless, extensive mixing had greater impact upon the Liberals than upon Orthodox: in every one of these cases the Orthodox with extensive social relations with non-Jews were more positively inclined towards Jewish ethnic distinctiveness than Liberals who mixed extensively.

On the other hand, it must be emphasised that the Liberal response does not seek completely to dissolve or extinguish ethnic identity and distinctiveness. To the contrary, it seeks to perpetuate it, but at a lower level of visibility than the Orthodox, rather than seeking complete conformity and the outright disappearance of Jews as an ethnic group.

How can we explain this Liberal response to its social situation? There is some evidence to indicate that it is guided by a belief that lessened ethnic distinctiveness will relieve the tension of Jews inherent in their social situation in a non-Jewish society. This can be found in Table 4.13 which deals with subjects' responses to the question of whether they thought it was harmful for Jews to stick together (Sense of Ethnic Tension). As it shows, Liberals were considerably more likely than the other groups to believe that it was harmful for Jews to stick together. Whereas about three in five among the Orthodox thought it was not harmful, three in five among the Liberals believed that it was.

Table 4.13 Religious Preference by Sense of Ethnic Tension (in percentages)

Religious Preference	Harmful for Jews to stick together	
	No	Yes
Orthodox (N = 312)	58	37
Liberal (N = 90)	38	57
Secular (N = 80)	46	52

Significant at ·001 level using chi-square test.

These findings must firstly be seen in the context of the subjects' social relations with non-Jews. As might have logically been expected, when we controlled for this variable in the cases of the Orthodox, Liberals and Seculars alike it was found that the greater the extent of social mixing with non-Jews the greater the belief that it was 'harmful for Jews to stick together', as shown in Table 4.14.

Table 4.14 Religious Preference by Sense of Ethnic Tension Holding Friendship with Non-Jews Constant (in percentages)

Religious Preference	Friendship with Non-Jews					
	None		Limited		High	
	Harmful if Jews stick together					
	No	Yes	No	Yes	No	Yes
Orthodox	68	32 (127)	65	35 (121)	37	63 (52)
Liberal	48	52 (21)	44	56 (36)	32	68 (28)
Secular	59	41 (27)	43	57 (30)	38	62 (21)

Thus we can say that there is a basic unity between behaviour and attitude; those who mix more with non-Jews are more likely to believe that it is harmful for Jews to stick together than those who do not mix. At a simple level, this explanation is satisfactory, and we can say that Liberals tend to perceive more harm in 'sticking together' because the predominant trend among them is for moderate to extensive mixing. This explanation, however, is not completely satisfactory. It does not tell us why at all levels of social relations and friendship with non-Jews, Liberals perceive more harm than Orthodox from Jews 'sticking together', and why a majority of Liberals who do not mix still believe that it is harmful for Jews to 'stick together'. Thus one must look further than the pattern of interaction with non-Jews in seeking to explain why harm is perceived in Jews 'sticking together'.

Part of the explanation is to be found in analysing what our subjects meant when they claimed that it would be harmful to Jews to 'stick together'. Unfortunately the Survey questionnaire did not probe our subjects' responses at this point and ask them to specify the harm that would ensue. Nevertheless, some indication of what they had in mind can be adduced from other parts of the Survey material. Perhaps the most striking is the relationship with perception of discrimination. As noted above, in general, the Orthodox and Liberals do not differ greatly in their perception of discrimination and belief that it is harmful for Jews to 'stick together'. However, when the latter relationship is examined for the Orthodox and Liberals separately, as in Table 4.15, striking differences between the groups emerge.

Table 4.15 Religious Preference by Sense of Ethnic Tension Holding Perception of Discrimination Constant (in percentages)

Religious Preference	Perception of Discrimination					
	Low		Medium		High	
			Harmful if Jews Stick Together			
	No	Yes	No	Yes	No	Yes
Orthodox	58	42 (100)	58	42 (91)	66	34 (111)
Liberal	52	48 (29)	39	61 (33)	28	72 (25)
Secular	56	44 (25)	48	52 (23)	39	61 (31)

Their perception of discrimination clearly has a different impact upon these groups' belief on whether it is harmful for Jews to 'stick together'. It makes little difference to the Orthodox who at all levels of discrimination strongly believe that it is not harmful for Jews to 'stick together'. For the Liberals (and the Seculars), precisely the opposite is the case: the belief that it is harmful for Jews to 'stick together' is positively related to increasing perception of discrimination. In other words, it seems safe to assume that for many Liberals and Seculars the harm that 'sticking together' engenders is in the realm of increased discrimination against Jews, and that therefore it should be avoided for fear of these consequences. Orthodox Jews, on the other hand, appear to be far less concerned at this possibility.

Tying these threads together, the findings indicate greater ethnic security among the Orthodox, and heightened tension and insecurity among Liberals regarding the place of Jews in a Gentile society. The question of ethnic security or insecurity is not whether there are in fact costs and disadvantages for Jews for 'sticking together', but that different sections of Jewry perceive the same situation very differently. Moreover, because Liberals *believe* that it is harmful for Jews to appear to 'stick together', they tend to de-emphasise many facets of Jewish distinctiveness in order to counteract these harmful effects, and to prevent possible discrimination, by in fact 'not sticking together'.

In short, what we are arguing here, is that a belief that it is harmful for Jews to 'stick together' because it may cause discrimination will tend to weaken the desire for ethnic distinctiveness. Because Liberals perceive greater harm in 'sticking together', they are consequently lower in their desire for ethnic distinctiveness. This is shown in Table 4.16.

Table 4.16 Religious Preference by Defence of Jewish Identity Holding Sense of Ethnic Tension Constant (in percentages)

Religious Preference	Harmful if Jews Stick Together					
	No			Yes		
	Defence of Jewish Identity					
	Low	Med.	High	Low	Med.	High
Orthodox	4	29	67 (184)	19	54	27 (118)
Liberal	26	54	20 (35)	52	42	6 (52)
Secular	11	40	49 (37)	76	19	5 (42)
Both groups significant at ·001 level using chi-square test.						

When the sense of ethnic tension is held constant the differences between the groups in relation to their concern for ethnic identity as shown in Table 4.10 have been considerably sharpened. In all groups, a belief that it is not harmful for Jews to 'stick together' heightens concern for ethnic identity, and a belief that it is harmful weakens that concern.

While half the Orthodox overall were high on defence of ethnic identity, among those who believed it was not harmful for Jews to 'stick together' two-thirds were high. One-tenth of Liberals were high and four-tenths low on defence of ethnic identity, but among Liberals who believed it was not harmful for Jews to 'stick together', one-fifth were high and one-quarter low. Among Seculars, the effect was even more startling.

Conversely among the Orthodox who believed that it was harmful for Jews to 'stick together' the proportion who were high on defence of Jewish identity fell to 27 per cent. Among the Liberals and Seculars, the proportions of those who were low on defence of Jewish identity among those believing that it was harmful for Jews to 'stick together' rose to 52 per cent and 76 per cent respectively, while the high defence proportion was more than halved in the Liberal case, and cut in quarter in the Secular case.

These figures suggest that concern for ethnic distinctiveness is lower among Liberals than among Orthodox, firstly, because a much greater proportion of the former perceive harm arising from Jews 'sticking together', and secondly, because this perception has a more direct effect on concern for ethnic distinctiveness among Liberals than among Orthodox. This becomes clear when we rank these groups in order of their concern for defence of Jewish identity. We find that the rank order is as follows:

Orthodox who do not perceive harm;
Seculars who do not perceive harm;
Orthodox who perceive harm;
Liberals who do not perceive harm;
Liberals who perceive harm;
Seculars who perceive harm.

The fact that Orthodox who do perceive harm and Seculars who do not perceive harm outrank Liberals who do not perceive harm suggests that the two factors operative here – concern for defence of Jewish identity, and ethnic security/insecurity – are also related in the opposite manner. Not only is it true that those who believe that it is harmful for Jews to 'stick together' respond by de-emphasising Jewish distinctiveness and lowering concern for the defence of Jewish identity, but the opposite process also obtains. Those who seek to maintain and promote Jewish ethnic distinctiveness and defend Jewish identity, are either prepared to pay the perceived costs of 'sticking together', or else, and more likely, believe that the costs and disadvantages of 'sticking together', without which ethnic distinctiveness cannot be maintained, are clearly outweighed by the gratifications and advantages of the latter. If this is true, we can predict that the marked differences between the Orthodox and Liberals in perception of harm to Jews (sense of ethnic tension) will tend to disappear as the degree of defence of Jewish identity is held constant. This prediction is most strikingly borne out in Table 4.17.

Two things stand out in Table 4.17. As the degree of defence of Jewish identity rises, so too does the response that 'sticking together' is not harmful to Jews, irrespective of religious preference. Even more striking is the fact that the differences between the Orthodox and Liberals are just about wiped out when defence of Jewish identity is held constant. In short, Jews who seek to further and defend Jewish identity are either prepared to pay the costs

Table 4.17 Religious Preference by Sense of Ethnic Tension Holding Defence of Jewish Identity Constant (in percentages)

Religious Preference	Defence of Jewish Identity					
	Low		Medium		High	
			Harmful for Jews to stick together			
	No	Yes	No	Yes	No	Yes
Orthodox	24	76 (29)	45	55 (117)	79	21 (156)
Liberal	25	75 (36)	46	54 (41)	70	30 (10)
Secular	11	89 (36)	65	35 (23)	90	10 (20)

of 'sticking together', or else see no harm in it at all, irrespective of whether they are Orthodox, Liberal or Secular. Conversely, those who do not seek to defend ethnic identity, are more likely to pay greater attention to the disadvantages, and perceive harm in Jews 'sticking together', irrespective of whether they are Orthodox, Liberal or Secular. The differences between these groups, then, stem from the fact that proportionately many more Orthodox than Seculars, and more Seculars than Liberals are prepared to ignore, or dismiss the disadvantages and costs of furthering Jewish identity.

The pattern of the Seculars reinforces our earlier suggestion that basically there were two types of Seculars: those for whom the absence of any Jewish religious commitment was paralleled by a low identification on all other aspects of Jewishness, and those who compensated for it or replaced it by a high degree of commitment to some other aspect of Jewishness, – Zionism, Yiddish [5] or emotional commitment. Their commitment to these elements of Secular Jewish identification is so strong that in Table 4.17 they outscore both the Liberals *and* the Orthodox in believing that it is not harmful for Jews to 'stick together'. The intensity of their response probably derives from a recognition that it is much harder to perpetuate commitment to Jewish ethnic identity in a pluralist society, once the religious element has been removed completely.

This Secular response also underlines the contrast between the Liberals and the other two groups. At the lowest level of concern for the Defence of Jewish Identity, Liberals are no more prepared to ignore or pay the cost of 'sticking together' than the Orthodox, and more prepared than Seculars, but in every case the vast majority of each group is not prepared to do so. At this level of concern, Liberal affiliation acts as a bulwark for some Jews in preventing a wholesale submission to the perceived disadvantages of 'sticking together'. In this it does precisely as well as Orthodox affiliation. What distinguishes the Liberals is the far greater proportion of its membership than that of the Orthodox in the lower categories of Defence of Jewish Identity, and the lower intensity of its response in the medium and higher categories as compared with Seculars. In seeking an explanation for this, one must turn to the institutional value system, which in the case of the Liberals, we argued above, was oriented towards social integration and conformity. They thus tread a narrow path between commitment to Jewish values and concerns, on the one hand, and an approach to non-Jewish society which is integrationist in ideology, and in keeping with this, actively involved in close social relationships with non-Jews, on the other hand. Most Orthodox and many Secular Jews are more ethnically-oriented in values and ideology, and seek to preserve Jewish religious and ethnic commitments. While neither negatively disposed to the outside world, nor more likely than Liberals to believe that it discriminates against them, these commitments are carried on together with limited rather than extensive social contacts with non-Jews. Widespread close social contacts are not sought (and generally discouraged) because of the potential threat they present to Jewish commitments, and consequently their complete absence does not provoke anxiety about 'sticking together', as it does among Liberals.

As in so many other areas, the problem for Jews in a free society is a battle between those who believe in the inner worth of the group and wish to perpetuate it ethnically and culturally, and those whose commitment to these internal goals is more or less, affected by the disadvantages of minority identity.

REFERENCES

1. On the historical aspects of the religious development of Melbourne Jewry after 1920 see P. Y. Medding, *From Assimilation to Group Survival* (Melbourne, 1968), pp. 76–84.

2. On the relation of Liberal Judaism then (Reform or Progressive Judaism in other countries) to Zionism, the State of Israel and to Jewish nationalism in the nineteenth and twentieth centuries, and in particular on its non-theological stance in this regard see I. Mattuck (ed.), *Aspects of Progressive Jewish Thought* (London, 1954). See also M. Simon, *Jewish Religious Conflicts* (London, 1950), chapters 11, 12, 13.

3. Similar findings have been reported in the USA by Sklare who found Reform Jews considerably less involved with Israel than Conservative Jews. See M. Sklare and J. Greenblum, *Jewish Identity on the Surburban Frontier* (New York, 1967), chapter 6.

4. On the institutional aspects of Liberals in Australia and their relations to the non-Jewish world, see Medding, pp. 76–97. For startling evidence on the integration-mindedness among Reform Jews in the United States as compared with Conservatives, and the amount of time spent in non-sectarian groups and activities see Sklare and Greenblum, pp. 172–8. On the missionary idea in Progressive (Liberal) Judaism which provides part of the theological basis for integration-mindedness, see Israel I. Mattuck, 'The Missionary Idea', in Mattuck (ed.), pp. 49–57; S. S. Cohon, 'Fundamental Concepts of Progressive Judaism' in I. Mattuck (ed.), pp. 60–9, esp. p. 69.

5. Because of the close connection of language with national origin and the heavy preponderance of non-Eastern Europeans among the Liberals, we did not examine the Yiddish language and culture loyalty of these groups as an element of ethnic distinctiveness. It is, however, relevant to note here that 33 per cent of the Orthodox and 26 per cent of the Seculars but only 1 per cent of the Liberals scored High on the Index of Yiddish language and culture.

5

Jewish Identification of Melbourne Jewry

Ronald Taft

Ethnic Identity

Ethnic identification can be regarded in its broadest sense as a person's attitudes concerning the relationship between himself and an ethnic group with which he is associated. These attitudes might involve beliefs about one's obligations to the group, the acceptance of behavioural prescriptions arising from membership in the group, feelings about belonging to the group and about participating in the formal and informal institutions and activities. Lewin has referred to a feeling of 'belongingness', which he defines as 'interdependence of fate'.[1] Cameron and Magaret define identification as 'reacting to the attributes of other persons, groups, objects and symbols as if these attributes were also one's own'.[2]

This incorporation into the self of the external attributes of other persons and objects implies that one's sense of identity is partially determined by one's group identifications. The reverse is also true; a person's identifications are partially determined by his sense of identity. A child learns early in his life that he has certain group identities – he is a son of his father, an Australian, a Jew, a resident of Carlisle Street, etc.; he also learns that certain role behaviour is expected from him by virtue of these identities. This is just a matter of cognitive learning, and there is no necessary emotional involvement in the group identity in the first instance. Such involvement tends to develop with experience. As Shibutani has described it, a person plays his roles according to the *meaning* of an object; that is, in accordance with its significance for his behaviour. But, in the course of performing these roles, the 'actor' develops an identification with the group which is associated with the roles. Because of the association of these groups with his self-concept they become invested with some of the same emotions and attitudes that are invested in the self itself.[3]

The intensity and quality of these involvements will depend on many factors. Partly, these feelings reflect the way in which 'significant' other people treat the person with respect to his identity.

But it is too simple to explain identification in terms of the reactions of other people: one would need to consider the influence of behavioural habits, imitation of 'heroes' (models), ideological congruity, an attempt to attain self-consistency, the role of the superego and guilt feelings, and various ego defences such as reaction formation, repression and denial. These processes could all serve to maintain and protect a group identification even when this identification is not one that brings obvious rewards to its members. For example, consider the case of a minority group member whose group is unfavourably regarded, or even unfavourably treated, by the majority group members of society. The minority group member, having already become identified with his original group, would not necessarily seek the apparent advantage to be obtained by switching his identification to that of the majority group. Firstly, he may not be permitted by either one or both of the groups concerned to change his membership from minority to majority and to attempt to shift his identification from one to the other might leave him in an undesirable marginal position. Secondly, he may not wish to change, even if he could, because of other reasons: he may have an ideological or value commitment to the minority group, as may be the case in a religious group such as Jews; or, he may believe that he has opportunities for self-expression as a member of a minority group which would be impossible in the majority group. He may also perceive his minority group membership as an advantage in many other ways; for example, there may be economic and prestige advantages to his full participation in the minority group life. Thirdly, the minority group members may have been indoctrinated, either by their own group or by the society at large, that loyalty is a high virtue, and consequently may feel guilty if they were to abandon their identification with the original group. The guilt feelings are especially likely to be strong when the majority group holds unfavourable attitudes towards the minority group. Fourthly, a person may be so deeply embedded in the life of his own group that, either he is not aware of the attitudes held by the majority group, or, even if he is aware of them, his communications with that group are too limited to make any changeover a practical possibility.

The reasons described above are relevant to the maintenance of ethnic identification among Jews, even when they live in an open society and are subject to only minimal discrimination and prejudice, as is the case in Australia. An initial childhood identification with Judaism or with the Jewish ethnic group, is expected, in most cases, to survive to adulthood, excepting for possible slow changes that may occur as a result of life circumstances and social pressures. Where there is a critical episode in a Jew's life such as anti-semitic persecution, enforced emigration or a mixed marriage, a sudden change in identification could occur. On the whole, however, ethnic identifications probably change more radically between generations than during the life-span of one individual. The viewpoint taken in the present treatment will be that generational differences need careful examination, in order to describe factors that influence ethnic identification in Jews.

Judaism as a Religion and as a Nationality

Both in terms of its own cultural values, and of its treatment by the various political regimes under which it lived, Jewry was often regarded as a separate nationality. This separate ethnic identity of Jews was reinforced in all parts of Europe in the last millenium by various manifestations of endemic anti-semitism, which often had the effect of strengthening the separate institutions of Judaism, and the adherence to them by individual Jews.

The typical way of life of Jews in Eastern Europe in the nineteenth century was characterised by the common religious practice, cultural separation and ethnic distinctiveness of the Jewish small town, the *shtetl*, and of the ghettoes of the larger towns. But by the twentieth century, the *shtetl* form of living accounted for only a proportion of the Jews of Poland, Russia and the Baltic States, since many of them lived in cities and to some extent participated intellectually in the non-Jewish world, whereby they were often subject to some degree of secularisation and assimilation to the more sophisticated Western culture. Many of the Eastern European-born members of the Melbourne Jewish community spent their childhood in Poland between 1910 and 1930. They were mostly city dwellers and were subject to civil requirements of secular education and proficiency in the Polish language. Consequently, the *shtetl* is the starting base for a consideration of their relationship to Jewishness only with respect to the life of their grandparents, or perhaps of their parents. Despite increasing secularism, the overall pattern was of widespread religous observance, among members of a separate community, who almost universally spoke Yiddish and regarded themselves – and were regarded by their neighbours – as belonging to a Jewish national minority.

Many of the same features also apply to Jews whose grandparents did not live in those countries where Jews were a separate nationality. Their religious background provided the unique cultural basis for a distinct ethnic identity, which spread universally by migration and by acceptance of the religious authority. The Jewish religion was not just a matter of a set of beliefs and prayer practices; even the part of Jewish life that is indisputably religious involves

the Hebrew language, sets of customs that have no religious imperative, formal association related to the protection and promotion
of the religion, and nostalgic reminiscences about a piece of territory which was regarded as the land that God promised to the Jews.
All of these aspects of the Jewish religion make it impossible to
sustain a complete distinction between being Jewish as a member
of a religious faith and being a member of an ethnic minority
with a sub-culture of its own.

*The Role of 'National' Background in the Ethnic Identification of Jews
in Australia*

Jews have lived in Australia since white settlement first occurred
at the end of the eighteenth century. Most of the Jewish immigrants
during the nineteenth century came to Australia from England, but a
substantial proportion of these were of German, Austrian, Hungarian
and Polish origin.[4] After 1880 increasing numbers came direct to
Australia from Eastern Europe, and in particular from Russia. The
vast majority of the Jews living in Australia today are immigrants, or
the children of immigrants, who arrived since 1921, and, in particular,
since 1938. Most of these stem from the Yiddish-speaking communities of Eastern Europe, although there is a substantial minority of
Jews from Germany, Austria, Hungary, Czechoslovakia, Britain,
Holland and France. Of the 11,000 Jewish families living today in
Melbourne, half come from Eastern Europe, a quarter from Australia
and Britain and the remaining quarter from Western and Central
Europe. In view of the importance attributed to the ethnic pressures
of the *shtetls* and ghettoes of the former Jewish Pale of Czarist
Russia, it is worth attempting to analyse the long-term origins
of the Jews of Melbourne. Judging by their numbers and the
histories of their families, it seems probable that 80 per cent of
their ancestors lived in the Pale of Settlement one hundred years
ago. The other 20 per cent stemmed from countries where Jews
were partially integrated into the life of their nation, and for them
the sense of Jewish nationality was weaker than that held by the
Yiddish-speaking Eastern Europeans. Less than 2 per cent of
these non-Yiddish-speaking Jews would have been of Sephardic
origin.

Generally speaking, the historical position of the Jews of Australia
as an ethnic group has been the same as that of the Jews of Britain;
that is, there has been a long period of economic and political
equality, and a considerable amount of social acceptance and
integration of the Jews into the general life of the country. In fact,
full legal and civic equality of Jews dates back even longer in
Australia than in Britain.[5] Thus today the typical Jew of Melbourne is a literate, middle class citizen of the Western World,

whose family had already evolved from the purely Jewish style of life in Europe itself, rather than in the New World. In other words, the starting point for the Australian experience of most Melbourne Jews is the second, third or even fourth generation removed from the Jewish ghetto, although there still are a few first generation types.

While accepting that in general Australian Jews have a separate and distinct ethnic minority group existence of their own,[6] we should not underestimate the variations that exist between individual Jews in Australia in the degree to which they participate in the corporate life of the Jewish community, and in the manner in which they express their participation. The purpose of this paper is to investigate the nature of these differences and their determinants. The major orientation of the analysis is based on the belief that in the community as presently constituted these differences reflect, in large part, the differing 'national' background of respondents. Since approximately 80 per cent of the Jews, of all ages, in Melbourne are immigrants to Australia or the children of immigrants, differences in national background assume particular importance. It has already been argued that the 'national' background of Jews who are of Eastern European origin can be described in terms of the Jewish ethnic way of life that was characteristic of their ancestors. Thus we can describe the ethnic status of a significant proportion of the Jews of Melbourne in terms of the number of generations since the family lived the *shtetl* or ghetto way of life.

Generational status, however, is not the only determinant of Jewish identification. National origin also plays an important part. The attitudes of a Jew towards his ethnic identity will be influenced not only by the traditions of his particular Jewish community of origin, but also by the attitudes of the surrounding non-Jewish community. As an example of the influence of internal traditions, the Jews of the Carpathian region of Hungary, Slovakia and Roumania are traditionally adherents of Chassidic movements, and the Jewish identification of Jews from this region may be expected to have a comparatively strong religious emphasis. As an example of the influence of the outside community on Jewish identification, Jews in the U.S.A. are more inclined to be voluntary synagogue members than they are in Western Europe because of the prevailing pattern of the population at large. On the other hand, Polish Jews tend to be either adherents of Orthodox congregations or to oppose religious participation on ideological grounds, thus reflecting the religious climate of Poland which overwhelmingly professes Roman Catholicism, but which has a vocal minority of confirmed atheists and anti-clericals.

A Comparison between Jews and Non-Jewish Immigrants as an Ethnic Minority in Australia

In a series of studies by the author on immigrants in Australia, ethnic identification has been treated as a position on a continuum between full integration with the immigrant group and full integration into Australian society.[7] For example, one of the measures of the identification of Dutch immigrants is, 'On the whole, do you feel yourself to be more Australian than Dutch by now?' Implicit in this approach is an assumption that the two identifications are mutually exclusive. While, in practice, this may be the case, if we consider being Australian or being Dutch as a very general type of identity, it is possible to be partly one and partly the other. Ethnic identification for immigrant groups is a matter partly of their degree of assimilation and partly of the particular aspect of assimilation under consideration. In a pluralistic society it is even possible to be highly identified with both nationalities as well as to be hardly identified with either. Thus, an immigrant may be proud to be a 'Dutch-Australian' or he may not be proud of being anything.

The ethnic identification of Jews in Australia is even more complicated if the Jew is an immigrant, or the child of immigrants, as most of them happen to be. A consideration of ethnic identification cannot ignore the influence of national origin as well as the strictly Jewish aspects of background. Where Jewish immigrants come from a region where Jews lived as a separate national minority, for example, in the Ukraine, the degree to which they become identified with Australia is likely to relate negatively to their Jewish ethnic identification rather than to their identification with the Ukraine. (It is also possible that they may be high or low on both Jewish and Australian national identification.)

But where a Jewish immigrant has come from a country where Jews have partially lost their status as a national minority, for example, in Britain and North Western Europe, assimilation to Australia resembles more the process among non-Jewish immigrants. That is, whether they become assimilated to Australia is partly related to the degree to which they adhere to their original nationality.

Irrespective of the immigrant's status on this national dimension, there are other aspects of Jewish identification which are largely unrelated to national or ethnic identification. For example, adherence to religion has little to do with identification with Australia, since religious pluralism is much more embedded in Australian cultural traditions than is national pluralism, although acceptance of the latter is probably growing. The relationship between assimilation to Australia and various aspects of Jewish identification will be pursued later in this chapter.

The Empirical Study

The Measurement of Ethnic Identification

In order to represent the subtleties of Jewish identification in the study of the Jews of Melbourne, we have adopted a multi-facet approach. In some previous studies, Jewish identification has been conceived as a single continuum on which any individual Jew may be placed according to whether his Judaism is strong or weak. This is too great an oversimplification and it provides no scope for representing different patterns of Jewish identification. Presumably, once the 'total Judaism' of the *shtetl* has broken down, some aspects of the culture will be retained in a form that is close to the original, while others will be assimilated to the norm of the general community. In order to examine this differential adherence to traditional Judaism, Jewish identification was analysed into seven areas which are discussed in detail in Appendix III. They are:

1 Defence of Jewishness as a separate and continuing entity *(Defence of Jewish identity)*
2 Primary group relations with Jews *(Social relations)*
3 Involvement in the formal Jewish community structure *(Communal involvement)*
4 Feelings of positive involvement with being Jewish *(Positive emotional involvement)*
5 Observance of, and involvement in the traditional Jewish religion and religious practices *(Religion)*
6 Support for the Yiddish language and Jewish 'folk-culture' *(Yiddish language)*
7 Identification with the State of Israel *(Israel)*

In addition to the seven separate aspects of Jewishness, the total of all areas was taken as an indication of the degree to which an individual Jew approximates the traditional Jewish way of life, although some of the areas, for example 4, 6 and 7 are not necessarily indicative of traditional Jewish ways in all Jewish groups. Thus Jews living in a *shtetl* a century ago would probably not have scored highly on a contemporary equivalent of aspect 7, Israel — even assuming that equivalent topics could have been developed at that time.

The Structure of the Indices

Table 5.1 presents the means and standard deviations of the 8 scales and the total Jewish identification score. If it had been possible to distribute the raw index scores symmetrically, the means of the seven Jewish identification indices would all have been 3.0 and

Table 5.1 Means, S.D. and Intercorrelations between the Identification Indices and Identification with Australia. For total sample (N = 504)*

Index	X	S.D.	1	2	3	4	5	6	7	8	9
1 Defence	3·0	1·6	—	·43	·24	·50	·49	·45	·44	·78	−·09
2 Social	3·7	1·8	·43	—	·10	·34	·15	·36	·36	·62	−·25
3 Community	3·3	1·4	·24	·10	—	·31	·44	·07	·20	·49	·19
4 Positive Emot. Involvement	3·2	1·5	·50	·34	·31	—	·45	·27	·38	·70	·00
5 Religion	2·9	1·6	·49	·15	·44	·45	—	·18	·30	·65	·13
6 Yiddish	2·8	1·9	·45	·36	·07	·27	·18	—	·37	·62	−·28
7 Israel	3·2	1·6	·44	·36	·20	·38	·30	·37	—	·67	−·30
8 Total identification	22·1	7·4	·78	·62	·49	·70	·65	·62	·67	—	−·15
9 Identification with Australia	6·4†	3·6	−·09	−·25	·19	·00	·13	−·28	−·30	−·15	—

* All correlations above ·13 are significant at ·05 level of significance
† Raw scores (adjusted)

the standard deviations 1.6. No attempt was made to re-distribute the Identification with Australia scale.

The intercorrelations between the indices are also presented in Table 5.1. The correlations between the individual identification scales and the Total is contaminated in that the scales were each included in the latter. Community Involvement was uncorrelated with Social Relations and with Yiddish Language, and its highest correlation (.44) was with Religious Observance. The highest inter-correlation occurred between Defence of Jewish Identity and Positive Emotional Involvement (.50) and the Defence scale corre-lated highly with all of the identification indices. In other words, no matter what type of Jewish involvement a respondent had, he was likely to advocate the preservation of Jewishness.

The Identification with Australia Index was positively related to Community and Religious Involvement, but negatively to Social Relations, Yiddish and Israel. The implications of these correla-tions will be discussed below.

The correlations are zero between Identification with Australia and the Defence of Jewish Identity and Positive Emotional Involve-ment in Jewishness scales, and positive with the Community In-volvement and Religious Observance scales. As part of their accep-tance of the Australian Way of Life, Jews appear also to accept a·need to be loyal to their own religious and communal institutions. There is, for example, a positive correlation of .20 (tetrachoric) between being a member of a Jewish organisation, and being a member of a general ('non-Jewish') organisation.

In order to clarify the relationships between the scales the corre-lation matrix was subjected to factor analysis. The aim of the analysis was to detect the attitude dimensions that underlie the identification variables; for example, could they all be accounted

Table 5.2 Factor Analyses of the Identification Indices

Cluster	Index	Factor Loadings			
		A		B	
		All respondents		Immigrant respondents arrived after age 10 yrs.	
		N = 504		N = 388	
		I	II	I	II
Jewish loyalty	1 Defence of Jewishness	55	51	68	34
	4 Positive emotional involvement	36	54	47	45
Jewish ethnic attachment	2 Social relations	56	17	54	04
	6 Yiddish language	58	14	62	07
	7 Israel	58	28	55	21
Formal attachment to Judaism	3 Community involvement	− ·01	56	11	54
Identification	5 Religious observance	15	69	33	64
	9 Identification with Australia	− ·50	28	− ·32	37

for by one dimension 'Jewish versus Australian Identification'? To avoid the contamination due to the co-presence of part and whole scales the Total Jewish Identification measure was omitted from the analysis. A principle components method of analysis was used and there were two significant factors.[8] After rotation (varimax), the indices loaded on the two factors as indicated in Table 5.2. In the interpretation, loadings of less than .20 were treated as being zero.

Factor I has its highest positive loadings on Social Relations, Yiddish Language and Israel. These three indices may be grouped under the title 'Jewish Ethnic Attachment', since they represent a seeking of identity through such basic relationships as ethnically exclusive friendships and intimacies, language and national affiliation. At the negative pole, there is a high loading on Identification with Australia, which reflects the negative correlations of this scale with the three indices of 'Ethnic Attachment'. Defence of Jewish Identity and Positive Emotional Involvement in Jewishness also loaded positively on the factor, while Community Involvement and Religious Observance, which might be paired as indices of 'Formal Attachment to Judaism', were unrelated to it.

This first factor, then, was marked at the positive pole by high Jewish identification in all facets excepting engagement in traditional Jewish religious observances and participation in the formal life of the organised community. Respondents who scored high on this factor tended to be less satisfied with life in Australia, less acculturated with respect to the English language and to have fewer emotional roots in Australia. The opposing poles of this factor, thus, represent the nationality dimension in which Jewish identification is contrasted with Australian identification.

When we look at Factor II (Column A) we note that this is marked by high loadings on the measures of 'Formal Attachment to Judaism' and by low ones on the measures of 'Ethnic Attachment'. Defence of Jewish Identity and Positive Emotional Involvement are both highly loaded on this factor, as well as on Factor I, but this time Identification with Australia comes out in the same direction as the measures of Jewish identification, instead of at the opposite pole. If we refer to the Defence and Positive Emotional Attachment indices as 'Jewish Loyalty', it seems that there are two forms of 'Jewish Loyalty' in this study: ethnic loyalty ('Folk Jewishness') and an attachment to formal Jewish institutions and religious customs. The latter type of loyalty appears to be consistent with participation in an acceptable segment of Australian society and reflects an aspect of Australian life in which pluralism operates. One of the items in the Positive Emotional Involvement is 'Do you have a (strong positive) feeling about being Jewish?' The analogous item for identification with Australia is 'Do you have a (strong positive) feeling about being Australian?' Further to the fact that Positive Emotional Involvement loads positively on both factors, it is interesting to note that the above two questions concerning feelings about being Jewish and being Australian correlate positively (+ ·20).

There is a positive loading, albeit a low one, of the Israel index on this second factor, but this loading may reflect the views of the minority of respondents who perceive Israel as the 'Promised Land' of the Bible, irrespective of their views of it as a Jewish secular nation.

The two factors thus present contrasting pictures with respect to identification with Australia. The first factor reflects a continuum in which an increase in identification with Australia is reflected in a decrease in Jewish ethnic identification. Factor I represents that part of Jewish identification which is analogous to the identification which an immigrant has either with his country of origin or with his new country. Thus the Social Relations scale represents identification with fellow nationalists; the Yiddish language scale represents identification with a national language and culture, and the Israel scale identification with their nation. In contrast, Factor II represents the aspect of Jewishness that is not directly analogous to any aspect of identification in immigrants.

Before concluding this section an objection to the analysis should be dealt with. The Identification with Australia Index could have a different meaning for those who have spent most of their lives in Australia than it has for those who immigrated as adults. For example, a respondent who was born in Australia would almost certainly obtain full points on the index for the nationality and knowledge of English items. To test the effect of this artefact, the analysis was repeated for the 388 respondents who migrated to Australia after age of ten years. The factor loadings are reported in Table 5.2, column B, are substantially the same as those found for the full sample of 504 respondents.

Types of Jewish Identification

In view of the differentiation between the facets of Jewish involvement, is it possible to designate different patternings of identification? Are there some Jews who express their involvement mainly by associating almost exclusively with a Jewish primary group (Social Relations), or by involvement in Israel, or by religious observance and so on? It is theoretically possible, for example, for a respondent to advocate strongly the continuation of Jewishness and Jewry (Defence of Jewish Identity) and yet not be deeply involved in any other facet of Jewishness.

In fact, the high intercorrelations that were obtained between the various indices suggest that the overall level of identification may be too high to make it possible to discriminate patterns in separate indices. Medding supports this argument when he states concerning his own study that '... the findings of the survey question the common assumption that the various forms of Jewish identification and expressions of group belonging have a separate existence of their own: that Jews either keep rituals and are religious, or are Zionists, or join Jewish organisations or have exclusively Jewish circles of friends. Our findings point in the opposite direction, to the existence of clusters of interacting and reinforcing attitudes, norms and behaviour patterns. While the theory of separate forms of identification may be true in certain specific cases (such as secular Zionists and Bundists), in general it may be said that these means of identification cling together.'[9] Nevertheless, the factor analysis of our study suggests that distinctions can be made between different types of Jewish identification and the results of such an analysis are given in the next section.

The Method of Typing the Respondents

Various attempts were made to classify the respondents into groups according to their scores on the measures of Jewish identification. Consideration was given to the absolute height of the identification, cross-classified according to the high and low points on the scales. On these variables alone there was such a variety of 'types of Jewish identification' that little information was gained by the groupings other than to bring out the diversity that exists among a group of·Jews.

An attempt was then made to classify the respondents in accordance with the factor dimensions and this was somewhat more successful. The respondents were first divided into four groups according to their status on the two 'Jewish Loyalty' scales (Defence and Positive Emotional Involvement).

A second classification of the respondents was then made in terms of the relative strength of the three 'ethnic' scales (Social, Yiddish and Israel) and the 'formal' scales (Community and Religion). With some respondents the former group was more marked, with others the latter, and in the remainder the two groups were balanced. This made it possible to divide the loyalty groups into subgroups according to whether they were predominantly Ethnic, Formal or Balanced. The low loyalty group did not provide enough variance to classify many of them into ethnic or formal, and they were divided into two sub-groups on other principle, namely, whether or not the respondent gave any answers that indicated a negative attitude towards Jewishness. When the respondent obtained a negative score on two or more of the items used in the indices, they were classified as Low Negative (LN), while the others were merely Low Loyalty (LL). Within the high loyalty group there was also insufficient variance to allocate many of the cases according to E or F, so they were divided according to whether they showed very high identification or not. The very high group scored 35 or more on the seven identification scales and were termed the Ghetto group, since they are highly integrated with almost every aspect of Jewish life.

The ten types of respondents are set out in Table 5.3. 44 per cent fell into the Medium High group, mostly with a predominantly ethnic outlook. Thus, the respondents whose loyalty is high are more likely to express their Jewish identification in ethnic rather than formal terms. The two extreme groups: the Low Loyalty Negative and the Ghetto types, each account for only 3–4 per cent of the respondents. A more detailed account of the characteristics of these two and the other eight groups follows.

To sum up the method of typing the respondents, they were first classified according to their degree of Jewish loyalty, and then

Table 5.3   Distribution of Types of Respondents

Total score on scales 1 & 4	Name of Group			N	Percentage
0–2	Low Loyalty	Negative	(LN)	17	3
		Other	(LL)	35	7
3–6*	Medium Low	Balanced	(MLE)	61	12
		Ethnic	(MLE)	57	11
		Formal	(MLF)	55	11
6–9˙	Medium High	Balanced	(MHB)	76	15
		Ethnic	(MHE)	101	20
		Formal	(MHF)	47	9
10–12	High	High Loyalty	(HL)	37	7
		Ghetto	(G)	18	4

* When the loyalty score was 6, the respondent was allocated to a group according to his overall identification level on the 7 scales.

they were typed according to the areas in which that loyalty was expressed, if at all.

Low Loyalty

LN. Low Negative (N = 17). These respondents are not only low in their scores on the Defence and Emotional indices, but they also express resentment concerning the behaviour of Jews or they actively advocate the weakening of Jewishness. Such expressions reflect negative opinions about Jewishness but do not necessarily reflect negative personal involvement. Negative responses in the Emotional Involvement area do indicate a personal resentment against Jewishness, for example, a person who answers 'What does being Jewish mean to you?' by saying, 'Only a burden! Judaism is an anachronism', is negatively involved. This type of response indicates 'self-hate', and eleven out of the seventeen LN respondents manifested some degree of this. A rating of the degree of negative involvement of the LN respondents resulted in the following: Strong 'self-hate', – three; Moderate, – three; Slight, – three; Ambivalence, – two; No 'self-hate', – six. Even were we to allow that some of the LN respondents who did not manifest negative involvement may have done so if probed more deeply, the proportion is still quite low in the sample as a whole — at most, three per cent.

The LN respondents are mainly Hungarians and Poles, who had little Jewish background, and little or no religious education. They came from families that were acculturated to the non-Jewish European middle class, and they nearly all had close relatives by marriage who were non-Jews, although only two of them were themselves married to non-Jews.

Most of the LN respondents had suffered severely from persecution during the Nazi period, and had subsequently lived for a short period under Communist regimes in Eastern Europe. They were thus mostly late arrivals in Australia, and were still struggling to regain the socio-economic position which their families had held pre-war. They tended to be dissatisfied with life in Australia and scored the lowest of all groups on identification with Australia, possibly because of their European cultural identification.

Despite their negative attitudes towards Jewishness, several of the LN respondents scored fairly high on certain scales; for example, a number of them reported that most of their personal friends were Jews, and that they felt more at home with Jews than with non-Jews. Others reported a moderate amount of religious affiliation.

If we consider the background of the LN group, their negative attitudes are not difficult to understand. They were highly acculturated Europeans who had been rejected because of the 'accident' that they were Jews. They derived little positive value out of being Jewish but they were not given any choice in their ethnic identity. A tendency to denigrate the Jewish side of their identity could thus be based on two factors: One, their suffering as Jews, and the second, the adoption of the frame of reference of a larger society which has rejected Jews and Judaism. Considering these two pressures, which have been widespread in the lives of many, if not most, of our 504 respondents, it is notable that the number who showed clear-cut self-hate is only nine. The following background material and characteristic responses to the question 'What does your being Jewish mean to you personally?' illustrate this type.

Resp. 086. Type LN. A Hungarian man who emigrated from Hungary to Israel in 1949 and to Australia in 1951. Speaks Hungarian at home.

'Trouble. I lived under German occupation in Hungary. That explains a lot. I suffered for being a Jew and I never believed that being a Jew is any different from any other religion so actually I suffered for nothing.'

Resp. 326. Type LN. Polish woman aged thirty-four. Emigrated from Poland to Israel in 1956 and after two years in a kibbutz went to Australia. Speaks Polish at home.

'It means bad luck. It is the basis of my complexes and neuroses.' Israel gives her 'a security feeling from a Jewish point of view.'

LL. Low Loyalty (N = 35). This group is much more accepting of Jewish identity, even though it resembles the LN group in being low in loyalty. In fact, many of the LL respondents participate actively in Jewish community life, although few of them claim more than a minimal adherence to the Jewish religion. They also tend to be quite low on the other Jewish identification scales.

The LL respondents are mostly Australian by birth, and the

remainder are mainly Germans, Austrians and Czechs who arrived in Australia as refugees before World War II. Few of them came from a Yiddish-speaking background. They received a Jewish education that was average in length for Melbourne Jews, and their general education was high average. Both their fathers' and their own occupational status was high. (It should be noted that the 'occupational status' of housewives is based on their husband's status.)

An interesting feature was that the LL respondents did not score as highly on the identification with Australia scale as might have been expected considering their background. The LL group seems to consist of Jews who do not strongly identify themselves with any nationality, and they are 'drifting' away from the Jewishness of their parents, rather than being attracted to anything else. Their children may be expected to drift even further, by a process of cultural erosion. A typical example is the following.

Resp. 316. Type LL. Man born in Holland, emigrated to Australia in 1949. Wife non-Jewish. Has no Jewish connections or involvements, but is not antagonistic.

'Nothing'.

Medium Low Loyalty

MLB. Balanced (N = 61). In addition to being rather low scorers on the Defence and Emotional scales, these tend to be low on all other Jewish identification scales, especially Religion and Yiddish. They were mostly born in Western or Central Europe, or, if not, they were born in Australia. Their fathers were somewhat above average for Jews in occupational level, and they themselves are average; in other words, they have lost some status through emigration. Their general educational level was good average, and their level of Jewish education somewhat below average. Few of them use Yiddish in conversation, and their level of identification with Australia is average for the total sample.

In short, the MLB group are about average for the sample in respect to most background variables excepting for their somewhat high socio-economic origins, and they are below average in all aspects of Jewish identification. They are characterised by the following respondent.

Resp. 203. Type MLB (but with ambivalence re loyalty). Polish woman aged fifty. Emigrated to Australia from Poland 1948, after being hidden in Warsaw for five years during the War. Fairly high involvement on all scales excepting Positive Emotional Involvement. Speaks Polish at home.

'A lot of trouble. I don't mind, but I have suffered. It's very hard to be a Jew – but I wouldn't convert.'

MLE. Ethnic (N = 57). Any Jewish loyalty possessed by this group is likely to be found in the area of Social Relations, but they are also not as low as the MLB group on loyalty to Yiddish and Israel. They have very little or no involvement in the Communal and Religious areas. This pattern means that their main positive association with Jewishness is represented by their almost exclusive preference for Jewish social contacts. This preference does not arise from ideological concern about preserving Jewishness so much as social habit. They tend to have come from Central or Eastern Europe as immigrants to Australia in the past few years and their language at home is mostly German, Polish or Hungarian, mixed with Yiddish. They have had a slightly below average level of general education and their occupational level is also comparatively low. They are not particularly satisfied with life in Australia, but they do not attribute any more anti-semitism to Australians than do other groups. Thus their high social exclusiveness cannot be attributed to fear of the outside world.

In summary, this group represents non-religious Jews from Poland (or in some cases from Central Europe) who have become partially acculturated to the Western World, but who still have a clear preference for social relations with Jews. In view both of their low level of activity in the formal Jewish community, and their comparatively low socio-economic level, they are probably rather passive in the conduct of their lives.

MLF. Formal (N = 55). In contrast with the MLE types, these seem to be more aggressive in their approach to life. They play an active part in the Jewish community and are moderately involved in the Jewish religion, but they mix to a considerable extent with non-Jews. They are predominantly male, and tend to be younger than other groups. They have high level occupations which represent an increase on the level of their fathers, and they seldom see themselves as working class. Their general education and their Jewish education is of a fairly high level. When asked 'What are the most important problems in the Jewish community?' the majority referred to the need for harmony. They nearly all speak English at home and were born either in Australia or in Germany and Austria. Their Identification with Australia is high and they are active in non-Jewish organisations.

These respondents are typical of the staunch supporters of Reform Judaism. Whatever Jewish loyalty they have is manifested in their association with the Jewish community and their participation in religion. The following cases typify their approach.

Resp. 013. Type MLF. Man of fifty-three, who was born in Poland but fled to England after the Nazi occupation. He is a professional, whose father was also a professional. Attends Reform synagogue fairly regularly. Prefers non-Jews to Jews socially and is fairly low on the other scales, especially Yiddish.

'Heritage, tradition – it doesn't really matter which.'

('What are the obligations of Jews in Australia towards Israel?')

'Like brothers to sisters.'

Resp. 267. Type MLF. Hungarian man aged forty-four, emigrated to Australia in 1950 and married English-born Jewess. Was in concentration camp. Graduated as a lawyer in Australia. Parents could speak Yiddish; respondent speaks English at home. Very low on all Ethnic scales and medium on both Formal ones.

'Being Jewish means a consciousness of belonging to a well-defined particular group. A cultural heritage.'

Later: 'I'm a European – Jewish – Cosmopolitan.'

Resp. 249. Type MLF. Born in Australia in 1914 of English parents. Active member of Reform congregation. Middle class businessman of working class origin. He scores high on Community and Religion, medium on Defence and low on the other four scales. He is very high on Identification with Australia.

'It's a way of life, a religion.'

Medium High Loyalty

MHB. Balanced (N = 76). In addition to the Loyalty scales, these respondents are also quite high on Social Relations and Religion, and above average on all of the other identification scales. They were either born in Australia or arrived from Eastern Europe before World War II. On all of the background measures they are remarkably close to the average for the full sample of Melbourne Jews.

MHE. Ethnic (N = 101). The main difference between the MHE and the MLE respondents is that the former express their loyalty strongly in the Yiddish and Israel areas, while the latter express it almost entirely in Social Relations. Like the MLE group, they too are low on the Communal and Religion scales. These MHE respondents were almost all born in Poland, and came to Australia after 1950. They mostly speak Yiddish at home, although nearly all can speak English. Their level of general education is the lowest of all groups, but their level of Jewish education is average. Both their social class of origin and their present class are low and their general assimilation to Australia is also low. They perceive less friendliness towards Jews among Australians than do most of the other groups, and they mostly consider that 'Combating anti-semitism' is the most important problem facing the Jewish community

The respondents in this group are twice as likely to be women as men. Like the other 'Ethnic' respondents, they are inclined to be passive rather than active in their approach to life.

The MHE type is the largest of all the groups designated here (20 per cent of the total sample) and it is characterised by high social segregation and high use of Yiddish, combined with low religious and communal participation. These respondents constitute a non-religious ghetto, but they are not without some reservations in their Jewish loyalty. Typical are the following cases.

Resp. 256. Type MHE. Polish woman aged forty-seven, emigrated in 1947 after spending War years in Poland. Yiddish-speaking. She is a staunch member of the *Bund*, a Polish-Jewish non-Communist but socialist organisation. She scores very high on the Yiddish, Positive Emotional Involvement and Communal scales, but is 'opposed to religion'. She is moderate on the Defence and Israel measures.

'It means belongingness. I have been brought up this way, my parents died for it and we have a tie to it by reason of our history and upbringing.'

Resp. 184. Type MHE. Polish man aged sixty. Emigrated to Australia in 1945 after living in Israel for three years. Naturalised in minimum time. Moderately high to very high on all scales.

'Being Jewish means everything for me, just everything. I would give my life for my nation. We gave the Bible to the World.'

MHF. Formal (N = 47). The moderately high Loyalty scores of these respondents are obtained because of high Positive Emotional Involvement with Jewishness rather than high Defence scores. They have particularly high Communal and Religion scores, but are below average on Social Relations, Yiddish and Israel. Thus, while they are strong on Jewish loyalty in certain ways, their total scores on overall Jewish identification are rather low. These respondents are mainly Australian, British or German-Austrian born, are high on Identification with Australia and almost all of them speak English in their homes. Their class of origin and general education was high average for the total sample, and have advanced themselves occupationally well beyond the level of their fathers. This group is the most successful economically of all of the groups, and, like the MLF group, they are mainly male, and seem to adopt an active approach to life.

The MHF group are 'successful' both within and outside of the Jewish group; they throw themselves into their activities with energy and are the backbone of the religious and formal communal institutions of the Jewish community, with the exception of those institutions that are organised around Yiddish language or Zionistic purposes. They also participate in non-Jewish organisations. Examples are the following.

Resp. 126. Type MHF. A young housewife born in Czechoslovakia just before the end of the War and emigrated to Australia at the age of five. She is a member of a strictly Orthodox community, is strictly religious and speaks Yiddish at home. She comes from a middle-class background. She is satisfied with life in Australia but is thinking of emigration to Israel. She is very high on the Religion scale but is only moderately high on the others. She is more concerned about the decline of religion than about the assimilation of Jews. Unlike many of the respondents, she is favourable to conversion of non-Jews to Judaism.

'Being Jewish means everything to me. It is my whole way of life.'

Resp. 505. Type MHF. Australian-born man of forty-nine, parents emigrated from Russia. Respondent is a professional, and his father was an upper middle-class business man. Is active in a Reform congregation, and scores moderately high on all scales excepting Social Relations and Yiddish.

'That's difficult to answer. It's very important to me. It means that I am the heir to a fine tradition and have the duty to preserve it and pass it on.'

High

HL. High Loyalty (N = 37). This group, by virtue of the method of discriminating them from the Ghetto group, are distinguished by the fact that their highest scores on Jewish identification occur on the Loyalty scales. They are low on the Communal and the Yiddish scales and are high on Social Relations, Religion and Israel. They are in most respects like the MHB group. Like the MHE respondents they are predominantly female, but are far more religious.

These HL respondents came from comparatively low-class origins, and also had comparatively low levels of general education, but they are now engaged in high level occupations, mostly in business and industry. They thus show the greatest upward mobility of all of the groups. This group, despite the fact that most of them were either born in Australia or arrived before World War II, are not highly identified with Australia, and remain somewhat suspicious about their acceptance by Australians.

Nearly all are the children of Yiddish-speaking parents, but in their homes they use English almost exclusively. They mix with Australians in business only and otherwise restrict their social contacts to other Jews. They support Jewish institutions of all types, but do not play the leadership role of the MHF respondents in the organised community. They see the most important problem facing the Jewish community as the need to combat the 'assimilation' (loss of identity) of Jews.

The Jewish identification of this group is dominated by their loyalty to Judaism, and by their overwhelming desire to preserve and perpetuate it, as seen in the following responses.

Resp. 283. Type HL. Polish woman immigrated to Australia at age of twenty-two in 1938. Husband is a Hebrew Teacher. Speaks Yiddish at home.

'You are very proud of being Jewish and want to share in their traditions.'

Resp. 021. Type. HL. Woman born in Australia of Australian parents, sixty years ago. Child married to non-Jew. Very high on Formal scales but moderately low on Ethnic. Strict religious orthodoxy (she was the only Australian falling into this category).

'My way of life. Almost my full life revolves around Judaism (holidays, Sabbath etc.).'

G. Ghetto (N = 18). As expected, these respondents are very high on every aspect of Jewish identification, and are low on Identification with Australia. They were all born into Yiddish-speaking homes, nearly all in Eastern Europe or Israel, and most of them arrived in Australia before World War II. They mainly speak Yiddish at home, and have had a long and intense Jewish education. Their class of origin was average but their present occupational level is below that of the total sample. In fact there is some real occupational decline in this group. They represent a passive, segregated group that would make little impact on the Australian community at large. Characteristic is the example below.

Resp. 350. Type G. Polish man aged fifty, emigrated to Australia in 1949. Naturalised Australian in 1954 but says that he would like to live in Israel. Speaks Yiddish at home. No contact with non-Jews, fairly traditional in religion (not strict) and very high on Defence, Yiddish and Israel scales. Is a member of Zionist Revisionist association (strongly nationalist).

'Because of suffering in concentration camps you feel proud to be a Jew.' (This reaction to camp makes an interesting contrast with that of respondent 086.)

(Israel mean to you personally?) 'Proud of it. It is good that we have a country of our own. It was bad when we didn't because look what happened in the War with all the concentration camps'.

Background Determinants of Patterns of Jewish Identification

We shall now consider the Jewish identification of the respondents in relation to certain background variables, such as sex, education and national background. To anticipate the findings, national background and number of generations from the *shtetl* and ghetto is the major contributor to the variance, and this will be dealt with at length. But first let us briefly consider the other variables.

Sex

The scores of males and females were very similar on most of the scales, and the total identification scores were virtually the same. The only scales on which there were any marked differences were Communal and Israel identification; the men were somewhat higher on the former, because they are more active in religious and other public affairs and they are more knowledgeable about the communal political organisations. The women were considerably higher on Israel identification; in the Melbourne Jewish community women support Israel very actively through the *WIZO* and related Zionist-oriented organisations, and, perhaps, their higher involvement is a result of the existence of these organisations. In view of the higher involvement of the women in Israel, it is not unexpected that they score lower on the Identification with Australia scale.

Education

The mean total scores for each level of education were as follows: Primary education only, 27.9; Secondary, 23.4; Some Tertiary, 22.2. Thus the higher the education, the less the Jewish identification. Those with only primary education are mainly immigrants from Eastern Europe, and 55 per cent of them are in the highly identified group; this compares with 25 per cent of those with some tertiary education.

In view of the fact that Australian-born Jews typically have high levels of education[10] it is important to examine in some detail the scores obtained on the individual scales by those who have engaged in post-secondary studies. The percentage of these respondents who fall into the low and high groups on the scales are presented in Table 5.4. The tertiary level respondents differ little from the others on the Communal, Emotional Involvement, Religion, Israel and Identification with Australia scales.

The tertiary level respondents are much less identified with Judaism in the Yiddish area, but this is probably largely a function of their national origins. They are also markedly lower on Social Relations with Jews, and perhaps by reflection, also on Defence of Jewish Identity. That is, a higher education seems to have only a small effect on most aspects of Jewish identification, excepting that they become less likely to be socially exclusive or to advocate exclusiveness in the interests of preserving Jewishness. This could

Table 5.4   Percentages of Low and High Scorers on the Identification Indices for Respondents with some Tertiary Education (Percentages for all respondents in parentheses)

	Defence	Social	Communal	Emotional	Religion	Yiddish	Israel	Total	Identification
Low	10 (6)	29 (17)	11 (12)	19 (14)	32 (25)	68 (46)	30 (23)	6 (6)	6 (7)
High	28 (39)	31 (43)	20 (16)	37 (43)	14 (19)	18 (37)	26 (31)	16 (25)	37 (33)

have the effect, in the long run, of the children of highly educated Jews having less concern about preserving Jewishness.

Socio-economic Class

Class was measured both objectively, with respect to the occupation of the head of the household, and subjectively according to the respondent's self-rating. By either criteria, the only effects on Jewish identification were that the higher class respondents were likely to be more highly identified in the Communal area and less on the Yiddish than the lower. They were also more highly identified with Australia. These trends could be entirely accounted for in terms of place of birth, and it is interesting to note that, overall, the influence of class is much less than that of education.

Age

There was no scale on which the age of the respondent made any difference. It should be remembered that all the respondents were heads of households, and if their unmarried children had been included in the study, age differences in identification would have emerged.

Family Life Cycle

While age was only minimally related to Jewish identification, the respondent's status as a parent was highly related. Following the lead of Sklare and Greenblum,[11] the respondents were classified as follows:

1. No children
2. Early childhood – all children under 9 years
3. Peak childhood – all children under 15 years
4. Late childhood – some unmarried children – 15 years and over
5. Children married – all children married.

Sklare and Greenblum concluded that religious observances were most common in families that were in the peak childhood stage, and lowest where the children were either pre- or post-school. These authors attributed their findings to the pressure on Jewish parents to transmit the Jewish heritage to their early teenage children.

The results of the Melbourne survey are presented in Table 5.5 for all of the indices. Some support is provided for Sklare and Greenblum's interpretation of their results; that is, Jewish identification, in general, is higher when the respondent has children over the age of nine years. Leaving aside the Yiddish scale which is largely a reflection of a Yiddish background, the first two stages

Table 5.5 Mean Scores on Indices according to Family Life Cycle

	1 No Children	2 Early Childhood	3 Peak Childhood	4 Late Childhood	5 Children Married
N	63	75	110	165	91
Defence	2·2	2·8	3·3	3·1	3·1
Social	3·2	3·3	3·8	3·9	3·8
Communal	3·0	3·3	3·3	3·3	3·4
Emotional	3·0	3·1	3·1	3·2	3·6
Religion	1·9	2·9	3·0	3·1	3·0
Yiddish	2·8	2·0	3·0	3·1	2·8
Israel	2·4	3·0	3·2	3·4	3·4
Total	18·5	20·4	22·7	23·1	23·1
Identification with Australia	6·2	6·6	6·6	6·2	6·2

in the family cycle were the lowest, with the 'no children' group even lower than the 'early childhood' group. The gradients were more marked on Defence, Social Relations, Religion and Israel, all of which are concerned either with the transmission of Jewishness, or, in the case of Social Relations, with preserving a Jewish atmosphere for the children by mixing socially with other Jews. On the other hand, the Communal and Emotional Involvement scales showed little increase in the later stages of the family cycle. It appears that the respondents' emotional attachments to Jewishness, or their involvement in Yiddish and in the Jewish community, are little affected by whether they have children or not. But in other respects, their Jewish involvement becomes considerably increased as their children enter their teens, especially with respect to the need to guard against the loss of the children to the Jewish people, as hinted at by the sharp increase in stage 3 on the Defence and Social Relations scales.

Thus, while Sklare and Greenblum's hypothesis that there is an increased awareness of the need to transmit the Jewish cultural heritage when children enter their teens was confirmed, this hypothesis should be supplemented by reference to the parents' realisation of the importance to Jewish continuity of trying to preserve their children's adherence to Jewish primary ties.

Generation and Nationality

It has been argued in the introductory section that ethnic identification in Jews is partly a function of the number of generations from the ghetto way of life, and partly of the country of origin. In the actual study, the measurement of generational status was difficult because of the problem of defining the ghetto generation in objective terms, and the incompleteness of the information that could be supplied by the respondents about their ancestors. The solution that was adopted was to employ the use of the Yiddish language as an index of closeness to the ghetto. This is a little crude as a measure but it is felt that it is fairly reliable and it has the advantage of providing a reasonably valid probe back two generations in that the ability or inability of the parents to speak Yiddish indicates something about the grandparents.

The following principles were adopted in classifying the respondents according to their background.

The 504 respondents were first classified according to their birthplace as follows:[12]

Eastern Europe N = 228

This consisted of 199 Polish-born, most of whom had emigrated to Australia after World War II, having been in concentration camps, or having spent the war years in Russia. The other countries represented were mainly Russia and Lithuania from which most of the respondents emigrated to Australia in the 1920s and 30s, with a few coming to Australia post-war after having lived in China. One-quarter of the total Eastern European group spent some time during the war in a Nazi concentration camp.

British N = 116

All persons born in English-speaking countries were described as 'British'. This included seventy-nine born in Australia[13] and thirty-one born in England; the other 6 were born in New Zealand, the U.S.A. and in other parts of the British Isles.

Others N = 160

This is a shorthand usage for all other categories of birthplace, including, in a few cases, non-European countries. Almost all of this group arrived in Australia after 1938, and mostly since 1945. 75 of the respondents were born in Germany or Austria, and 52 in Hungary or Czechoslovakia. The remainder were born in a wide variety of countries, such as Holland, France, Egypt, Singapore and Israel. The latter accounted for only 14 respondents, although it might be noted that altogether another 57 of the 360 respondents who were born in Europe came to Australia after having lived in Israel for varying periods.

Generation by Birthplace

E1. N = 122. Those born in Eastern European countries who use Yiddish at home. They may sometimes use other languages — mainly Polish, but if they speak Yiddish at least partially, they are classified as E1s. The E1 group will be referred to as first generation, although it is probable that in most cases they have already moved well away from the classical ghetto way of life. Most of these respondents were not traditional in their religious observances, and in fact only 30 were both Yiddish-speaking and traditional in religion.[14] These latter respondents, representing only 6 per cent of the entire sample, are the true first generation group, but they are too few to be nominated as a separate group.

E2. N = 84. The second generation Eastern European Jews were defined as those who can speak Yiddish but seldom or never do so at home. The fact that they know Yiddish is taken as *prima facie* evidence that their parents had spoken it at home when they were children, or that the respondents had mixed closely with other people who did speak Yiddish. While this inference may not be correct in all cases, it seems to be a reasonable enough working principle.

This second generation group excludes 22 Eastern European-born who could not speak Yiddish, four of them with parents who also could not. In view of the degree of drift from the ghetto way of life of these Jews, they all have been classified with the third generation Other group (see O3 below). Support for this classification was provided by the fact that the results of the survey for this group of Eastern Europeans was similar to the other O3 respondents.

British

B2. N = 68. Those who were born in English-speaking countries of parents who were able to speak Yiddish, were also regarded as second generation, and were in some ways comparable with the E2 group.

Approximately one-half of these respondents claimed to be able to speak Yiddish themselves, but only three of them, all born in England, actually ever use it in their homes, apart from possible occasional phrases. Most of the parents of the B2 respondents emigrated from Poland or Russia to England or Australia in the first third of the twentieth century, although some of the parents were born in Britain or Australia in Jewish districts where Yiddish was commonly spoken, in the British equivalent of the modern Eastern European ghetto. Some of the respondents in the B2 group were themselves also brought up in such a district.

B3. N = 48. Unless both of the respondent's parents were able to speak Yiddish, he was classified as B3. The few cases where only one of the parents could speak Yiddish were included in this third generation group after it had been established that the mixed group resembled the other B3 respondents in their responses more closely than the B2 group. This is consistent with an observation made in the 'Lakeville' study by Sklare and Greenblum,[15] that more typically 'American' opinions prevailed in the respondents who were of mixed American and foreign parentage.

Some of the B3 group might be better described as fourth generation (or more) rather than third, but, since it is probable that many of them had grandparents who could speak Yiddish, it seems to be best to treat them as third generation rather than fourth in the absence of more information.

Other

O2. N = 62. Like the B2 group, these respondents had two parents who could speak Yiddish, irrespective of whether they themselves could speak it. In fact two-thirds of these O2 respondents claimed to be able to do so, but only 13 of them actually used it at all in their homes.

The O2 group consisted almost entirely of three types of people. About one-quarter of them were the children of Jews who had emigrated from Eastern European countries in the first third of the twentieth century (or earlier) to the large Central and Western European cities of Vienna, Antwerp and Berlin. In these places the children learnt the vernacular languages and participated to some extent in the general life of the Western world. Another half of the O2 respondents were born and raised in the Yiddish-speaking areas that formed part of the Eastern regions of the old Austro-Hungarian Empire, for example, Galicia, Transylvania and Slovakia. These respondents make an interesting comparison with those who were raised in Eastern Europe, in that they almost universally use the vernacular rather than Yiddish in their everyday life. However, they are more traditional in respect to religious customs than the E1 respondents.

The remaining 14 respondents were born in Israel of Eastern European ancestry. In Israel they also used the vernacular language (Hebrew) and became partially assimilated to the ways of the western world: they have been included in the O2 group because they resemble the members of this group more than any other in their attitudes. Whenever they have distinct characteristics of their own, this will be mentioned in the discussion.

O3. N = 120. The Jews from Europe whose parents did not know Yiddish constitute the group that is the most adapted to the European, middle class way of life. In most cases, they are much more than three generations removed from ghetto living, and especially in Germany and Holland, their ancestors participated for more than a century in the general life of their country,

Table 5.6 Scores on Indices according to Birthplace and Nationality. (With exception of X̄ and S.D. all figures are percentages.)

		Total sample	E 1	E 2	B 2	B 3	O 2	O 3
	N =	504	122	84	68	48	62	120
1 Defence								
Low		6	1	2	3	6	2	17
High		39	63	40	47	23	47	11
X̄		3·0	3·9	3·2	3·3	2·4	3·5	1·7
S.D.		1·6	1·3	1·5	1·6	1·4	1·5	1·3
2 Social								
Low		17	5	12	19	42	10	27
High		43	63	42	32	24	55	26
X̄		3·7	4·6	3·8	3·3	2·6	4·2	3·0
S.D.		1·8	1·4	1·7	1·7	1·9	1·7	1·8
3 Communal								
Low		12	10	13	2	11	7	22
High		16	13	12	21	26	17	13
X̄		3·3	3·3	3·1	3·8	3·6	3·5	2·8
S.D.		1·4	1·3	1·4	1·1	1·4	1·2	1·6
4 Emotional Involvement								
Low		14	9	12	4	17	8	30
High		43	61	47	47	27	51	30
X̄		3·2	3·7	3·4	3·3	2·9	3·5	2·5
S.D.		1·5	1·4	1·5	1·2	1·3	1·4	1·5
5 Religion								
Low		25	22	31	7	11	13	43
High		19	22	14	22	19	33	5
X̄		2·9	3·2	2·6	3·5	3·2	3·8	2·0
S.D.		1·6	1·6	1·6	1·2	1·3	1·8	1·4
6 Yiddish								
Low		46	2	32	46	85	39	87
High		37	96	33	24	2	15	4
X̄		2·8	5·2	2·9	2·4	1·3	2·7	1·3
S.D.		1·9	0·9	1·5	1·4	0·8	1·5	0·8
7 Israel								
Low		23	6	12	27	61	13	36
High		31	50	52	21	6	30	14
X̄		3·2	4·1	3·9	2·8	1·8	3·6	2·5
S.D.		1·6	1·3	1·5	1·6	1·4	1·4	1·5
8 Total Identification Score								
Low		6	0	2	2	11	2	20
High		25	56	19	22	6	36	2
X̄		22·0	27·9	22·9	22·4	17·6	24·7	15·7
S.D.		7·4	4·5	5·9	6·0	6·3	6·6	5·7
9 Identification with Australia								
Low		7	11	15	4	0	3	5
High		33	8	25	67	85	26	25
X̄		6·4	5·5	5·9	7·5	8·2	6·3	6·4
S.D.		1·8	1·6	2·0	1·5	0·8	1·5	1·6

as well as in Jewish life. The O3 group included 60 respondents who were born in Germany and Austria, 26 born in Hungary and Czechoslovakia, and 29 in other parts of Western and Eastern Europe. This group also included five respondents who were born in Asia or North Africa into families of Sephardic origin and for whom the Ashkenazic way of life in Europe was quite foreign.

The results for the six groups on the various measures of Jewish identification have been set out in Table 5.6. The means have been given for each index and, in addition, the percentages of each group who fall into the low and high extremes on the indices. The cut-off points for these extreme groups were set arbitrarily to approximate in the case of 'low' scorers virtually no Jewish identification in that area, and, in the case of the 'high' very strong identification.

First Generation

E1. (Eastern European-born, speak Yiddish at home.)

These tend to have had lower middle or working class origins in Poland, but are upwardly mobile in Australia. The females mostly have only primary education, and the males early secondary. Their standard of Jewish education, also, is only average.

With respect to Jewish Identification, the E1 group is the strongest of all groups, and more than half show very high identification. They are particularly high on Defence, Social Relations, Israel and Yiddish. It is not surprising that they are almost all high on the latter since they speak Yiddish as their vernacular. This also tends to segregate them socially, although they are nearly all able to speak English if required.

They are moderately high on Positive Emotional Involvement, and 57 per cent have very strong positive feelings about being Jewish. To them being Jewish typically means either being part of a nation, or having a particular religion. However, they are not particularly religious in the sense of participation in worship or having religious feelings, and only one in eight of them observes the Sabbath strictly. But they are high in the observance of religious customs, such as Passover, Yom Kippur fasting, and the dietary laws. In these respects their religion is 'sacramental' rather than 'moralistic'.[16]

The weakest manifestation of Jewish identification in the E1 group is with respect to the Melbourne Jewish community, although even here the positive outweighs the negative. Only one half belong to a Jewish religious congregation. More than half of the E1 respondents fall into the MHE type (moderately high loyalty to Judaism with ethnic rather than formal orientation, see Table 5.7).

Their identification with Australia is below average for the total sample, although very few are really low in their identification,

Table 5.7 Principal types of Jewish Identification found in each national and
generational group.*

Group	Types (in order of frequency)				
E 1	MHE	MHB	MLE	HL	
E 2	MLE	MHB	MLB	MHE	
B 2	MHB	MHF	HL	MLB	MLF
B 3	MLF	MLB	MHF	MHB	LL
O 2	MHE	MHF	MHB	MLE	
O 3	LL	MLB	MLF	LN	

* The types that appear in more than 10 per cent of
the respondents in the group are set out in order of
frequency. Those appearing in over 20 per cent are
underlined, and those appearing in over 40 per cent are
underlined twice.

and only 14 per cent are dissatisfied with life in Australia. They
belong to a few Australian organisations, are comparatively slow to
become naturalised, and are inclined towards emigration to Israel.
Their political preference in Australia is strongly pro-Labor.

Second Generation

E2. (Eastern Europe, do not use Yiddish at home, but can speak it.)
This group differed in their origins from the E1s in that their
parents in Eastern Europe were middle class, and they themselves
had more often completed a secondary or even tertiary education.
On the other hand, their Jewish education was also rather weak.
The E2 group were markedly upwardly mobile economically and
were most successful in business. Nevertheless, like the E1s, they
preferred the Labor Party and held liberal political views. Typically,
this group were born in Poland, lived in Europe or Israel during
World War II and emigrated to Australia after the war. They
tended to be younger than the E1 respondents.

The Jewish Identification of the E2 group, while fairly high, is
well below that of the E1s, and they are notably low on religion.
They are the lowest of all but the O3 group on religious observance;
one-third have virtually no religious loyalty to Judaism, and strict
observers of the Jewish religion are comparatively rare in this
group. Although they are not respecters of traditional Judaism,
they are also not followers of Reform. Only one in ten attends
Reform service. The E2 group also tended to be low on the other
Formal identification scale, Communal Involvement; they are even
less identified in this area than are the E1s. Only one-quarter of
the E2 group are active members of Jewish organisations, and
only one in eight is really involved in formal Jewish communal life.

Unlike the E1s, the E2s do not compensate for their religious
and communal apathy by a high identification with Yiddish culture.

However, they match the E1s in their high involvement with Israel; one half of the E2 group are highly involved in this area, and most of them would like to live in Israel if they were to leave Australia. They are also fairly high on the two Jewish Loyalty scales, especially Positive Emotional Involvement on which nearly one half score very highly.

Most of this group fall into the Moderately High and Moderately Low types, and they are either Ethnic or Balanced. The most common type is MLE, as opposed to MHE which predominates in the E1 group.

To sum up the Jewish Identification of these second generation, Eastern European-born respondents, they are moderately involved in Jewish life, but much less so than the first generation Eastern Europeans. By implication they are much less involved than their own parents, especially in the areas of religion and the Yiddish language. The Jewish involvement of the E2 group is overwhelmingly national; that is, an involvement with Israel.

In respect to the direction of their national involvement, the E2 respondents tended to be only moderate in their integration into Australian life, even though most of them speak English at home (many of them speak Polish also). Few of them are highly satisfied with life in Australia, and only 58 per cent of them unreservedly wish to spend the rest of their lives there.

B2. (Born in Australia or Britain, of Yiddish-speaking parents.)

These respondents typically, but by no means universally, had humble origins in a 'Jewish district', such as the Carlton area of Melbourne, or the East End of London. Here they obtained a fairly solid Jewish education and a general education to advanced secondary school or tertiary level. Their upward socio-economic mobility has been marked and they now hold high-level occupations. They are satisfied with life in Australia and are well integrated into general Australian life. They report that they have experienced very little anti-semitism during their lives, nor do they perceive that there is much discrimination against Jews in Australia. The general picture of their adjustment to life then, seems to be a relaxed one as far as their dual status as both Australians and Jews is concerned. Their political and social attitudes tend to be somewhat conservative, although not as much as their occupational level might indicate.

How do the B2 respondents stand with regard to their Jewish Identification? In this respect they make an interesting comparison with the E2s. Considering their family histories, the B2s and the E2s could be cousins, and often are in fact. The major differences are that the two groups of respondents were brought up in different cultural environments and they had entirely different experiences as Jews, the E2s having suffered and the B2s not. In view of the fact that the E2s were subjected to extreme anti-semitism, and also that they were raised in the Jewish traditional areas of Poland, it might be expected that their Jewish Identification would be more intense. Looking first at the 'Total identification scores' there is virtually no difference between the E2 and B2 groups. But these totals are made up in different ways. The Loyalty scales, Defence and Positive Emotional Involvement, are similar excepting that the B2s include practically no low scorers. The Jewish Loyalty of the B2s is quite high; they are quite concerned about the need for Jewish continuity, and there are practically none who could be termed disloyal. However, they are much lower than the E2s on each of the Ethnic identification scales, Social Relations, Yiddish and Israel. On the latter scale the B2s even include more very low than high scorers.

In contrast, the B2s are considerably higher than the E2s on the Formal scales, Communal and Religion. With few exceptions, the former are involved in the community; half of them are active members of a Jewish organisation, which means that they are regular attenders or committee members of at least one secular Jewish organisation. Their congregational membership is also high, and virtually all of them attend religious services on occasions. Three-quarters of them make some recognition of the advent of the Sabbath and 82 per cent of them fast on Yom Kippur. One-fifth are affiliated with Reform congregations but the vast majority attend newly established orthodox ones. Two identification types predominate, MHB and MHF, and there is also an important proportion whose loyalty falls into the HL type. The remainder are mainly MLB and MLF.

To sum up this group, the B2s are an economically successful, upwardly mobile group, who are loyal to Judaism, and who identify themselves strongly with the Jewish religion and communal organisations. Returning to the question of differences between the E2s and B2s, some of these cannot be attributed to the greater anti-semitism, and disruption of their lives experienced by the former. It is difficult to ascribe the lower religious affiliation and higher Yiddish preference of the E2s to these experiences, and these differences must be explained in terms of cultural influences. However, the lower Social Relations and Israel scale scores of the B2s and the higher Communal Involvement may be attributable to the fact that they were brought up in an atmosphere of acceptance, security and continuity and could therefore more readily become integrated into the Australian community at large. The low Jewish ethnic identification of the B2s is matched by their high level of identification with Australia.

On the question of the comparative effect on Jewish attitudes of national culture versus the effect of disruption of life, it is interesting now to look at the third second generation-group.

O2. (Children of Yiddish-speaking parents, respondents are non-British and not born in Eastern Europe.)

With only a few exceptions, the O2s suffered extreme deprivation and danger as Jews during the Nazi period. Their class origin was typically lower middle class, and they have maintained that same level in Australia; thus they do not share the strong upward mobility of the E2s or the B2s. Ironically, they have an even higher educational background than these other two groups, and also they have a high level of Jewish education. This group, on the average, represents the latest of all Jewish immigrant groups to arrive in Australia, but their Index of Identification with Australia has already reached the average, and they are moderately satisfied with life in Australia. They are the most likely of all of the Jewish groups to be non-Labor in their political preferences, possibly as a result of their experience with Communist regimes in Europe.

How do the O2s compare with the E2s and B2s in their pattern of Jewish Identification? While their scores on the Loyalty scales are similar to the other two groups, their Total Identification scores are considerably higher. One-third of the O2s come into the category of high identification, and only 2 per cent into the low one. The relatively highest contribution of the individual scales comes from the Religion index on which the O2 group is the highest of all. One-third of the O2 respondents are strictly traditional in their religious observances, which places them well above any other group. 84 per cent of the O2 group fast fully on Yom Kippur, compared with 59 per cent of the E2s. With respect to religion, the O2s resemble the B2s more than they do the E2s, and this provides further evidence that it is cultural factors rather than personal disruption that determines scores on this scale. Something of the same is true of the other Formal scale, Communal Involvement, on which the O2s fall in between the E2s and the B2s.

On the Ethnic scales, the O2s show a variant pattern. They are very high on the Social Relations index, manifesting a high preference for associating with fellow-Jews; this might be a bi-product of their high religious orthodoxy, which affects their associations with non-Jews to dietary restrictions and restrictions on travelling on the Sabbath. With respect to Israel, the O2s also fall in between the E2s and B2s, and 30 per cent of them are strongly involved with Israel. Most of them would go to Israel if they left Australia. Finally, their scores on the Yiddish scale are also low, and very few of them are involved with the Yiddish language.

With respect to the latter, it is worth noting that even those who themselves come from the Yiddish-speaking areas of Hungary and Czechoslovakia tend not to use it as their vernacular. What they derive most from their upbringing is a strictly Orthodox religious tradition, and these Jews form the backbone of the newly-established, strictly-Orthodox congregations in Melbourne.

The O2 group is fairly heterogeneous in its national background and this is reflected in the variance of the scores on some of the scales. On the Total identification score it is the most variant of all groups. This is also the case on the Religion index; apart from the strict observers, there is also a minority who are opposed to religion. The heterogeneity of the group is reflected in the fact that there is no single type that stands out. Most of them, however, fall into the three moderately high loyalty types (MHB, MHE and MHF) or the MLE type.

A special comment should be made about the characteristics of the 21 per cent of the O2 respondents who were born in Israel. These are more similar to the other O2s than they are to any other of the groups, but there are some important differences. The proportion of high and low scores is roughly equivalent for the Israelis and the other O2s on the two Loyalty scales and on the Social Relations scale, but, on the other scales, the Israeli-born are considerably higher. One-half of the Israelis score high on the Religion scale, which makes them higher than any other group, but, even without the Israelis, the O2s would still remain high on religious identification. One-third of the Israelis are high on Communal Involvement and Yiddish, and two-thirds on Israel, and without them the O2s would be very low on these three scales. The Total Jewish Identification scores of the Israelis average 29.2 which is higher even than the E1s but the remaining O2s still average 23.4 without the Israelis, and this is exceeded only by the E1 group.

Third Generation

O3. (Born in non-English-speaking countries; parents cannot speak Yiddish.)

The bulk of this group, from Germany, Austria, Hungary and Czechoslovakia, were refugees from the Nazis and have had considerable experience of anti-semitism. They were of upper middle-class origin, with very high educational level, often with degrees or diplomas. Their present socio-economic level tends to be lower than it was before emigration, and their subjective class identification is often below the level of their present occupation.

In contrast to any of the first or second generation groups, the O3 respondents frequently had close relatives who were married to non-Jews. Their own identification with Australia was average and they were somewhat dissatisfied with Australia, but two-thirds of them intend to spend the rest of their lives there. Politically they tend to be slightly pro-Labor.

Coming now to their Jewish Identification, their total score is the lowest of all groups; only 2 per cent score highly and 20 per cent score low, by far the highest number of low identifiers of any group. They are consistently low on all scales, and are comparatively the lowest of all groups on Defence, Yiddish and Religion. For example, 43 per cent are not at all opposed to mixed marriages, only 11 per cent are in favour of teaching Yiddish to Jewish children, and only 63 per cent ever attend religious services. If they are affiliated with a congregation it is likely to be a Reform one. Few of the O3s have strong Jewish loyalty, and 30 per cent are classified as having virtually no positive emotional involvement with Jewishness. It will be recalled from the earlier discussion on types of Jewish identification, that a substantial proportion of those manifesting hostility concerning their Jewish identity were members of the O3 group.

Their identification scores are not as low, comparatively, on the Social Relations, Communal Involvement and Israel indices as they are on the others. For example, they tend to have mostly Jewish friends, but this may be a result of mixing with other immigrants who came to Australia with them and who have similar backgrounds. Over half are members of Jewish organisations and nearly half of them are active members. In this respect the organisations are likely to be fraternal (Bnai Brith) or welfare organisations. Again, their moderate attachment to Israel may be connected with the fact that they are refugees, and many of them have close relatives living there. However, one-third have no feelings of attachment to Israel at all. The most common identification types occurring in the O3 group are LL and MLB — in other words, they are gently drifting away from a positive identification. The LN and MLF types are also common.

To sum up, the O3s are by far the lowest of all groups in their attachment to Jewishness. Few of them take any sort of protective attitude towards it, and one might expect that the Jewish identification manifested by their children would be very weak. Before leaving the O3 group it should be remarked that the group with whom they contrast most is O2. This contrast is most marked in the areas of the Religion and Loyalty scales. The divergence between the two groups demonstrates the paramount importance of the Yiddish-speaking index of generational status, as compared with a simple classification according to national birthplace.

B3. (British-born of non-Yiddish-speaking parents.)

The B3s have the highest class of origin of all the groups, but, nevertheless, they also show upward mobility themselves. Three-quarters of the B3s are proprietors, managers or independent professionals. One-third of them attended universities, and more than 10 per cent of the males are medical practitioners. Their level of Jewish education is moderate only, and it is lower than the B2s.

They are very much integrated into Australian life, and are very satisfied with it. The majority of them belong to non-ethnic organisations, they have many non-Jewish friends and there are many marriages to non-Jews in their families. They nearly all report that they have experienced little anti-semitism during their lives.

The B3 respondents are low on most aspects of Jewish identification, but not as low as the O3s. Unlike the latter, the B3s tend to be above average on the Formal scales. They are comparatively high on the Communal Involvement scale and they have the highest rate of membership of Jewish organisations. They are also fairly high on religious identification, and certainly much higher than the O3s. 89 per cent have some identification with the Jewish religion, and more than half observe Yom Kippur and the Sabbath. The majority of those affiliated with a congregation are Reform, but there are also many who are affiliated with the older Orthodox congregations.[17]

While few of the B3 respondents are strongly involved emotionally with Judaism, there are also few who are actually lacking in loyalty. Four-fifths of them believe that Jewishness plays an important part in their lives, almost all of them would like their grandchildren to be Jewish and three-quarters are opposed to mixed marriages. The B3 group is particularly low on the three Ethnic scales, on each one of which it has the lowest average score of all groups. A large majority have virtually no identification at all with Israel, and only one in six would go to live there if they left Australia. When they are asked 'What does your being Jewish mean to you?' they tend to answer 'Belonging to the Jewish people or nation', but when asked 'What does Israel mean to you?' they usually say 'A place of refuge for homeless Jews' or 'Nothing'.

The most common identification type in the B3 group is MLF, and most of the others are accounted for by the two balanced types (MLB and MHB) and the LL types. They resemble the O3 group to some extent, excepting that there are many more moderately high, and fewer low, loyalty types in the B3 group.

To sum up, the B3 respondents exhibit moderate Jewish loyalty or, at least, are not disloyal, and their identification is with community and religion rather than with Ethnic areas. They are strongly Australian, and have little interest in Israel.

Second and Third Generation Australian Jews

Having completed the review of all of the national groups, we will conclude the presentation of results by an analysis of the Australian Jews according to their generation in Australia. This will enable us to look specifically at possible changes that may take place with time, with a consequent opportunity to predict changes that may take place in the community in the future.

For this analysis we have used a sample of 116 of the respondents who were entirely or mainly educated in Australia. Of these, 79 were actually born in Australia, and the other 37 arrived here before their tenth birthday. For purposes of the analysis they have been divided into those whose two parents were British- or Australian-born (N = 40); those whose two parents were foreign-born (N = 63), and those of mixed parentage (N = 13). All of these respondents were living in Australia before 1940, and almost all of the foreign-born parents came from Eastern Europe. The findings for the three groups are presented in Table 5.8.

The small group of mixed parentage falls in between the two others on almost all measures, and will not be further considered. We shall compare the 'Foreign' and the 'British' groups in order to study the trends as increased Australianisation occurs. In this respect, it is noted that the British respondents are considerably higher on identification with Australia, and must for all intents and purposes be regarded as fully Australian.[18] One by-product of their Australianisation is their conservative voting preferences (91 per cent vote Liberal) which are consistent with their high social class position. Unlike the foreign generation, 56 per cent of whom support the Labor Party despite their own middle-class membership, the British subjects vote more like other Australians of similar class background.

On the Jewish Identification indices, the British are slightly higher than the Foreign or Communal, but there is little difference on this index or on the scores on the other Formal identification scale, Religion, although the patterns of item responses on the latter are somewhat different. This will be analysed below in more detail.

The Loyalty and the Ethnic scales all show a rather steep decline from the Foreign to the British groups, most of all on the Yiddish and Israel scales. On these latter scales, there is very little Jewish identification at all on the part of the British respondents.[19] As far as the British-Australians are concerned, Australia, or perhaps England, is the only country with which they are involved, and Israel constitutes just another country, with which there are certain historical connections. They are rarely antagonistic to Israel, but

Table 5.8　Australian-Educated Respondents' Scores on Indices and Related Questions. (With exception of X̄ and S.D. all figures are percentages.)

		Foreign Parents	Mixed Parents	Brit. Parents
	N =	63	13	40
Defence				
Low		3	8	5
High		49	31	25
X̄		3·4	3·3	2·4
S.D.		1·6	1·9	1·4
Social				
Low		21	31	40
High		29	23	23
X		3·3	3·0	2·6
S.D.		1·7	1·8	1·8
Communal				
Low		3	15	5
High		16	23	30
X		3·6	3·6	3·8
S.D.		1·1	1·4	1·3
Emotional involvement				
Low		3	15	20
High		51	46	33
X̄		3·5	3·1	2·9
S.D.		1·3	1·4	1·4
Religion				
Low		10	15	10
High		24	8	20
X̄		3·5	3·0	3·2
S.D		1·4	1·4	1·3
Yiddish				
Low		45	68	83
High		32	15	2
X̄		2·6	1·6	1·4
S.D.		1·5	1·0	0·8
Israel				
Low		22	23	65
High		30	23	0
X̄		3·3	2·6	1·5
S.D		1·6	1·6	1·1
Total Identification				
Low		2	15	8
High		24	10	6
X̄		23·1	19·7	17·8
S.D		6·6	8·0	6·3
Identification with Australia				
Low		2	0	0
High		57	85	90
X		7·2	7·7	8·4
S.D		1·6	0·8	0·7

the Zionist sentiment of the past fifty years seems almost to have passed by them without much influence on their emotions.

Even though the scores of the British respondents are lower than the Foreign on the Loyalty scales, they, nevertheless, show considerable Jewish loyalty. Only one in five is lacking in Positive Emotional Involvement and almost all of them desire that Jewishness should be preserved and continued. It is noticeable, however, that whereas more of the Foreign Australians feel 'very strongly' about their Jewish identity than feel 'very strongly' about their Australian identity (45 per cent versus 30 per cent), the order is reversed in the British-Australians (30 per cent versus 57 per cent). Significantly, the mixed group are equal at 46 per cent each. In addition, the British respondents are much more socially integrated with non-Jews and belong to many more non-ethnic organisations than do the Foreign, but the mixed group is closer to the latter than the former on these indices.

So strong is the pull of the Australian way of life on the highly identified British Jews that their identification with Jewishness seems to have taken a form that is fully consistent with the Australian value system. Thus, the strictly ethnic, and exclusionist aspects of Jewishness are played down. Jewish identification is channelled into the religious area, almost exclusively. Herberg has argued, in the case of America, that religious affiliation can provide a means for a Jew to bridge the gap between his Americanisation and his desire to preserve his Jewish heritage.[20] The position in Australia is similar to that in America in this respect.

Within an Australian context, affiliation with a congregation, attendance at services, observance of moderate abstinences (Fasts) and the recognition of the Sabbath and common festivals are fully acceptable forms of religious behaviour. On the other hand, customs that enhance separation are discouraged; examples are strict dietary laws and strict Sabbath observance, which seriously interfere with social relations with non-Jews, and the exclusive use of Hebrew in religious services which serves to exclude the non-Jew from participation. Thus, 50 per cent of the British-Australians are affiliated with Reform Judaism, and most of the remainder attend older congregations which, while nominally Orthodox, are somewhat 'Anglicised' in their procedures (e.g. choir, prayers and sermons in English, and maintenance of decorum).

The move from religious Orthodoxy to Reform has been noted in many studies of the respective generations of Jews in America.[21] As Kramer and Leventman have argued for American Jews, Australian Jews have learned to make distinctions between the sacred and the secular which were unknown in the ghetto. At the same time they are still loyal Jews, and engage in a search for religious forms capable of perpetuating their identity. The second generation, as described by Kramer and Leventman, carry out this search, while they are establishing a favourable position in the American economy, but they live a social life largely confined to their own community in a 'gilded ghetto'. This second generation corresponds to the Foreign Australians in the present study. The third generation in Kramer and Leventman's study corresponds to the British-Australians, and according to those authors they find that they can be both Jewish and successful in the larger society, and they feel no need to shed a religious affiliation that does not restrict their life chances. Their relationship to Judaism is 'sentiment rather than commitment', but they still retain the desire to perpetuate Jewish identity.

The high communal involvement scores of the British-Australians need some discussion. Why are more than half of them active in Jewish organisations, when this would seem to involve separatism? Presumably, this activity arises from the respected position which they hold in the Jewish community. Kurt Lewin has discussed the tendency for Jewish communal leadership to be placed in the hands of marginal persons who have status in non-Jewish circles. Thus the British-Australian is well placed for communal leadership. As a rule, however, his activities within the community follow a different pattern from those of a typical Jew of foreign background. The British-Australian is likely to be active in sporting, non-Orthodox religious, fraternal, educational and social organisations, but seldom Orthodox, Yiddish or Zionist activities, or any activities involving commitments to World Jewry rather than to local Jewish interests. The Jewish communal activities pursued by the British-Australian can be regarded as a part of the Australian scene, and as contributing towards Australian life. On this argument it seems likely that the leadership of Jewish schools, other than those devoted to propagating extreme Orthodoxy, will also pass eventually into British-Australian hands.

What of the future of Jewish identification in Melbourne?

The generation described above as British-Australian consists of some third generation and some of later generations. It is possible that the fourth generation rather than the third is the critical one, and that the future of Jewish identification depends more on them than on the third. Discussion of this complex problem is taken up in chapter 13 dealing with the children of our adult respondents. But while projections about the future are fraught with uncertainty, certain firm conclusions with important future implications do stand out with regard to the adults in our survey. These seem to fall into two main points.

The first is that a considerable degree of Jewish loyalty appears to survive persecution and the minority status of the Jews. Even where, as in Australia, complete assimilation and loss of Jewish identity could probably be achieved, if desired in one or two generations, there appear to be few Jews who actually seek this. Some degree of Jewish loyalty is to be found in most of the adult Jews of Melbourne irrespective of their life experiences, or background.

The second major point is that the form which Jewish loyalty takes is not a function just of country of birth, but also of closeness to Jewish ethnicity. In the first and second generations, the dominant aspect of Jewish loyalty is the concern for Jewish survival, and the preservation of certain ethnic modes of behaviour, but as 'Australianisation' increases, there is a growth in affiliation with the organised Jewish community and with a modified form of the Jewish religion. Whether the adherence of future generations to these 'formal' aspects of Judaism will suffice to preserve Jewish life or Judaism in any form, is an open question. This will depend to some degree on such intangibles as whether the majority Australian viewpoint places any value itself on Jewish survival, and whether the present accepting attitude of non-Jews for Jews continues.

A further intangible factor is connected with the future status of the State of Israel, its security, its relationship with Australia and its future appeal to the Jews of the Diaspora.

REFERENCES

1. K. Lewin, *Resolving Social Conflicts* (New York, 1948), p. 187.
2. N. Cameron and A. Magaret, *Behaviour Pathology* (New York, 1951), p. 60.
3. T. Shibutani, *Society and Personality* (Englewood Cliffs, 1961).
4. The demographic history of Australian Jews is related in C. A. Price, *Jewish Settlers in Australia* (Canberra, 1964).
5. See I. Getzler, *Neither Toleration nor Favour: The Australian Chapter of Jewish Emancipation* (Melbourne, 1970).
6. This has been argued in P. Y. Medding, *From Assimilation to Group Survival* (Melbourne, 1968), p. 15.
7. R. Taft, *From Stranger to Citizen* (London, 1966).
8. These were the only factors with an eigen value of one or more.
9. Medding, p. 270.
10. From a separate study of Jewish youth in Melbourne reported in chapter 13, it appears that well over 60 per cent of current adolescents will undertake tertiary level education.
11. M. Sklare and J. Greenblum, *Jewish Identity on the Surburban Frontier* (New York, 1967), p. 73ff.
12. It may seem to be more meaningful to classify the nationalities according to where the respondents lived for most of the early part of their lives, but this would create practical problems of both definition and measurement.
13. While only 79 respondents were born in Australia, 116 of them already lived there by the time they were ten years old.
14. Even in the first generation of Yiddish-speaking immigrants who went to the USA early in the twentieth century, it is probable as Liebman has pointed out, that substantial numbers had already abandoned the traditional life of the *shtetl* or ghetto in favour of secularism. The majority of the immigrants were culturally rather than religiously traditional. See C. S. Liebman, 'Religion, Class and Culture in American Jewish History', *The Jewish Journal of Sociology*, Vol. 9 (1967), pp. 227–41.

15. *Ibid.*, p. 339.

16. This is consistent with Sklare and Greenblum's distinction, *ibid.*, p. 89ff, in which the sacramental religious observance is described as a transitional stage between strictly religious attitudes and the secular.

17. There are no Conservative Jewish congregations in Australia, but some of the older Orthodox ones have introduced practices associated in America with Conservative congregations, such as mixed choirs, and English translations of some prayers.

18. Several pieces of evidence point this way. In an unpublished study in Perth, Tauss found that Jews of British parentage did not differ from other Australians on the Taft 'Australianism' scale, which is a scale of typical Australian opinions. (See Taft, *From Stranger to Citizen*.) In the present survey, the proportion of the 'British' group of Australian Jews who are satisfied with life in Australia, and who would like to spend the rest of their lives here, compares with that of other Australians. (See Taft, *op. cit.*, pp. 40–1.)

19. The data were collected just before the War of June 1967 and there is evidence (see chapter 7) that involvement with Israel increased as a result of the War. However, this increase occurred more in those of a foreign rather than a British background.

20. W. Herberg, *Protestant–Catholic–Jew* (Garden City, 1960), p. 31.

21. See for example J. R. Kramer and S. Leventman, *Children of the Gilded Ghetto* (New Haven, 1961); S. Goldstein and C. S. Goldscheider, *Jewish Americans* (Englewood Cliffs, 1968), and Sklare and Greenblum, *op. cit.*

6

*Yiddish in Melbourne**

Manfred Klarberg

Until recent times it was common for Jewish communities to develop their own dialect of the local language whether it was Persian, Arabic, Spanish, or German. To communicate ideas related to Jewish culture, words and phrases not readily available in the local language were often borrowed from Hebrew. The growth of distinct forms of speech also helped to distinguish the Jews from their neighbours. Thus, two major social functions of language – solidarity and separation – contributed to the development of Yiddish.[1]

Since the emancipation of the Jews of Europe in the last century a search developed for the major factor of Jewish identity. Religion, language, culture, and nationalism were all suggested in various forms both singly and in combination. One approach in Eastern Europe postulated that Jews could become an integral part of the new secular society while still maintaining Jewish identity through the Yiddish language and its secular culture. Even many who rejected this approach vehemently, the Orthodox Jews, and the Zionists, still spoke Yiddish – the vernacular of Eastern European Jewry. Yiddish was brought to Australia and developed by the trickle of Jewish immigrants from Eastern Europe before 1939 and the much larger intake after 1945.[2] However, no study of Yiddish language maintenance within the Jewish community has yet been undertaken.

Scope of Investigation[3]

For a full survey of the level which Yiddish maintains in Melbourne today, one would have to investigate the whole of the Jewish community's language habits – in homes, businesses, social clubs, synagogues, and religious and secular day schools. However, only the institutional environment is considered here, because it is the predominant setting of social activity. The 1967 Survey disclosed that over 25 per cent of Melbourne Jews spoke Yiddish at home, about 55 per cent claimed various degrees of knowledge of Yiddish, while the remainder

* This is a revised version of my article which appeared in *The Jewish Journal of Sociology* (June 1970), pp. 59–76.

were children of non-Yiddish-speaking parents. The last group represents those who are not of immediate Eastern European descent.

There are two groups in the community which maintain organisations in which Yiddish is used extensively: the ultra-orthodox[4] and the secular. Among the ultra-orthodox, the frequent personal contact resulting from daily synagogue attendance and other religious observances tends to strengthen language maintenance, thus creating factors not present in most immigrant groups. On the other hand, the members of the secular sector identify themselves as belonging to a Jewish culture which expresses itself principally through the medium of the Yiddish language. There seems, therefore, to be particular justification for studying this sector, not least because these secular Jewish groups maintain a number of distinctive Yiddish cultural institutions, – schools, library, theatre and clubs – which are also patronised in varying degrees by the Jewish community at large. In addition to these institutions, I considered it important to include both the Victorian Jewish Board of Deputies and Jewish Press, which serve all sections of the Jewish community and follow a policy of using both Yiddish and English.

Interviews conducted with the leading personalities in these institutions yielded important information and insights. Publications were also obtained; however, it became apparent that the importance of Yiddish lay more in its use as a spoken language than as a literary medium.

The Yiddish Schools

The oldest Yiddish school, Peretz School, was founded in 1935 in Carlton, an inner industrial suburb, where most of the Jewish immigrants concentrated between the wars. In 1938 the present headmaster[5] took over; the school then had 35 pupils. It expanded steadily, moved to its present spacious premises in 1956, and in 1961 reached its peak enrolment of 262 pupils. This rise in enrolment is in inverse proportion to the trend of the Jewish population in the area during the period 1947–61. The Jewish population of the inner, eastern, and northern suburbs from which the Peretz School drew its pupils, fell not only proportionally (from 31.7 per cent to 14.2 per cent), but even absolutely (from 4,650 to 4,200).

The growth of the Peretz School was, then, unrelated to overall population figures. It must be explained by the trend not uncommon in poor immigrant areas in all countries.[6] While the older and better integrated settlers moved elsewhere, they were replaced by newcomers who found that the area provided them with readily available Jewish communal facilities, cheap rent and proximity to the city centre which made it easy to travel to work. These people, mostly D.P.s from Eastern Europe, had spent the post-war years in the ghetto-like environment of the refugee camps. There they used Yiddish as the lingua franca, irrespective of whether Yiddish or some local national tongue had been their first language at home. The Peretz School found so many supporters among them, that despite reduced Jewish population, school enrolment actually increased.[7] After its peak of 262 pupils in 1961, enrolment dropped to 110 in 1968, as a result of the exodus of the new immigrants as soon as they were financially able to move.

With the growth of the Jewish population south-of-the-Yarra, a need was felt for the teaching of Yiddish. A committee of interested parents in St Kilda founded the Sholem Aleichem School in 1946. Teachers were drawn from graduates of the Peretz School and trained by its headmaster, and also from among Polish immigrants. Co-ordination and ease of transfer were achieved via a uniform syllabus, designed to provide supplementary Yiddish education at primary and secondary level for pupils receiving their general education elsewhere. By 1960 the Sholem Aleichem School reached its optimum level of 200 pupils, allowing the full span of eleven classes to function, and has maintained it since.

The overall number of children receiving Yiddish instruction had dropped between 1960–8 from 450 to 300. This constitutes about 5 per cent of all Jewish children who attend Melbourne Jewish educational institutions either part-time or full-time, as compared with 3 per cent in the United States.[8] This is not surprising since the Melbourne Jewish community has a higher proportion of post World War II immigrants than American Jewry.

Teaching of Yiddish

The children attend for three hours every Sunday morning. Some indication of its appeal is that teenagers preparing for School Leaving and Matriculation examinations attend regularly, even though they can obtain no formal credit for their work. Conversation between the youngsters during breaks is exclusively in English. In the first four grades (6–10 years age-group), the children are taught Yiddish through conversation and using American books. Bible stories in Yiddish provide an introduction to Jewish culture. In grades 5–7, textbook language-learning is continued, but extracts from Yiddish literature are also used. Some of the Prophets are read in Yiddish translation. Jewish history from Biblical times to the present day is also taught in the upper grades.

The standards of fluency and cultural awareness are well demonstrated in a wall-newspaper at each school; regular contributions by pupils to the Yiddish press, and occasional school publications. In fact, the standard of written expression is high, and spelling is good partly because of the simplicity of the spelling system.

Syntactical faults seemed more common, and appeared to be chiefly due to interference from English.

On special occasions the schools stage functions where pupils recite, sing and perform plays in Yiddish. They often participate in public Jewish community functions, such as the annual Warsaw Ghetto Revolt commemoration, and in Yiddish items at the annual Israel Independence Day celebration.

Generational Patterns among the Pupils

A questionnaire was administered to the 11 students in the highest class of the Sholem Aleichem School. Aged fourteen–seventeen years, 5 of them were born in Australia, 4 in Poland, and 2 in Israel. Their parents were all born in Eastern Europe (19 in Poland, and 3 in adjoining countries). They arrived in Australia between 1948 and 1962. The responses indicate that the parents almost invariably speak to each other and to their children in Yiddish, and often the children also reply in Yiddish. However, 8 of them speak to their brothers and sisters in English – 5 always did, and 3 mainly did. One claimed to speak Yiddish 'always', yet 'mostly' English; one speaks an 'other language', while one has no sibling. The replies seem to indicate that they will probably speak English in their own homes, and that they will not pass Yiddish on to their children. Since this group is the 'hard core' of Yiddishists, the outlook for the future of the language is not very promising.

Jewish Press and Literature

Press

Gilson and Zubrzycki[9] state that the only study of the Jewish press in Australia was published in 1913. Up to the year of that study,[10] all Jewish publications had been in English. *The Australian Jewish News* was founded as *Australier Leben* in 1931; it was a Yiddish publication, and became bilingual under its present name two years later. *The Australian Jewish Herald,* founded in 1870, first added a supplement in Yiddish in 1946. It was called *The Australian Jewish Post* and took some years to reach the scale of *The Australian Jewish News* Yiddish section. Thus during the war years and immediately thereafter, *The Australian Jewish News* monopolised the Yiddish market, and so gained an advantage over its rival, becoming the leading Australian Jewish newspaper; and reaching practically every Jewish home. *The Australian Jewish Herald,* after changing hands a number of times, ceased publication in 1968.

Being weekly publications, the Yiddish and English sections of *The Australian Jewish News* supplement the daily press in their coverage of events of specifically overseas Jewish interest, particularly of matters concerning Israel. General Australian news is absent from both sections, indicating that the editors expect their readers to be informed by the daily press; the Yiddish reader, then, is assumed to be bilingual. The main difference between the Yiddish and the English sections is that the English section consists mainly of reports of communal happenings and organisational activities, the Yiddish section includes political comment, ideological debate, and literary criticism, reflecting marked consumer demand. While both the readers of the English and Yiddish sections can, and do, read the daily papers, those whose first language is English require *The Australian Jewish News* purely as a social notice-board. Those whose first language is Yiddish, and who must make an effort to read the news in the daily papers, prefer to read cultural matters in their mother tongue.

The Australian Jewish News, it should be noted, is not secular Yiddishist, but addresses itself to all sections of the Jewish community. There are Melbourne and Sydney editions of both the English and Yiddish sections. The Melbourne edition serves all states other than New South Wales. The following are the circulation figures supplied by the paper in June 1968:

| Melbourne edition: | English 9,500 | Yiddish 4,000 |
| Sydney edition: | English 6,100 | Yiddish 1,000. |

In addition to the weekly *Australian Jewish News,* there are two quarterlies – *Der Landsman* which has been published by the Federation of Australia *landsmanshaften* since 1965, and a Bundist publication called *Unzer Gedank. Der Landsman* contains articles on Israel, the Holocaust in Europe, short stories, essays and reviews.

Literature

Many books have been published in Yiddish in Australia. Some authors, such as Herz Bergner, have been translated into English. An interesting piece of Australiana is a Yiddish translation of a Hebrew travelogue[11] which describes a visit to Australia and New Zealand in 1861–2 after the Gold Rush.

The First Australian-Jewish Almanac appeared in 1937, and a second one in 1942. *The Third Australian-Jewish Almanac*[12] appeared in 1967. With the exception of one article in Hebrew, it is a compendium of Yiddish cultural activities, including analyses of Jewish life in Australia written by Australian writers, and by visiting overseas writers, and 'Stories, Poems, and Drama'. However, as in the United States,[13] the local scene has had a strong influence on writers, and there is an essay in the *Almanac* on the Aboriginal problem.

These books must find their market overseas, and even locally, by private sale: the three Jewish bookstores in Melbourne report selling only 'two or three' Yiddish books annually. Yiddish records, however, are extremely popular.

Kadimah

The Kadimah is the central organisation for the furthering of Jewish culture. It was founded in 1911 to provide a forum for Jewish debates, cultural activities, and to set up a 'national' library. Its fifty-sixth annual report (in Yiddish and English) shows its important contribution to cultural life. Concerts and lecture evenings are arranged on numerous occasions; memorial evenings are held for important departed leaders of Yiddish cultural life. In 1967, the library held a total of 8,743 books – 5,770 in Yiddish, 2,379 in English, and 594 in Hebrew. There are still over 100 active Yiddish readers but the number of books read fell from 920 in 1966 to 767 in 1967. Not a single new member joined in 1967 and although there are 1,379 subscribing members listed, membership is falling. The library is open twice a week. It has bought a cinema close to the Sholem Aleichem School in Elsternwick – a southern suburb – and in October 1968 moved from its premises in Carlton. If we assume that there is a parallel between the situation in the United States and in Australia, the Kadimah librarian's hope that the move to the south will revitalise his library might not be realised. Fishman, who deals mainly with a community of second-generation immigrants, hardly mentions Yiddish libraries.[14] A swing to Anglo-Jewish culture, envisaged by some, would appear to be the only prospect of Kadimah's continued activity.

Yiddish Theatre

The Kadimah provides a major Yiddish cultural service through its David Herman Theatre Group. There are usually two seasons annually, each of 10–12 performances. Plays performed include original Yiddish scripts, as well as translations from English and Hebrew dramatists. The group consists of local Yiddish actors and other theatre enthusiasts. They also stage occasional performances at the Jewish Home for the Aged, and for other charitable purposes. The needs of this group governed the Kadimah's choice of a cinema for its new premises. It is supported by over 3,000 regular patrons.

Yiddish Clubs
The Bund, Zukunft, Skif

The Bund was founded in 1897 as one of the many socialist groups in Russia. It soon broke with the extreme Left, and has since been the sworn enemy of the Communists. Its ideology consists of two basic doctrines. These are, first, that Jewish culture can be maintained, based on the belief that 'Yiddish can flower in any place where Jews live', and second, the political doctrine that 'socialism is the best form of government'. The Bund conducts various cultural evenings, talks, discussions, and readings, and encourages Zukunft – a group of university students and young adults – to do likewise. In addition to the normal range of cultural and political topics which are debated by intelligent young people, Zukunft meetings often discuss topics related to Jewish affairs. However, with the exception of discussions on Yiddish literature, all meetings are held in English. The reason, I was informed, is that 'it would take us twice as long to say what we think in Yiddish'. This is an example of a sociolinguistic phenomenon of interest. When Yiddish came to Australia, it had not developed the style necessary to deal with the discussions of the milieu in which these young people gained their experience. As they are not sufficiently at home in the language to develop it, they feel the need to use English. On subjects of Yiddish literature, however, they feel Yiddish to be the better vehicle of expression.

The members of Zukunft lead a young group called Skif, where Yiddish is officially encouraged (but, in fact, not used at their weekly meetings). I was told that at summer camps which the organisation runs, the daily parade and announcements are conducted in Yiddish. Internal publications are mostly in English, and the Yiddish programme for a cultural evening to be presented by the gronp for their elders was transliterated into roman type.

Landsmanshaften

There are numerous associations known as *landsmanshaften,* which are joined by immigrants hailing from a common town in Poland.[15] These hold occasional cultural functions and fund-raising activities, and many of them conduct an annual memorial evening on the anniversary of the Nazi slaughter of their townsfolk and relatives. All their functions are conducted in Yiddish.

The Victorian Jewish Board of Deputies

The Victorian Jewish Board of Deputies is the 'roof organisation' of the Jewish community, to which are affiliated most Jewish organisations. The Bund is not officially represented, but the Yiddish schools and Kadimah are, and further, as a result of the election of direct representatives by members of the Jewish public who care to register as voters by paying a levy, a number of Bundists are on the Board. The 'Yiddishist' group form quite a strong vocal

bloc. When, in 1948, the Board embarked on its greatest enterprise, the establishment of Mount Scopus College[16] – a day school
which was intended to cater for the children of all sections of the
community – this group was strong enough to enforce the provision of Yiddish as an elective subject. In fact, the school soon
abandoned Yiddish classes because of insufficient demand.

Delegates to the Board may address it in Yiddish, which a
number regularly do. In such cases an English translation is given.
Thus at Board meetings where Jews of many backgrounds come
together, Yiddish seems to have a quite definite social function.
While the older generation of immigrants may use Yiddish simply
in order to express themselves with greater freedom, the young
people, who express themselves better in English, often deliberately use Yiddish phrases in order to identify with the Eastern
European tradition.

Discussion

It is noteworthy that there is a considerable overlap among the
Yiddish organisations. Most of the members of Zukunft are graduates of the Yiddish schools. The secretary of the theatre group is
a sub-editor of the Yiddish section of *The Australian Jewish News;*
the headmaster of the Peretz School is a member of Bund, while
some of the contributors to *The Australian Jewish News,* and many
of the above, will be found among the delegates to the Victorian
Jewish Board of Deputies. These people form the core of the
Yiddishist groups.

This leads us to a hard-core-periphery analysis:

Yiddish weekly paper circulation	4,000
Yiddish theatre patrons	3,000
Yiddish library members	1,379
Yiddish school pupils	300
Active Yiddish book borrowers	100

It is very difficult to determine to what extent the Yiddish section
of *The Australian Jewish News* is read. In some families, it is likely
that two or more of the older members will read it. In others, it
may hardly be glanced at – according to the 1967 Survey, 30 per
cent claim to read it. The figures for theatre patrons, on the other
hand, are more accurate. However, one requires much less linguistic
ability to understand a Yiddish play than to read a Yiddish newspaper. Library membership entitles one to vote at annual meetings,
so that it may indicate political affiliation rather than cultural
activity. The active Yiddish book borrowers and the Yiddish
school pupils, though two generations apart, clearly belong to
what an informant described as the 'hard core'. These same people

are to be found among the leaders of the Bund and its youth organisations.

It is interesting to note that in the United States Yiddish has fared worse than other comparable immigrant languages.[17] Perhaps the competition with Hebrew, as the language which Jewish schools have traditionally found it necessary to teach, is a factor. A more basic factor is the 'low' status of Yiddish as a language. Rarely has a secular institution of higher learning used Yiddish as the language of instruction. A few secondary schools did, but this situation existed only for a short period in some countries by virtue of the provisions for ethnic minorities in the Treaty of Versailles, which were ignored more often than not. Furthermore, it is nowhere a language of government. A number of informants were apologetic about the use of Yiddish. One, a columnist in the defunct *Australian Jewish Herald,* pointed out that 'after all, English is also a language which has developed from a number of languages'.

Finally, it seems that in Melbourne, Yiddish is relative to the size of the Jewish community, better known and more widely used than is the case in the United States. This is because a greater proportion of the Jewish community consists of first generation Australians, while the problem of adjustment is still with us. However, in view of its non-use by the younger generation, even of the hard-core, it could well be that it is losing ground faster than it did in the United States among all but the ultra-orthodox group. Only when a distinct way of life exists is there need for a language which can give expression to the unique experiences of the group. Ethnic group survival depends on the presence of a multitude of factors. A minority whose other behaviour patterns conform with the majority will soon abandon its linguistic distinctiveness. Among the ultra-orthodox, then, investigation is likely to show greater fluency in Yiddish, and the more active use of the language among members of the younger generation.

REFERENCES

1. Cf. G. Hammarstrom, 'Zur socialektalen und dialektalen Funktion der Sprache', *Zeitschrift fur Mundartforeschung*, Vol. 24, Nos. 3/4, 1967.

2. See chapter 2 for details of immigration figures. See also P. Y. Medding, *From Assimilation to Group Survival* (Melbourne, 1968) for a general analysis of the development of the Melbourne Jewish community since 1920, and the historical detail about the role of Yiddish.

3. This study records the situation as at November 1968. I wish to acknowledge my gratitude to Mr B. Jernudd, who supervised my research at Monash University. I have also to thank Professor J. A. Fishman who read this paper in manuscript, making valuable suggestions, and Mr U. L. Kaploun whose advice on style was greatly appreciated.

4. 'Ultra-orthodox' is used for those Jews who take their orthodoxy seriously as described by J. A. Fishman, *Yiddish in America* (The Hague, 1965), pp. 57–63.

5. At one time Director of the Jewish section of the Latvian Government Education Department.

6. C. A. Price, *Jewish Settlers in Australia* (Canberra, 1964).

7. This increase may be partly explained by the post-war 'baby boom'.

8. Fishman, *op. cit.*, p. 25.

9. M. Gilson and J. Zubrzycki, *Foreign Language Press in Australia* (Canberra, 1967), p. vii.

10. P. J. Mark, *Jewish Press in Australia Past and Present* (Sydney, 1913).

11. Jacob Safir, *Iben Safir* (Yiddish edition), (Melbourne, 1950).

12. *Third Australian-Jewish Almanac*, Kadimah (Melbourne, 1967).

13. Fishman, *op. cit.*, p. 35.

14. Fishman, *op. cit.* There is no section devoted to libraries. The YIVO library is mentioned in passing on p. 44, and the Los Angeles Yiddish Culture Club library on p. 47.

15. The only non-Polish group known as *landsmanshaft* is one combining all Latvian and Lithuanian Jews.

16. By 1968 this college consisted of a central primary and secondary school and three branch primary schools. Total enrolment was approaching 2,000.

17. Fishman, *op. cit.*, p. 69 and p. 72n.

7

The Impact of the Middle East Crisis of June 1967 on Jews in Melbourne

Ronald Taft

In an article on 'Israel and American Jewry', Hertzberg[1] reports on his impressions of the unprecedented feelings of involvement in the June 1967 Crisis on the part of American Jews from all walks of life. From contemporary reports in the Jewish press, it appears that the response of Jews throughout the non-communist world was similar to the U.S. pattern, if not even more zealous. According to these reports there was an impressive wave of rallies of support for Israel, unprecedentedly large contributions of funds and volunteering of services. Subsequent reports also reveal that Jews in Eastern Europe and the Soviet Union were aware of the events, were mainly sympathetic to Israel's cause despite official hostility to it, and derived a great morale boost from Israel's success. The response in Melbourne was no exception. Out of a community of 34,000 Jews of all ages, 7,000 attended a public rally before the outbreak of War to express their moral support for Israel, and 2,500 attended a youth rally. Altogether 700 young persons volunteered to go to Israel and these were mainly students who were risking a whole academic year (March to November in the Antipodes).

This chapter reports on a survey that was conducted a week or two after the War in order to investigate the reactions of a sample of the original respondents in the 1967 Survey.[2]

Overall Emotional Reactions to the Crisis

The interview schedule asked the respondent for his reactions and those of members of his household to the Crisis in three separate stages: before the outbreak of open warfare; during the War; and immediately after the victory. In order to investigate the salience of the Crisis the interview opened with the question 'What do you think is the most important problem facing the Melbourne Jewish Community?' This was asked before any hint was given concerning the theme of the interview.

The responses to all of the questions (which are detailed below) were combined into two overall ratings: ego involvement and intensity of emotional reactions.[3]

The distribution of ratings are set out in Table 7.1. The modal rating on ego involvement was 4 ('a fair amount of personal involvement'). This implies that the respondent changed his daily routine in order to keep up with the news, and that his preoccupation with the Crisis led to neglect of his normal interests. Such respondents possibly reported thinking about whether they should volunteer their services to help Israel's cause. The ratings of 5 and 6 were used conservatively, even though more than one-third of the respondents received them. To 'earn' 5, respondents had to provide ample evidence that their lives were disrupted by the fact that Israel was being tried. Typical comments of respondents receiving a rating 5 were: 'Didn't bother trying to work during that week',

Table 7.1   Overall Ratings on Ego Involvement in the Crisis and Emotional Intensity of Reaction to it (in percentages)

	Random Sample (N = 54)	Augmented Sample (N = 68)
Ego involvement		
1. No interest at all	0	0
2. Casual interest without involvement	0	0
3. Slight involvement but somewhat superficial	4	9
4. Moderately involved	52	50
5. Considerable involvement	39	37
6. Very intense involvement	6	4
Emotional intensity		
1. Nil or slight emotional reaction	9	15
2. Definite emotional reaction	49	49
3. Intense emotional reaction	41	36

'Had fits of crying', 'Was distressed that I am too old to volunteer', 'Attended several rallies to support Israel and worked on emergency committees'. A rating of 6 was preserved for extreme cases. Typical comments: 'The attack on Israel was like my hand was cut off', 'After victory I felt like I had recovered from a severe illness', 'I felt shock – a feeling of both death and life', 'Didn't sleep or eat', 'Israel and I want peace'.

The respondents were also asked whether 'they were surprised at their own reactions to the Crisis'. Only 15 per cent said that they were surprised, and another 6 per cent were not sure. A typical remark of a 'surprised' respondent was 'I was surprised how much I wanted to listen to the news'. Another respondent, who said than Israel means 'very little' to him, said, 'I found myself giving more money than I ever thought I would give to anything'. An inspection of the responses of 'surprised' respondents in the 1967 Survey suggests that typically they were persons whose interest in Israel had been fairly low before the Crisis, although they usually had other emotional links with Jewishness, such as religion, Jewish friends or Yiddish language.

To sum up, the most notable results on ego involvement were the extremely small numbers who were only 'slightly involved', even in the sample augmented by those favouring assimilation; and the comparatively high number of those who were 'considerably involved'.

The ratings on emotional intensity were not independent of those on ego involvement; i.e. persons who showed intense reactions tended to be rated higher on ego involvement, and those who showed little emotional reaction tended to be low on involvement. But there were exceptions; there were respondents who became emotionally unbalanced by the Crisis, but were far more concerned with themselves than the world events, and there were others – typically males – whose interests were completely absorbed by the Crisis, but who remained quite cool. 90 per cent of the respondents in the random sample showed a definite emotional reaction, and almost half of these showed an intense reaction. There were no sex differences in these reactions which were probably determined by the respondent's ego involvement in the Crisis and by his or her temperament.

Some Specific Reactions to the Crisis

Let us now look at some of the topics that were considered in assessing the overall reactions to the Crisis.

Salience. 'What do you think is the most important problem facing the Melbourne Jewish Community?' 26 per cent of all respondents in the random sample mentioned Israel. This compares with only 5 per cent in the original study before the War. The 74 per cent of the respondents who did not mention Israel included many who were highly involved in the Middle East Crisis, but they either just did not perceive this as a problem facing the *local* Jewish Community, or they believed that there were more salient problems. The most commonly mentioned problem was that of keeping harmony within the Community. This was mentioned twice as often as it was in the 1967 Survey, while problems connected with assimilation were mentioned only half as often. It would be reasonable to attribute the changes in the salience of these problems to the effect of the Crisis.

Involvement in the Crisis before the War broke out. The interviewers asked the respondents to describe how they felt about the Crisis before the War broke out and whether they became concerned about the safety of Israel, and if so, how much. The responses were rated using the procedure described below, and these are set out in Table 7.2.

The results indicate that most Jews felt themselves drawn into the Crisis before the battles started. It should be noted that a rating of 'involvement' implies that the respondent was concerned about the threat to Israel and not just world peace generally. The results are not surprising when we consider the number of Jews attending public rallies of support before the War (see above). The one respondent who did not know about the Crisis was visiting his homeland in Eastern Europe at the time, and did not notice any news reports on the matter.

Table 7.2　Involvement in the Crisis Before the Outbreak of War (in percentages)

Degree of Involvement	Random Sample	Augmented Sample
Unaware	0	1
Indifferent	2	6
Some interest	2	3
Moderate involvement	6	4
Considerable involvement	15	15
Considerable involvement *and* concern for safety of Israel	76	71

Dependence on news. Every one of the respondents in the random sample claimed that they followed the news 'much more' than normally (with the exception of one elderly woman whose English wasn't good enough).

Seeking social contacts. Respondents were asked whether they sought out the company of other Jewish people and of members of their family. 26 per cent answered 'much more than usual' and another 20 per cent 'a little more'. This means that nearly one-half of the respondents sought more social contacts as a result of the Crisis.[4]

Attendance at rallies and religious services. Nearly half of the respondents claimed to have attended at least one rally on behalf of Israel, and half of these (i.e. one-quarter) attended two or more. On the other hand, only one in nine attended a religious service that they might otherwise not have attended.

Donations. 96 per cent stated that their household had given a donation to the Israel Appeal and 92 per cent claimed that they had contributed more than usual.

Volunteering services. 'Did you have any thoughts at all about volunteering your services to help Israel in any way?' Volunteering was not confined to offering to go to Israel, but it included such services as collecting money or interviewing volunteers. The responses are summarised in Table 7.3.

The respondents were also asked whether any members of the household had actually volunteered to go to Israel. 11 per cent of

Table 7.3 Volunteering Services to Help Israel*
(in percentages)

	Random Sample
No thought of volunteering	65
Fantasy thoughts, but no action	13
Serious consideration	6
Actually offered services	17

* Not necessarily to go to Israel.

all households contained at least one volunteer, according to the claims made by the respondents.[5] Details will be given below of volunteering by children of various ages.

Variables associated with the Degree of Ego Involvement

What are the determinants of whether a particular respondent was highly involved or not in the Crisis? To investigate this a number of background and opinion variables were analysed in relation to the degree of ego involvement, and the statistical significance of the relationships was tested by using either bi-serial correlations or χ^2.[6]

Results of the Analyses

There were no age differences, nor sex differences, other than the possibly suggestive finding that all three respondents who scored the highest rating on involvement were women. There was an interesting relationship with socio-economic class. A positive correlation of .33 between class level and involvement was highly significant.[7] Businessmen (and their wives) and those in professional occupations tended to be much more involved than were those in lower-level occupations. There was no relationship to voting preferences in Australian politics, nor with feelings of satisfaction with life in Australia.

Place of birth was not a significant determinant of involvement, although there was a tendency for those born in Eastern Europe to be more involved in the Crisis than were others. The relationship is statistically significant when those whose mother tongue was Yiddish is compared with the remainder.

It might be thought that social integration with non-Jews – commonly called 'assimilation – would reduce the respondent's involvement in the Crisis. As a rough objective measure of this integration, the respondents were classified according to whether they had a mixed marriage in their immediate family, including themselves. The 16 respondents concerned did not differ from the others on involvement; if anything, they were more involved in the Crisis than were those with no mixed marriages. Another measure of integration, the composite scale of Identification with Australia, was also unrelated to involvement in the Crisis.

It was thought that those who believe that there is a good deal of anti-semitism in Australia would be more involved in the Crisis than those who did not. This time there was a significant correlation of .25, but it was in the opposite direction to the prediction. That is, the more a respondent perceives Australians as friendly towards Jews, the greater his involvement in the Middle East Crisis. On the other hand, the more anti-semitism that the respondent has personally experienced in his whole lifetime — wherever he may have lived — the higher his involvement, but the highly involved respondents were, typically, Yiddish-speaking persons who had arrived in Australia after World War II, having suffered under the Nazis.

Have the more involved respondents had more contact with Israel than the less involved? Strangely enough the answer is 'No'. There is no relationship at all between degree of involvement and ever having visited or lived in Israel, or having close relatives and friends living there. Involvement, thus, is definitely not affected by familiarity with the Middle East or by personal ties with the inhabitants of Israel.

Participation in Zionist movements also showed little relationship with involvement in the Crisis (see Table 7.4). Respondents were asked to indicate their degree of participation on a 5-point scale, ranging from 'no participation at all' to 'Zionist activities were paramount in my life'. Ratings were made for three life periods: before eighteen years, as a young adult and now. There was no relationship at all with Zionist participation before eighteen; there were twelve respondents who had been completely absorbed in Zionism, and of these only two scored 5 (see Table 7.4 for the meaning of these ratings). There was a trend for those who participated in Zionism as young adults to be more involved in the Crisis, but this trend was significant only at the .10 level. There was no relationship between present-day Zionist participation and involvement. Not one of the three respondents who scored the highest on involvement in the Crisis had ever been associated with Zionist movements, while three out of the six scoring lowest had been so associated (see Table 7.4).

Table 7.4 Degree of Participation in Zionism in Whole Life and Degree of Ego Involvement in the Crisis (N = 68)

Zionist participation at any stage of life	Degree of ego involvement			
	Slight (3)	Moderate (4)	Considerable (5)	Very Intense (6)
Nil or slight	3	21	11	3
Fair to very considerable	3	13	14	0

It appears that participation in Zionist activity could be an 'avocation' that has little to do with deep feelings about the State of Israel.

Finally, what is the relationship between Jewish involvement and involvement in the Crisis? In the 1967 Survey, the respondents were scored on seven composite indices each representing a facet of Jewish Identification.[8] These facets are listed in Table 7.5 together with their correlations with ego involvement in the Crisis.

Table 7.5 Correlation between Identification with Various Facets of Jewishness and Degree of Ego Involvement in the Crisis (N = 68)

Indices	Bi-serial correlation
Defence of Jewish identity	·45
Social relations	·16
Community institutions	·45
Positive emotional involvement	·53
Religion	·48
Yiddish Language	·34
Israel	·52
Total identification score	·59

All of the indices are positively correlated at a high level of significance with the exception of the Social Relations scale which bears only a slight positive relationship. This scale refers to proportion of friends who are Jewish and relative feelings of ease in the company of Jews and non-Jews. This low relationship is consistent with the lack of relationship mentioned above between involvement and mixed marriages in the family. The findings for the Social Relations scale suggest that social influences from other Jews played little part in the development of feelings of involvement.

The highest correlations with individual scales were with Identification with Israel and Positive Emotional Involvement in Jewishness; and the Total Identification score obtained by summing up all the scales had the highest relationship with degree of involvement for any measure in the study. Not surprisingly, the five respondents who indicated some signs of self-hate (e.g. 'I wish that I hadn't been Jewish') were all in the lower groups on involvement, i.e. rated 3 or 4. But even these showed some degree of involvement.

By way of summary, it might be useful to describe the cases which fell into the two extremes on involvement. It should, however, be borne in mind that those described as 'low' on this were in fact somewhat involved, albeit fairly superficially. In fact, five of the six 'low' respondents admitted to being more involved in the Crisis by virtue of their Jewish background than was the average Australian.

The three most highly involved respondents (rated 6) were all females whose mother tongue was Yiddish, and who had come to Australia after suffering under the Nazis during the War. They were all considerably involved in Jewishness and two of them were particularly religious. All three reacted to the Crisis with intense emotions, and they each showed signs of mistrust of Gentiles in general; for example, one would not put a *Mezzuzah* on her door in case of trouble. On the other hand, they were all sympathetic to the Arab people. None of them had ever participated in Zionist movements, but they all had many close relatives living in Israel. One of the three scored fairly low on the Identification with Israel scale largely because, before the Crisis, she considered that money should be spent to keep local youth from assimilating rather than to build up Israel. After the Crisis she changed her mind about the relative importance of these two needs.

In contrast to the above, all of the six who were the least involved in the Crisis were fairly low in their Jewish identification in general, and especially with respect to Israel. Strangely, they tended to be above average in their identification with local Jewish community institutions; that is, they were aware of, and participated in, these institutions even though they had practically no other Jewish attachment, not even a formal religious one. To speculate, perhaps these low involvement respondents have learnt how to participate in an activity without giving anything of their emotions or of themselves. In support of this, only two of the six reported any emotional reaction at all to the Crisis, and this was not intense. The distribution of the other variables with respect to the low involved group was similar to that of the sample as a whole, excepting that three of them were born in Australia, and only one spoke Yiddish. The latter was also the only one who had experienced much anti-semitism in her life. Four of them, however, believed that there is a considerable amount of anti-semitism in Australia.

Effect of the Victory on the Respondents' Behaviour, Attitudes and Jewish Identification

Apart from an open-ended question on the respondent's emotional reactions to Israel's victory, there were two questions on whether the victory had any effect on his behaviour and outlook on life. The responses were rated strictly, being counted positive only if some lasting change was implied, and not just a feeling of rejoicing. The analysis is set out in Table 7.6.

The findings suggest that almost all of the respondents felt that the victory had some lasting effect on them although typically this was described as an increase in self-esteem or feelings of well-being. In one-quarter of the cases the effect was to increase feelings of attachment to Israel or Jewishness.

Table 7.6   Effect of Israel's Victory on the Respondents' Behaviour and Outlook on Life (in percentages, N = 54)

	Random Sample
1. No lasting effect (apart from temporary emotional reactions)	8
2. More positive attitude to Israel	9
3. More positive attitude to being Jewish	19
4. Boost to self-esteem, happiness (not just momentary)	48
5. Strengthened character or moral outlook	4
6. Suspicion or resentment of non-Jews; mourning of Jewish dead	12
7. Negative attitudes towards Israel or Jews	1

Some of the comments of the respondents are worth quoting:

'The War made me think that no one is absolutely safe, maybe not even in Australia.'

'The Jews of Israel can now feel free. No one can touch them. Let them live!'

'This war was like a compensation for the slaughter of all those Jews in Europe. I now know that if we would have had guns then, we would have done the same to the Germans as we have done to the Arabs now.'

The results quoted so far are based on the respondents' own descriptions of the effect of the War on them.

An objective measure of changes in attitudes due to the Crisis can also be made by comparing certain questions that were asked in both the 1967 Survey and follow-up study.

It has already been pointed out that there was an increase in the salience of Israel as a problem of the Melbourne Jewish Community.

A further question asked: 'What does your being Jewish mean to you personally?' Typical answers mentioned belonging, ancestry or a way of life. In the original survey only 2 out of 68 referred to being members of a nation or people and in the follow-up survey this had increased to only 3. In the original survey, 32 respondents mentioned feelings of pride or belonging, and in the follow-up the figure was 29. In the original study, 5 respondents gave answers suggesting that their being Jewish was a matter of indifference to them, or, even, something negative, for example, 'it only means suffering'. In the follow-up study the corresponding figure was 5. Clearly the Crisis did not change the answers to this question.

Another question asked 'What does the State of Israel mean to you personally?' Responses were rated on a 5-point scale, ranging from 'unfavourable response' to one indicating 'exceptionally strong positive identification'. The ratings on the 1967 Survey are presented in Table 7.7, together with the changes that occurred in the follow-up study. The percentage of persons who were clearly ego-involved with Israel (rating of 4 or 5 – See Table 7.7) rose from 51 per cent before the Crisis to 75 per cent after it. It will be noted that three of the four highest ratings dropped from 5 to 3, but this could be due merely to conservatism in making the ratings, for example, the response 'A homeland for Jews' might, or might not be intended to include the respondent himself. In any case, respondents who scored the maximum in the original study, could not increase their scores. Ignoring those scoring 1 or 5, we have 61 cases, of whom 27 increased their favourableness,

Table 7.7 'What Does Israel Mean to You Personally?'
Comparison between Original and Follow-up Surveys

	1967	Increase +2	Increase +1	No change 0	Decrease −1	Decrease −2
1. Unfavourable response	1			1		
2. Indifferent	4		3	1		
3. Favourable, but no ego involvement	27	1	17	9		
4. Some positive ego involvement	30		6	18	6	
5. Very strong positive ego	4			1	0	3
Total	66*	1	26	30	6	3

Total Change +14

* Two respondents did not answer the question.

6 decreased and 28 remained the same. The trend is highly significant.[9] This finding is consistent with the contention that the Crisis led to increase in the positive involvement of Jews in Israel. The change was especially marked in the case of respondents who had viewed Israel before the Crisis as something good for Jews in general, but had not felt personal involvement.

We can apply a similar treatment to two measures of involvement in Judaism. The first is the question 'Does your being Jewish play an important part in your life?' and the second, the respondents' positive or negative feelings about being Jewish. On both these objective measures of change, there were significant increases in the degree and the depth of Jewish Identification.

Involvement of the Children

The respondents were asked about their children's reactions to the Crisis. These were rated by independent raters on the degree of involvement manifested and the results are set out in Table 7.8 according to the ages of the children. There was complete agreement between the two raters in 94 per cent of the cases. The group aged sixteen to twenty-four years were by far the most involved, two-thirds of the population of this age were rated as 'considerably' or 'very intensely' involved, and, according to the parents' reports, 16 per cent of this age group actually volunteered to go to Israel.[10]

Judging from the information supplied by the parents, it appears that the late teenage and early adult groups were at least as ego-involved in the Crisis as their parents, if not more so. Their involvement may have been considerably influenced by the fact that at

Table 7.8   Degree of Involvement of Children (expressed as percentage of all children in the age group living at home)

	up to 10 yrs	11–15 yrs	16–24 yrs
Not aware of crisis	25	0	0
Indifferent or only slight involvement	54	27	13
Moderately involved	14	47	19
Considerable or intense involvement	7	27	68
N =	28	15	31

these ages they either were at school or university with other Jews or were otherwise in close contact with Jewish groups.[11]

DISCUSSION

We have established that there was a widespread, almost universal, absorption in the Middle East Crisis of June among the Jews of Melbourne. This absorption took the form of extreme concern about the safety of Israel, emotional upsets, obsessive seeking of news, constant discussion of events and taking spontaneous actions to support Israel's cause. While some of these reactions occurred in mild form among non-Jewish Australians, — especially obsession with news — the reactions of the Jews were much sharper. 90 per cent of the Jews who were surveyed believed that their reactions to the Crisis were different from those of non-Jewish Australians, and another 5 per cent were not sure.

The degree of involvement of emotions and self in Israel's struggle was quite intense in almost half of the adult Jews surveyed. This involvement began during the Crisis following Egypt's closing of the Gulf of Akaba, and its effects were still present after Israel's victory, in 90 per cent of the cases. The most ego-involved Jews were those who were born in Eastern Europe in Yiddish-speaking homes, who had suffered under the Nazis and who had prospered economically since coming to Australia after the War. Some commentators have been impressed by the effect of the Crisis on Jews who were on the periphery and we also found such cases of 'conversion', but the strongly involved people were, on the whole, those who already were rather fully identified with Jewishness before the Crisis. This applied particularly to ego involvement with Israel as a state; those who were the most ego-involved with

Israel beforehand became the most involved in the Crisis. The War had a definite effect on most of the respondents; generally this took the form of a boost in pride, but in several cases it also strengthened their attachment to Jewishness and to Israel. It was notable, however, that neither personal contacts with Israel nor participation in Zionist activities were related to a respondent's degree of involvement in the Crisis. In fact, whether or not a Jew participated in Jewish community life did not seem to have a great deal of relevance, although it had some; such participants were to be found at each extreme on involvement in the Crisis. Involvement was more a matter of attitudes than of either behaviour or of formal integration into the Jewish community.

Informal social relations and integration with other Jews played little role. The involvement was not the result of social pressures, but was a spontaneous and individual reaction. This interpretation is supported by the fact that the attendances were astounding at the rallies before the outbreak of fighting. These rallies were announced in the press with only a few days' notice and there was little time for peer pressures to operate — with the notable exception of younger people attending school or university.

This spontaneous wave of feeling was a most unusual phenomenon when it is considered that it occurred with respect to a country other than that in which the people concerned were domiciled. The studies reported in this paper can do little to explain the phenomenon. All we can do here is to describe it and to leave it to speculation to explain. One could speculate, for instance, that the continued existence of Israel as a nation had accustomed Jews to its presence, and that an affiliative attitude had gradually been built up towards it. When this country was threatened, these unconscious attitudes came to the fore and overwhelmed the person, sometimes to his surprise. Another possibility, not necessarily contradictory to the previous, is that there has been an increasing feeling among Jews that it is better to fight for one's life than to try to save it by co-operating with one's predatory enemies. This feeling is embodied in uneasy feelings about the Jews of Europe under the Nazis, and admiration for the Warsaw Ghetto fighters. As a result, there was an immediate defensive reaction to threat and a feeling of support for Israel's intention of standing up to her enemies. The earlier quotation of comments by respondents on the effect on them of the June War is suggestive in this regard. At the same time it was comparatively easy for the Jews of Melbourne to 'enjoy the luxury' of being highly involved in the Crisis, especially the wealthier ones who had the leisure and independence to do so. On this occasion the surrounding society was very sympathetic to the Israeli cause, and, from other responses we know that most of the respondents were aware of this. This might explain why those who were more highly involved in the Crisis also perceived the Australian environment as a friendly one.

Whatever the explanations offered, it seems most likely that the June Crisis had an effect on the Jews of Melbourne that will be felt for a long time to come.

REFERENCES

1. Arthur Hertzberg, 'Israel and American Jewry', *Commentary* Vol. 44 (August 1967), pp. 169–73.

2. The random sample was drawn from those originally surveyed in the 1967 Survey. Because the proportion of respondents not identified with Judaism was low, it was decided to augment the number of non-identified respondents by selecting at random a number who were not opposed to mixed marriages. See *The Jewish Journal of Sociology*, Vol. 9 (December 1967), for fuller details of these procedures.

3. Details of rating procedure can be found in *The Jewish Journal of Sociology*, Vol. 9 (December 1967), pp. 243–62, in which a fuller version of this article originally appeared.

4. This compares with findings reported by P. B. Sheatsley and J. B. Feldman, 'The Kennedy Assassination: Preliminary Thoughts and Emotions', *Public Opinion Quarterly*, Vol. 28 (1964), pp. 189–215.
According to these investigators, 54 per cent of their respondents felt like talking to someone about the assassination after they heard about it, and 37 per cent actually did so.

5. Converting this figure to the Melbourne Jewish population as a whole, this would produce something like 1,300 volunteers, making an allowance for multiple volunteers in the one household. This compares with a figure of 750 official volunteers in the community, to which should be added persons who just went to Israel without going through the official volunteer scheme. The data obtained in the sample survey are almost certainly a considerable overestimate, possibly influenced by the definition of a volunteer. The official concept is someone who signed a volunteer form, but the householder's concept was probably someone who said that he had decided to volunteer.

6. Bi-serial correlations have been used wherever possible. These were preferred to product moment correlations because of the comparatively few cases, and because of the narrow range of the scores on most variables. In each bi-serial correlation, the dichotomised variable was the one with the poorest distribution with respect to range and normality.

7. With 68 cases, a correlation of ·24 is significant at the ·05 level of probability and a correlation of ·31 is significant at the ·01 level.

8. The construction and scoring of these scales is described in detail in Appendix III.

9. Using the Sign Test to compare the increases with the decreases, the difference is significant at the ·001 level.

10. An analysis of the official volunteer application forms indicates that there were 490 from persons aged sixteen to twenty-four years. This constitutes approximately 9 per cent of the total numbers of Jews in these ages. Thus the respondents' reports represent a considerable overestimation (cf. footnote 7).

11. The most involved ages were those between nineteen and twenty-two. Of this group 11·5 per cent actually volunteered for Israel. More than half of the Jewish population of these ages are full-time students.

PART 3

The Jew in Australian Society:
Political and Social Integration

8

The Perception of Discrimination

Michael Liffman

Probably the most important and distinctive fact of Jewish life over the past two thousand years has been the inevitable status of Jews as a minority group in a larger community – a minority group in terms of its perception of itself, and its perception by the 'host' community, in terms of its small numbers, and its status as a community whose origins and traditions have generally been regarded as differing in significant ways from those of the dominant, and therefore 'host' culture.

This fact – the implications of which are so obvious as to require no discussion – is relevant to any study of Jews in Australia, in that one of the crucial dimensions of the Jewish community's existence in an Australian community will be its perception of its relations with that community. The actual nature of a minority group's interaction with its larger environment – which is, of course, basic to any study of either the minority group or the host environment – is both a cause and a result of the way in which that group perceives its environment; and it is the nature of this perception which is the subject of the present chapter.

From the outset, it becomes clear that the local Jewish community, while in no way alarmed, is somewhat sceptical of the reputed easy-going tolerance of the Australian community. When asked their opinion as to the extent of anti-semitism in Australia, only 3 per cent of the sample felt that it was non-existent, 30 per cent estimated 'a little', a further 33 per cent answered 'some' and 25 per cent suspected the existence of 'a fair amount'. Only 7 per cent felt that there was 'a great deal' of anti-semitism in Australia. 30 per cent of the sample claimed to have personally experienced anti-semitism in Australia, almost exclusively in the form of 'insult or threat'. Asked to rate the friendliness of the average Australian to most Jews, 8 per cent rated Australians 'very friendly', 38 per cent rated them 'friendly', and 42 per cent rated them 'in-between'. 4 per cent claimed that Australians were, in fact, 'unfriendly'.

Clearly, then, the Jewish community does not feel wholly at ease in the Australian environment. Such a finding would seem both predictable and understandable, even if only in terms of past experience and history, and suggests obvious questions as to which people are the most likely to perceive discrimination, and why, and the extent to which this tendency depends on, and further affects, the nature of an individual's Jewish identity and his inter-action with his non-Jewish environment.

The data resulting from the major survey made possible considerable exploration of this area, based on the 'Perception of Discrimination' Index[1] and the relationship between scores on this, and other data.

In hypothesising about the nature of some of these relationships, it might appear that the most obvious single factor influencing the degree of a person's perception of discrimination would be the actual, objective experiences of discrimination that a person has had. However, in assessing these experiences and drawing conclusions from them, a person will be acting on perceptions and judgements which will presumably depend, not only on his actual experiences, but on a number of other circumstantial and personal factors. Because an individual perception of discrimination is a subjective response of this sort, a number of difficulties arise.

From the outset, causal relationships in this area are impossible to establish. This is because hypothetically predictable and statisti-cally confirmable relationships may be spurious because they may depend on a variety of circumstances which are differently per-ceived and acted upon by individuals, in terms of factors which were not elicited by, or extracted from, the interview schedule. Or, restated in less behaviourist terms, people's reactions to circum-stances are ultimately the function of an autonomous and unique personality, and it may be false to seek, as well as impossible to find, generalised explanations for these attitudes.

This is compounded by the fact that where correlations can be shown, statistically or hypothetically, it is sometimes difficult to determine the nature and direction of any causal link which might exist. The nature of a subjective attitude such as a tendency to perceive discrimination is such that it could either be a cause, or an effect, of a certain characteristic with which it appears to be statistically correlated. Thus, a finding that those who feel the highest discrimination are those who score highest on 'defence of Jewish identity' is consistent with two alternative broad pro-positions (1) that their high discrimination perception results from their high awareness of the Jewish component of their identity (and they therefore have a greater expectation of, and sensitivity to, discrimination); (2) that their high discrimination perception results in a need for reassurance and protection from threat, which is found in a strong and reinforcing commitment to a Jewish identity. To further complicate the matter, the threat posed by a strong perception of discrimination might be equally effectively responded to by a negation of that part of one's identity which induces it – i.e. one's Jewishness. In fact, as will be seen, all these situations can be found in the data.

This suggests, as stated above, that many of these apparent suggestions are at best second-order explanations, which themselves depend on further factors, or that they are entirely misconceived and no explanation can be offered.

The subjective and unreliable nature of the notion of discrimination perception is aggravated by the nature of the questions which made up the index. People's ideas as to what amounts to discrimination may vary so that behaviour which to some people is highly anti-semitic may, to others, be only mildly so. This may in part account for the fact that Australia-born Jews see far more discrimination in this country than do people who were in Europe during the War. This relativity of standards as to what amounts to discrimination is an important factor in the picture which people have of discrimination; but inasmuch as it has not been able to be separated from, but remains a hidden part of, people's expressed perception of discrimination, it serves to confuse rather than inform.

If the individual's actual experience of anti-semitism is to be regarded as the primary influence on his perception of discrimination, it would follow that this relationship would appear in the findings concerning the respondents' war-time experience, country of birth, etc. In fact, however, rather than indicate any direct relationship the findings indicate the importance of these subjective processes whereby the individual acts upon his own experience in arriving at an assessment of discrimination in this country. Thus, there was a clear tendency for those who had been in Nazi-occupied Europe at any time (including those who had been in concentration camps), to perceive less discrimination in this country than those who had not had this experience, as shown in Table 8.1.

Table 8.1 Amount of Anti-Semitism Experienced by Perception of Discrimination (in percentages)

Amount of Anti-Semitism Experienced	Perception of Discrimination		
	Low	Medium	High
Nazi Experience			
Any Concentration Camp (N = 76)	28	26	43
Nazi-Occupied Europe after 1940 (N = 130)	29	36	30
No Nazi Experience			
Nazi-Occupied Europe before 1940 (N = 74)	30	36	31
Other Great Amount (N = 18)	27	27	43
Moderate Amount (N = 26)	25	11	60
Slight Amount (N = 98)	23	33	42

Totals in this and subsequent tables may not add up to 100 per cent owing to the computer cutting off the decimal point.

It may be then, that the experiences of these people, which must, in almost every area, have been a more extreme experience of anti-semitism than that of any other group, had led them either to be unaware of anti-semitism in this country in comparison with what they have known, or, to judge such anti-semitism as they have experienced here as being relatively insignificant.[2] Thus the effect of extreme experience seems to be, not to create a high sensitivity to, and expectation of, anti-semitism, but rather to establish a standard of what amounts to discrimination which results in a fairly modest (and probably realistic) assessment of the Australian situation.

Significantly, of those who have not had experience of Nazi anti-semitism, there was a suggestion that the greater the amount of anti-semitism which they claimed to have experienced in their lives, the greater was their perception of discrimination in this country. It may be then, that in the absence of a definite and objectively undeniable extreme experience of anti-semitism, a feeling that an individual has experienced a 'great amount' of anti-semitism may be a subjective, relative (and possibly unreliable) judgement which is as much suggestive of a general and self-fulfilling expectation of discrimination as of the actual experience of it.

This apparent tendency of those who have experienced the persecution of Nazi-occupied Europe to be less aware than others of discrimination in Australia is also reflected in the findings relating perception of discrimination to time of arrival in Australia. Those who arrived in Australia between 1940 and 1959 were slightly less likely to perceive strong discrimination than those who arrived between 1920 and 1939 and presumably had been able to avoid the most extreme conditions of the Nazi persecution.

Interestingly, those who tended to perceive the most discrimination in Australia were not migrants at all but those born in Australia. This finding is strongly confirmed when perception of discrimination is related to country of birth, as in Table 8.2. Here there is a clear tendency for those people born in Australia (and

Table 8.2 Perception of Discrimination by Country of Birth (in percentages)

Country of Birth	Perception of Discrimination		
	Low	Medium	High
Australia & New Zealand (N = 81)	25	30	42
Israel (N = 14)	14	42	42
Poland (N = 199)	28	32	37
Germany/Austria (N = 75)	32	36	29
Russia (N = 16)	43	25	30
Hungarian/Czech. (N = 52)	47	25	24
Great Britain (N = 35)	50	25	22

New Zealand) to perceive discrimination more strongly than any other group.

This seems a particularly interesting finding, running as it does counter to the logical expectation that those people coming from countries with the worst record of anti-semitism would be the most sensitive to discrimination. Instead, while to some extent this tendency prevails within migrants from European countries, those people perceiving the most discrimination in Australia are themselves Australians. Part of the explanation may lie in fairly obvious factors. Australian-born Jews tend to have more contact, in their daily life, with non-Jews than do immigrant Jews – to this extent, at least, they are likely to encounter more instances of anti-semitism. Furthermore, immigrant Jews may choose to attribute such discrimination as they are aware of to their status as foreigners rather than Jews; this option is not open to Australian Jews. Due to their greater understanding of the Australian language and idiom, Australian Jews are more likely to notice the sort of subtle, low-keyed discriminatory remark or incident which would escape the attention of the newcomer less familiar with the Australian style.

The relativity of standards as to what amounts to discrimination is no doubt very important here. Living in a society which is regarded as being free from the traditional sources and expressions of anti-semitism, Australians are probably struck by a hostile remark or an isolated incident which would be regarded by a European Jew as being trivial or commonplace.

But not only is the Australian more aware of such occurrences because of their relative infrequency and his lack of experience of more significant expressions of discrimination; he is more concerned by them. As an Australian by birth he presumably identifies himself with Australia more than does the immigrant Jew, but as a Jew he is aware of his status as a member of a minority group and the consequent possibilities of anti-semitism. Clearly this could result in a heightened anxiety, and a consequently greater sensitivity to discrimination.[3]

Another effect of this dual identity might be that some Australian Jews find that, as Australians, one way in which they retain their Jewish Identity in a situation where pressures towards assimilation and loss of Jewish Identity are strongly felt, is to feel that assimilation must be resisted, or is not an available alternative, because of the hostility of the general community.

It has been suggested above that one of the reasons for the difficulty in establishing plausible causal relationships between differing attitudes and circumstances, and the propensity to perceive discrimination, is that even where correlations do appear to exist, their nature is such that causal relationships could be shown, hypothetically at least, to work in various directions and to various effects. It is this fact that renders one of the most interesting findings of the survey somewhat inconclusive. In a number of those scales which broadly measure 'Jewishness' in various areas, there exists a general tendency for a low 'commitment' to 'Jewishness' to be associated with a low perception of discrimination, and similarly, for a high commitment to Jewishness to be associated with a high perception of discrimination. The difficulty arising out of these not unpredictable findings is that explanation for their apparent relationship can be argued in different ways. The association of low commitment to areas of Jewish concern with low perception of discrimination supports the hypothesis that those who (for whatever reason) see little discrimination in the community are therefore less likely to have awareness of their Jewishness imposed upon them by the outside world, and are less likely to seek protection from that world in a close and comforting identification with a Jewish community. However, contrary to this, it could be argued that a lack of commitment to 'Jewishness' (for whatever reason), reflects, or causes, a general lack of salience of Jewishness as part of an individual's view of the world, which may well result in a tendency not to perceive or recognise discrimination.

Similarly, the association of high Jewishness with high perception of discrimination, could be seen as indicating either the effect of high Jewishness (however derived) on perception of discrimination, or the effect of high perception of discrimination in attitudes to Jewishness.

This relationship can be seen in the Index of Religious Involvement and Observance (but with the interesting exceptions of the very lowest and highest scores on the scale) as shown in Table 8.3. This scale is a useful indication of the nature of an individual's conscious commitment to an important aspect of his Jewish Identity, and as such appears illustrative of the relationship under

Table 8.3   Perception of Discrimination by Religious Involvement and Observance (in percentages)

Religious Involvement and Observance	Perception of Discrimination		
	Low	Medium	High
0–2	31	25	40
3	34	37	27
4	27	41	28
5	30	28	38
6	31	23	43
7	26	36	35
8	43	32	21

consideration. The relationship could also be seen, although it was often fairly slight, in the Indices of Social Relations with Jews, Defence of Jewish Identity and Positive Emotional Involvement in Judaism, all of which deal with slightly different components of a person's overall Jewishness. These are presented below in Tables 8.4, 8.5 and 8.6.

Table 8.4 Perception of Discrimination by Social Relations with Jews (in percentages)

Social Relations with Jews	Perception of Discrimination		
	Low	Medium	High
Low (N = 153)	36	34	30
Medium (N = 136)	29	37	34
High (N = 215)	32	28	40

Table 8.5 Perception of Discrimination by Defence of Jewish Identity (in percentages)

Defence of Jewish Identity	Perception of Discrimination		
	Low	Medium	High
Low (N = 110)	39	28	33
Medium (N = 196)	31	33	36
High (N = 198)	30	33	37

Table 8.6 Perception of Discrimination by Positive Emotional Identification with Judaism (in percentages)

Positive Identification with Judaism	Perception of Discrimination		
	Low	Medium	High
Low (N = 174)	33	36	31
Medium (N = 205)	32	30	38
High (N = 125)	31	32	37

Of these three, the relationship was most apparent in the Social Relations scale, which measured the extent of the respondents' social contact with non-Jews; the pattern remained clear in the Defence scale, which investigated the extent to which respondents valued and wished to maintain their formal identity as Jews, and was much weaker in the Emotional Involvement scale which sought to measure the more subjective and elusive factor of the individual's own reaction to the fact of his Jewishness.

The general picture, then, is that awareness of discrimination increases with awareness of Jewishness. However, one interesting qualification must be made to this statement. In a number of areas it appears that those people at the lowest point of the attitude scale, i.e. those people with the lowest commitment to Jewishness, break down into two groups of unusually low, and unusually high perception of discrimination. Thus they deviate from the general pattern inasmuch as considerable proportions of the low Jewishness section perceive high discrimination, in addition to the considerable number who, in accordance with the general pattern, perceive low discrimination. This is particularly the case with the Religious Involvement and Observance scale and the self-rating on religiousness questions, where opposition to religion is clearly associated with a high perception of discrimination. This suggests that an extremely low commitment to Judaism may, in accordance with the general explanation advanced above, be a cause, or a result, of low perception of discrimination; but also that low commitment to Jewishness may be a result of a very high perception of discrimination in the community, and a consequent desire to reject that aspect of one's identity which appears to elicit this response. It is this latter logic which may explain this apparent tendency for a high proportion of those rating lowest on Jewish religion scales to perceive high discrimination, in spite of the general pattern of low Jewishness to be clearly associated with low discrimination perception.

At the highest extreme of these two scales measuring commitment to Jewish religion, a similar tendency is apparent. Contrary to the more general pattern, those people expressing the highest commitment to religion perceive, in unusually high proportions, only low discrimination. This may be explained by the suggestion that in some cases an extremely strong commitment to a Jewish identity provides a protective and insulating sense of group solidarity and closeness which does not allow the intrusion of feelings of threat from a largely irrelevant outside world.

The general picture, then, is a complex and unhelpful one. The attitude a person has to his Jewishness may determine the way in which he sees the outside world, or it may be determined by it. The relationship can operate in a number of ways, and the data do not allow any specific hypotheses to be tested. The general tendencies are fairly constant and predictable, and suggest that the extent of a person's perception of discrimination varies with the extent of his identification with Jewishness.

In addition, there is a tendency for extreme commitment to, or rejection of, Jewishness, to be associated with extremes of discrimination perception, in a way which suggests that a number of interesting relationships may operate in this area. (Lack of relevant data, however, prevent further exploration of these possibilities, particularly in view of the very small numbers of people [in absolute terms] who fall into these extreme response categories. This latter fact also suggests that the reliability of these figures may not be high.)

Table 8.7 Perception of Discrimination by Defence of Jewish Identity Holding Country of Origin Constant (in percentages)

Country of Birth:	Australia/N.Z.			British Isles			Poland			Germany/Aust.			Hung./Czech.		
							Perception of Discrimination								
Defence of Jewish Identity	Low	Med.	High	Low	Med.	High	Low	Med.	High	Low	Med.	High	Low	Med.	High
Low	35	35 (20)	30	80	0 (5)	20	27	35 (26)	38	45	29 (31)	26	50	17 (18)	33
Medium	22	26 (31)	52	59	29 (17)	12	26	29 (72)	45	28	41 (29)	31	42	37 (19)	21
High	23	33 (30)	44	31	31 (13)	38	33	33 (101)	33	20	40 (15)	40	53	20 (15)	27

An important fact arising out of this pattern is that while the relationship of people's perception of discrimination to their attitudes to their Jewishness is clearly evident, it remains very much subsidiary to another different variable – that of country of birth. As shown earlier, one of the most striking relationships is that between country of birth and perception of discrimination. Nevertheless, the relationship between Jewishness and perception of discrimination persists when country of birth is held constant, as in Table 8.7. Thus comparison of Australian-born with subjects born elsewhere on the Defence of Jewish Identity scale shows that, while within most countries the general relationship of Jewishness to perception of discrimination prevails (i.e. perception of discrimination increases with Jewishness), the earlier finding that Australian respondents rank highest on discrimination perception is also confirmed strongly.

Another significant relationship arising out of the findings is between occupation and discrimination perception, where it appears that the higher the level of a person's occupation (according to the conventional criteria employed in such assessments), the higher the amount of discrimination perceived.

Table 8.8   Perception of Discrimination by Occupation (in percentages)

Occupation	Perception of Discrimination		
	Low	Medium	High
High Managerial and Professional (N = 112)	24	33	40
Lower Managerial and Admin. (N = 146)	31	32	32
Skilled Supervisory non-Manual (N = 143)	31	34	31
Lower non-Manual (N = 28)	38	21	38
Skilled Manual (N = 45)	35	31	32
Unskilled Semi-skilled Manual (N = 20)	45	30	25

Again, the data permit little more than speculation about the reasons for this. Higher occupation Jews have more contact with non-Jews in the course of their professional activity and thus presumably experience, and are aware of, a greater amount of discrimination. Professional, managerial and business occupations, by their nature, are more competitive, and could be expected to create tension which might be expressed, or perceived, in discriminatory terms. Australians are more strongly represented in the higher occupations, and therefore the greater tendency of those occupations to perceive discrimination is in part a reflection of the tendency of Australian Jews generally to perceive higher discrimination. People in higher occupations tend to be greater organisation 'joiners', and this fact may be reflected both in higher membership of Jewish communal organisations and congregations, and in a more general higher awareness of a Jewish Identity, which in turn, as has been seen, is related to a greater awareness of discrimination. People in higher occupations have generally had more years of education, and, although the figures for the total sample are somewhat inconclusive on this point,[4] there is a strong tendency for perception of discrimination to increase with length of education for those born in Australia, the British Isles, and Germany and Austria. (Explanations for this fact appear rather elusive; but in many ways the highly educated sample will be the same as the high occupation sample and the same factors are likely to be operative.)

In exploring patterns of discrimination perception, it appears difficult to construct an overall picture. It appears that the extent to which a person will perceive discrimination in the community is a personal response arising out of a combination of a number of factors. In part, the propensity to perceive discrimination may be a direct result of a person's experiences or situation – thus a person whose Jewishness is an important part of his identity will tend to be more aware of discrimination; as will a person whose occupation brings him into greater friction engendering competition with non-Jews. In part, it will be a result of the way in which a person's experiences act upon his expectations of discrimination, and his standards as to what constitutes discrimination. Thus the Australian Jew, used to a relatively benign environment, is more aware of anti-semitism here than the ex-concentration camp inmate. In part, a person's propensity to perceive discrimination may be not only a result of a person's history and individuality, but also a determinant of a person's situation. High perception of discrimination may constitute a threat which is reduced by a strong commitment to a Jewish identity, or an anxiety which results in a rejection of that same commitment.

Only one confident conclusion can be drawn. The way in which members of a minority group – or at least a long-suffering minority group like the Jews – see the outside society, is neither the collective and united voice of the group, nor necessarily a reliable indicator of the attitude or behaviour of that society. It is both a personal and collective assessment telling as much, at least in the short-term, about the past of those making it, and the nature and variety of individual reactions to a collective experience, as about the present in response to which it is made. The way in which a minority group perceives the world is one of the important dynamics of the interaction between such a group and the world, and like all such dynamics can only be usefully understood if viewed with respect and empathy for all participants in the total context in which it occurs.

REFERENCES

1. See Appendix III for its construction and constituent parts.

2. See R. Taft and J. Goldlust, 'Jewish Refugees in Melbourne', *Australian and New Zealand Journal of Sociology*, Vol. 6 (April 1970) pp. 28–48, for evidence indicating that they are fairly typical of the population in other respects.

3. It could be argued that an alternate reaction to this anxiety would be to refuse to admit the existence of anti-semitism in Australia. Why is this reaction not apparent in the responses of the Australian-born Jews? Is the existence of anti-semitism in Australia so demonstrable as to be undeniable, even by those who might want to deny it?

4. The Polish section constitutes an important exception here, as perception of discrimination does not increase with education for them.

9

Factors Influencing the Voting Behaviour of Melbourne Jews

Peter Y. Medding

GENERAL THEORIES OF PERSISTENCE AND CHANGE IN ETHNIC VOTING BEHAVIOUR

The Assimilation Theory

This theory asserts that occupational, educational, and geographic mobility lead to a change in ethnic voting patterns. These forms of mobility, it is argued, lead to a decline in feelings of ethnic identity and cohesion. Thus, as ethnic values change and become those of the general population, and as ethnic socio-economic class rises, their voting pattern should come to approximate the similar native class-voting distribution.[1] (It should be noted that this can only apply to an initial Left voting pattern.)

Two counter-theories have been proposed, the mobilisation theory of Wolfinger, and the non-assimilation theory of Parenti.

Counter-theory A: The Mobilisation Theory

This asserts the opposite to the former – that ethnic voting may become stronger as socio-economic class rises. This is because entry into the middle class enables the ethnic group to mobilise its political resources behind ethnic candidates. Political skills and political resources, are, it is being suggested, middle-class skills and resources. In other words, there occurs a major increase in the political salience of ethnicity, due to the appearance of middle-class ethnic political leaders and candidates, balanced tickets and so forth. And it is generally more likely that these will come to the fore in the party that has hitherto been most closely allied with the ethnic group – the Left party.[2]

Counter-theory B: The Realist Non-Assimilation Theory

This bases itself upon the distinction, well known to sociologists, between acculturation and structural assimilation. It suggests, firstly, that acculturation itself is never complete: new values may be adopted without completely replacing the old. We have discussed

141

this in detail in chapter one: in short, we can say that ethnic cultural values may be maintained side by side with the adoption of those common to the general population and continue to influence political preferences. (This is, of course, a statement of the cultural pluralist position.) Similarly we pointed out that ethnic identification need not wane with upward social mobility as suggested in the assimilation theory, and may even get stronger.[3]

JEWISH POLITICAL TRADITIONS AND CULTURE

The traditional voting pattern of Jewry has been for parties on the Left. In Europe the Left and Centre-Left parties enjoyed Jewish support owing to their liberal and internationalist positions, and their more willing acceptance of Jews and Jewish rights. The parties on the Right were associated with discrimination, anti-semitism and fascism. This historical preference for Left parties, particularly in Eastern and Central Europe has also been shown to have continued in the United States where Jews have been predominantly Democrat since 1932. The historical and traditional preference has been reinforced by Jewish liberal values, and by feelings of discrimination.[4]

One of the more puzzling questions has been the relation between Jewish values, and the intensity of ethnic identity, with this voting choice. That is to say, was Jewish Left voting a result of history, tradition, continued minority situation, discrimination and social unease among Gentiles (negative ethnic factors), or did it stem also from positive ethnic involvement and specific ethnic values? Thus Fuchs has argued that Jewish values predispose Jews to liberal political attitudes and that liberal political attitudes lead to Left voting.[5] But this theory is difficult to sustain. For example, the connection between Jewish values and political liberalism has never been demonstrated with any degree of certainty. Moreover it has been found that the most religiously involved Jews, those supposedly the most involved in and influenced by the ethnic values, have been the least Left-of-Centre.[6] It may be, of course, that these values are carried by those not religiously involved, whilst the latter are more influenced in their political behaviour by the salience of other values, albeit Jewish ones.

THE POLITICAL SALIENCE OF ETHNICITY FOR JEWS IN AUSTRALIA

Historical events in Australia have made some aspects of the above issues sharper. In the 1930s and 1940s the Liberal Party and its forerunner the United Australia Party, and their leader Mr Menzies, were openly accused of anti-semitism, which was deemed to be fairly active on the Conservative Right and seen in discrimination in exclusive elite, social, business and golf clubs, and in the exclusion of Jews from the Melbourne Stock Exchange. This, in spite of the fact that the only Jewish parliamentarians were politically on the Right. Conversely, Labor gained support through Dr Evatt's key role at the United Nations in the establishment of Israel, and through Mr Calwell, who as Minister of Immigration, made possible Jewish migration after the war.

Twenty years of continuous Liberal rule have blotted out some of the memories of these past contributions. Moreover, many Jews migrated to Australia after the Liberals came to power in 1949. Their political experience, and that of their fellow-ethnics already here, was that the Liberal government continued Jewish migration, gave strong support to Israel, and to the plight of Soviet Jewry. Liberal Prime Ministers and various other Ministers have been publicly and ceremonially honoured by the Jewish community, and they have responded fulsomely (see Mr Gorton's statement in chapter 1). The result was that there no longer seemed to be any differences between the parties as regards their attitude to Jewry.

A limited amount of research has been carried out in the past in Melbourne seeking to examine Jewish voting preferences. Thus in 1947 Taft found that 75 per cent of his sample of Melbourne Jews who were prepared to state how they voted supported Labor.[7] Similarly, Medding found that in 1958 and 1961 approximately two-thirds of Melbourne Jews supported the ALP.[8]

Our 1967 Survey provided a further opportunity to examine some of these questions, particularly the effects of increasing acculturation and socio-economic mobility, and the changed historical conditions for Jews in Australia and overseas upon their political preferences.

These general observations gave rise to the following hypotheses for empirical investigation and analysis:

1. That Jews will be predominantly Left-of-Centre in their voting choice, which would represent the continuation of the traditional ethnic voting preference (EVP);
2. That EVP will be directly related to European origin;
3. That EVP is directly related to the degree of ethnic insecurity and perception of discrimination in Australia (negative ethnic group involvement);
4. That EVP is directly related to political liberalism;
5. That EVP is directly related to religio-ethnic identification (positive ethnic group involvement);
6. That as socio-economic status rises EVP will decline;
7. That Australian birth leads to a decline in EVP;
8. That EVP will decline as the degree of structural integration increases;
9. That EVP will decline as the degree of cultural integration and degree of satisfaction with Australian life increases.

FINDINGS

The Predominance of Left-of-Centre Voting

For this to hold, we would have to find that more Jews vote Labor than Liberal. As we can see from Table 9.1, this is so for both men and women, although the Labor vote is barely stronger than that for the Liberals.

Table 9.1 Voting Preference at 1966 Federal Elections of Melbourne Jews by Sex Compared with Victorian Population (Gallup Poll, February 1967) (in percentages)

Vote	Males	Females	Total	Gallup Poll
ALP	40·8	42·8	41·9	36·1
LCP	40·4	38·7	39·5	48·3
DLP	1·3	1·5	1·4	7·0
Other	0·4	1·1	0·8	1·1
Don't know, Informal, Not voted	2·6	2·2	2·4	2·0
Not registered	4·7	4·8	4·7	
Not answered	9·8	8·9	9·3	5·6
N	(235)	(269)	(504)	

ALP Australian Labor Party (Labor)
LCP Liberal Country Party (Liberal)
DLP Democratic Labor Party

When we compare the Labor and Liberal preferences by excluding all other responses we find that the Labor vote captures a bare majority of voters as shown in Table 9.2.

Table 9.2 Vote by Sex (in percentages)

	ALP	LCP	N
Male	50·4	49·6	(191)
Female	52·5	47·5	(219)

To see this predominance of Labor voting in proper perspective, it is useful to compare this distribution with a Gallup Poll survey for the same period as shown in the last column of Table 9.1. This demonstrates that the Jewish support for Labor is clearly in excess of that for the general Victorian population.

Not only is Labor voting among Jewry higher than among the general population, it must be also noted that this occurs despite the higher socio-economic status of the Jewish sample as evidenced by Table 9.3. Whereas less than one-tenth of the general population are to be found in the two highest occupational groups, just over half of Melbourne Jews were situated there.

We may thus conclude that Melbourne Jews are more favourably disposed to Left-of-Centre political parties (the ALP) than the rest of the general population, and that this is so despite a strikingly

Table 9.3 Comparison of Socio-economic Distributions of General Victorian Population and Melbourne Jewry (in percentages)

	Melbourne Jewry	Victorian Population (Gallup)
Professional & High Managerial	22·2	4·4
Small Business	29·0	3·7
White Collar	33·9	24·1
Skilled Workers	8·9	32·3
Unskilled, Semi-skilled	4·0	24·2
Farm Owners	—	5·6
Farm Laborers	—	2·3
Others, Don't Work	2·0	3·3
N	(504)	

higher socio-economic status which ought to dispose them to be predominantly Right-of-Centre. We have therefore established the continuation among Melbourne Jewry of the traditional EVP for Left parties. (Below we shall return to the relationship of socio-economic status to voting, and we will examine its influence upon EVP more closely.)

That EVP will be directly related to European origin

The empirical evidence verifying this hypothesis is shown in Table 9.4.

Table 9.4 Vote by Country of Origin (in percentages)

Country of Origin	ALP	LCP
Poland (N = 161)	65	35
Germany/Austria (N = 63)	56	44
Hungary/Czechoslovakia (N = 40)	35	65
Significant at ·001 level using chi-square test		

The figures bear out our hypothesis for Poland, and Germany/Austria. Jews born in Hungary and Czechoslovakia, on the other hand, are predominantly Liberal in their voting support, which replicates a previous finding.[9] Jewish support for Left parties was strongest in Eastern Europe, and Germany and Austria, and was brought to Australia by the migrants from those countries. It was strongly reinforced by the experience of the 1933–45 period when Jews in Europe suffered from the Fascist Right-Wing Nazi persecution and the attempted Final Solution. For Jews from Hungary and Czechoslovakia, however, the fear of Communism, forcing their immigration from there, was super-imposed upon this historical memory, and has left its impact in a flight from Left-wing politics (including the ALP) because of its supposed associations with Communism. This came out strongly in the interviews.

That EVP will be directly related to the degree of ethnic insecurity and perception of discrimination in Australia (negative ethnic group involvement)

This hypothesis was tested by an Index of Perception of Discrimination (see Appendix III). This measure clearly demonstrated the correctness of our hypothesis of a direct relation between perception of discrimination and Left-of-Centre voting, as shown in Table 9.5.

Table 9.5 Vote by Perception of Discrimination (in percentages)

Perception of Discrimination	ALP	LCP
Low (N = 129)	40	60
Medium (N = 132)	53	47
High (N = 149)	60	40

Significant at ·01 level using chi-square test

That EVP is directly related to political liberalism

As a measure of political liberalism involving humanitarianism, and attitudes to problems with overtones of colour and race we used a single question, 'Do you think the Government should allow Asian immigrants into Australia on the same basis as European migrants?' While no strong claims can be made for a single question as an index of overall political liberalism (if such an index can be constructed), it does discriminate strikingly between Labor and Liberal supporters as shown in Table 9.6, demonstrating that political liberals are more likely to vote for a Left party. To put these figures in proper perspective it might be noted that approximately 25 per cent of a nation-wide sample in 1967 supported the immigration of Asians on equal terms to Europeans, as compared with about 56 per cent for our sample.[10]

Table 9.6 Vote by Political Liberalism (in percentages)

Asian Migration	ALP	LCP
Same as Europeans (N = 227)	60	40
Not same as Europeans (N = 152)	40	60

Significant at ·001 level using chi-square test

That EVP is directly related to the degree of religio-ethnic identification (positive ethnic group involvement)

Subjects were rated on an Index of Religious Involvement and Observance (see Appendix III). Table 9.7 shows that the predicted relation is not proven and that there is an inverse relationship between Religious Involvement and Observance, and Labor voting.

Table 9.7 Vote by Religious Involvement and Observance (in percentages)

Religious Observance		ALP	LCP
Low	(N = 97)	62	38
Medium	(N = 234)	50	50
High	(N = 79)	43	57

Significant at ·05 level using chi-square test

A number of factors explain this finding. Among those with a low level of Religious Observance, generally speaking secular Jews, are to be found many who regard themselves as ideologically committed to socialism of both Bundist and Zionist varieties. Religion and secular socialism are thus alternatives. This group heavily weights the low religious observers towards Left-of-Centre voting. On the other hand, amongst religiously observant Jews such factors as opposition to atheistic socialism, and communism, general conservatism and reluctance to change, help to produce this Right-of-Centre response. Thus when we took an even stricter test of religious observance, strictly Orthodox Sabbath observance, we found that 67 per cent in this group voted Liberal (N = 30). In Melbourne, moreover, certain leading Rabbis have publicly expressed support for incumbent Liberal politicians who have assisted the religious educational institutions with which they are connected, and this too must have had some impact.

That as socio-economic status rises the degree of EVP will decline

Our earlier figures suggested that Jews as a whole, despite relatively high socio-economic status, are predominantly Left-of-Centre. But these overall figures do not tell us anything about the effects of socio-economic status upon voting. While the group as a whole may be predominantly Labor, there might be widespread variations between different socio-economic groups. As shown in Tables 9.8 and 9.9, this is in fact the case: Labor voting declines as socio-economic status (as measured by occupation, and by class

Table 9.8 Vote by Occupation for Melbourne Jews compared with February 1967 Gallup Poll* (in percentages)

Occupation	Melbourne Jews		Gallup Poll	
	ALP	LCP	ALP	LCP
Professional, Higher Managerial (N = 97)	38	62	16·6	83·4
Administrative (Small Business) (N = 130)	48·5	51·5	35·8	64·2
Non-Manual (White Collar) (N = 131)	56	44	32·6	67·4
Manual (Skilled & Unskilled) (N = 45)	78	22	55·8	44·2

Significant at ·001 level using chi-square test

* Recalculated to exclude those voting otherwise.

Table 9.9 Vote by Class Self-identification for Melbourne Jews compared with May 1967 Gallup Poll* (in percentages)

Class Self-Identification	Melbourne Jews		Gallup Poll	
	ALP	LCP	ALP	LCP
Upper (N = 51)	37	63	21	79
Middle (N = 268)	47	53	35	65
Lower (N = 73)	78	22	61	39
Significant at ·001 level using chi-square test				

* Recalculated to exclude those voting otherwise.

self-identification) rises. This finding is directly contrary to at least one study in the United States, which found that Jews with higher socio-economic status were more Left-of-Centre than those with lower socio-economic status.[11]

Again to put these findings in proper perspective it is useful to compare the figures for occupation and class self-identification with Gallup Poll figures. While we have shown that the tendency to vote Labor declines as occupational status and class self-identification rise (corresponding to a similar general relationship in most industrial societies), it should be noted at the same time that Jews differ markedly from the general Australian population in the way in which this relationship develops. This is seen clearly in Tables 9.8 and 9.9.

The differences are unmistakable. The point at which a majority of Jewish voters prefers Labor is higher up the socio-economic scale than among the general population. Among Jews the Labor vote is close to half in the small business section, whereas the same group in the general population is only 30 per cent in favour of Labor. Moreover, the Labor vote, even when less than a majority, is considerably higher among Jews than among non-Jews at all socio-economic levels. This should not detract from the major finding, however, that voting among Jews *is* influenced by socio-economic status, even though the socio-economic status must be higher among Jews before the EVP ceases to be predominant.

That Australian birth leads to a decline in EVP

This follows from our assumption that the salience and relevance of the Jewish political experience in Europe which helped to produce predominantly Left-of-Centre voting, has waned in Australia. This is borne out by our finding that 36 per cent of those born in Australia/New Zealand voted ALP and 64 per cent LCP (N = 70). To be kept in perspective this should be compared with Table 9.4 on page 145.

That EVP will decline as the degree of structural integration increases

By structural integration we mean the degree of entry into personal friendship with non-Jews. The assumption is that the more that Jews come into contact with non-Jews the more likely they are to adopt the political stance of the rest of the society, which is far less Labor inclined. As a result EVP will decline. On the other hand, Jews who restrict their social friendships to other Jews, that is, are not structurally assimilated, will find their EVP being reinforced within the cultural and friendship boundaries of the ethnic group. Table 9.10 clearly bears out this hypothesis.

Table 9.10	Vote by Friendship with Non-Jews (in percentages)		
Non-Jewish Friendships		ALP	LCP
None	(N = 155)	60	40
Limited	(N = 169)	53	47
Extensive	(N = 86)	35	65
Significant at ·01 level using chi-square test			

That EVP will decline as the degree of cultural integration and satisfaction with Australian life increases

This was tested by an Index of Identification with Australia (see Appendix III). The assumption is that as Jews identify more with Australia, their voting will take on more of the characteristics of the surrounding society, which in our case should lead to increased Liberal voting. This assumes of course that political issues are not perceived as ethnically salient, or relevant, nor closely related to political party choice, and that there is little or no difference between the parties in their attitude to Jews or issues of direct Jewish political interest. It assumes also that EVP is strongest during the earliest period of residence in a new country, when the degree of acculturation is at its lowest. Table 9.11 bears out these assumptions.

Our analysis to date has proceeded at the fairly uncomplicated level of separately checking a number of hypotheses relating to

Table 9.11	Vote by Identification with Australia (in percentages)		
Degree of Identification		ALP	LCP
Low	(N = 55)	76	24
Medium	(N = 214)	56	44
High	(N = 141)	35	65
Significant at ·001 level using chi-square test			

voting preference. In so doing we found that certain factors were associated with the tendency to maintain the EVP and vote Labor, whilst others were associated with the breakdown and decline in EVP and the consequent Liberal preference. We now turn to a second level of analysis which will consist of further examination and testing of these findings by holding other variables constant, and particularly by investigation of situations where individuals were simultaneously subject to conflicting variables, e.g. high perception of discrimination and a high degree of identification with Australia. Although we held all these variables constant in turn, in addition to others, such as age, sex, and education, we shall report only those findings which alter the original relationships and not those which maintain or reinforce them in the predicted directions.

National Origin

Briefly recapitulating, we found that Poles and Germans/Austrians tended to vote Labor, while Australian-born and Hungarians and Czechoslovakians voted Liberal.

One of the first questions that arises in relation to this finding is the durability of the traditional EVP. Does it erode in one generation, or does it take longer? That is to say, do all Australian-born exhibit a greater propensity to vote Liberal, irrespective of how long their forebears have been in Australia, and from where they came? Table 9.12 sheds considerable light upon these questions.

Table 9.12 Vote by Birth in English-speaking* Country Holding Parents' Country of Origin Constant (in percentages)

Subjects English-speaking Birth	ALP	LCP
Both Parents born in		
Eastern Europe (N = 32)	53	47
English speaking Country (N = 37)	11	89
Significant at ·001 level using chi-square test		

* This includes all those born in Australia/New Zealand, Britain and other English-speaking countries. Altogether there were 85 subjects born in Australia/New Zealand, and 35 born in Britain and other English-speaking countries. We felt free to combine them at this juncture to test the above relationship, for two reasons: first, exactly the same proportion of the second group, 36 per cent (N=28), voted ALP as among Australian/New Zealand-born; and second, the European Jewish political experience was equally removed from all of them.

Table 9.12 can be taken at two levels. We may say simply that the traditional East European preference for Left-of-Centre parties is not eroded completely in one generation: it seems that it takes two or more generations for this to occur. But at a deeper level these figures represent the continuation and maintenance of the East European preference for Left-of-Centre parties. The English-speaking children of English-speaking parents had little contact, if any, with the traditional EVP. Many of them, moreover, belong to that group of 'Anglicised' Jews of predominantly British and German origin who came of age in Australia and Britain in the 1920s and 1930s, and who sought to be 'more British than the British'. Politically, this manifested itself in a strong Right-of-Centre voting preference. Some of their leading members in Australia (Sir Archie Michaelis, the Hon. H. I. Cohen and Colonel H. E. Cohen) were Right-of-Centre parliamentarians. In many other ways, too, they sought to minimise ethnic distinctiveness, so that they were most unlikely to maintain any traditional Jewish ethnic political preference.[12]

The English-speaking children born of East European parents, on the other hand, although less strongly Left-of-Centre than those born in Eastern Europe, are still more likely to vote Labor than Liberal in about the same proportions as German and Austrian Jews. Put in other words, the traditional voting patterns have maintained themselves among the new generations born in Australia, and birth in Australia alone is not sufficient to erode that preference.

Other major qualifications to these findings come when levels of friendship with non-Jews, degree of identification with Australia, perception of discrimination, political liberalism, and occupation were held constant, as we see below in the following tables.

Table 9.13 Vote by Country of Origin Holding Level of Friendship with Non-Jews Constant

| Country of Origin | Friendship with Non-Jews | | | | | | | | |
| | None | | | Limited | | | High | | |
	ALP %	LCP %		ALP %	LCP %		ALP %	LCP %	
Australia/N.Z.	38	62	(13)	39	61	(31)	31	69	(26)
Poland	68	32	(78)	66	34	(67)	44	56	(16)
Germany/Austria	64	36	(22)	59	41	(27)	36	64	(14)

Table 9.13 shows that at all levels of friendship with non-Jews, Jews born in Poland and Germany/Austria, are consistently higher in their EVP than are Jews born in Australia. On the other hand, however, where there is extensive structural integration with non-Jews, the preference for Labor among Poles and Germans/Austrians declines, and national origin is no longer associated with majority Left-of-Centre support.

Table 9.14 demonstrates that for Poles and Germans/Austrians, EVP is maintained at all levels of identification and despite the

Table 9.14 Vote by Country of Origin Holding Identification with Australia Constant

Country of Origin	Degree of Identification with Australia								
	Low			Medium			High		
	ALP %	LCP %		ALP %	LCP %		ALP %	LCP %	
Australia/N.Z.	—	—*		69	31	(13)	27	73	(55)
Poland	82	18	(38)	62	38	(95)	50	50	(28)
Germany/Austria	—	—*		56	44	(36)	52	48	(21)

* Too few cases for analysis.

predicted decline in Labor voting as degree of identification increases, a majority in both groups still votes Labor. The Australian-born response is interesting. The High Identified group behaves as predicted, but is at the middle level that a problem arises. This group is higher in ALP support than the other national groups with a similar degree of identification. A possible explanation for this phenomenon is that Australian-born Jews, in a situation where the vast majority of their fellows are in the High Identified group register a strong ALP vote as a protest against their feelings of dissatisfaction about life in Australia and relatively lower degree of cultural integration. This dissatisfaction would perhaps be more strongly felt than among European migrants whose level of expectation is lower. This is reinforced by the fact that English-speaking born of East European parents make up over three-fifths of the Medium Identified group, but less than one-fifth of the High Identified group.

When levels of discrimination were held constant the national groups behaved as predicted. Poles were consistently above 50 per cent in their Labor voting, and Australian-born consistently below it. The major exception is the German-born group where a low perception of discrimination breaks down EVP and we find only 41 per cent of this group voting ALP (N = 22). So too, when political liberalism was held constant, as shown in Table 9.15.

Table 9.15 Vote by Country of Origin Holding Political Liberalism Constant

Country of Origin	Same as Europeans			Asian Migration Not same as Europeans		
	ALP %	LCP %		ALP %	LCP %	
Australia/N.Z.	32	68	(31)	33	67	(33)
Poland	71	29	(100)	56	44	(45)
Germany/Austria	66	34	(35)	41	59	(27)

The major exceptions to predicted behaviour are German-born who oppose Asian migration, among whom the traditional EVP was broken down and less than a majority supported the ALP. These two findings together suggest that German-born Jews can be divided into two groups. There are firstly those for whom discrimination against Jews is still salient, and for whom the ideals of political liberalism are still highly relevant. As might be predicted this group remains staunchly Left-of-Centre in its voting. On the other hand there is a second group for whom discrimination is no longer salient, and who are not politically liberal and amongst these the traditional EVP has disappeared.

Finally, when occupation was held constant, the expected voting differences were found within all national groups, with the exception of Polish-born in Professional and High Managerial occupations. Here occupational mobility had produced a decline in the traditional Labor preference, to the extent that only 41 per cent of this group voted Labor (N = 27), which was little more than the Australian-born Professional and Managerial group.

Perception of Discrimination

Here our findings were unambiguous; when every other variable was held constant the Labor vote consistently increased as the perception of discrimination increased. This suggests strongly that arguments linking Left-of-Centre EVP with negative ethnic group identification, minority feeling, and insecurity are valid.

Political Liberalism

We found above, a direct relationship between liberal attitudes to Asian migration and ALP voting. This relationship was maintained as each variable in turn was held constant, with only one exception, the Australia-born. Here political liberalism made no difference; among those supporting Asian migration 32 per cent voted ALP (N = 31), whilst 33 per cent of those opposing Asian migration voted ALP (N = 33). This fits in with our previous argument that the degree of acculturation and Australian birth is likely

Table 9.16 Vote by Political Liberalism Holding Birthplace of Subject and Parents Constant

	Subject Born in English-speaking country Parents Born in					
	Eastern Europe			English-speaking Country		
	ALP %	LCP %		ALP %	LCP %	
Asian Migration						
Same as Europeans	62	38	(13)	19	81	(16)
Not same as Europeans	47	53	(17)	0	100	(19)

to alter traditional ethnic political values in the direction of greater similarity with the general population.

But further refinement is introduced when we compare the responses of those born in English-speaking countries, of East European parents, with those of English-speaking parents, as shown in Table 9.16.

Table 9.16 makes it clear when parents' place of birth is held constant, political liberalism still does make a difference in the predicted direction, and is positively related to Labor support. On the other hand, support for the Right among Jews whose parents were born in English-speaking countries is nevertheless so overwhelming that the quantitative impact made by political liberalism is negligible, and hardly increases the size of the pro-Labor vote.

Religious Observance and Involvement

Our earlier analysis suggested that ALP voting declined as the degree of religious involvement and observance increased. When our other variables were held constant this relationship was maintained except in two instances – among the Australian-born and the highly identified with Australia. This is indeed surprising as both these variables ought to operate in the direction of reducing the propensity to vote Labor. In both cases, the opposite occurred: and when these were held constant Labor voting increased. However, in the case of the Australian-born, as with other similar cases, when divided according to parents' place of birth, the predicted relationship was reinstated; that is, within each group an increase in religious observance was positively related to a declining Labor vote. Those whose parents were born in English-speaking countries were overwhelmingly pro-Liberal with about 90 per cent in the medium and high religious observance categories voting that way.

When degree of identification with Australia was held constant Labor voting decreased as degree of religious observance increased, except in the case of the High identified. Here approximately two-thirds at each level of religious observance supported the Liberal party. This high level of support for the Liberals seems to represent a ceiling beyond which increasing religious observance does not provide any further reinforcement. It should also be noted that there is a very high proportion of Australian-born among the High identified.

Socio-Economic Status

Here we found that ALP voting declined as occupational status and class self-identification rose. This relationship held when other variables were held constant except in the case of national origin.

The relationship between occupation and vote held consistently for those born in Poland but it made no difference among the Australian-born where there was a consistently low ALP vote. The figures for self-identification of class confirm these findings: the ALP vote increased as class declined for Polish-born, but not for Australians or Germans. This forces us to qualify our earlier finding about the impact of class upon EVP. The revised finding would be that class position, as it rises, brings about a decrease in the predominance of Left-of-Centre voting among Jews born in Poland (the largest single group of adult Jews in Melbourne), but that class is less important among Jews born in Germany/ Austria and Australia. That class does operate among Polish Jews is of importance in relation to overseas findings about the non-influence of class on Jewish voting patterns. But at the same time while rising class position decreases the propensity to vote Labor among Polish-born Jews, each of these occupational groups is well in excess of the comparative group in the general population. The fact that occupational mobility seems to have little impact upon the voting patterns of our German/Austrian-born subjects reinforces our previous analysis that perceptions of discrimination, feelings of anti-semitism and seeing things in class terms (irrespective of objective class position) seem to be the distinguishing features of this group.

Structural Integration

It will be recalled that we found an inverse relationship between Labor voting and degree of friendliness with non-Jews. The relationship was maintained in all cases when other variables were held constant, except for qualifications that must be made for degree of identification, and occupation, as seen in Tables 9.17 and 9.18.

Table 9.17 Vote by Friendship with Non-Jews Holding Degree of Identification with Australia Constant

Friendship with Non-Jews	Degree of Identification								
	Low			Medium			High		
	ALP %	LCP %		ALP %	LCP %		ALP %	LCP %	
None	89	11	(28)	56	44	(90)	46	54	(37)
Limited	65	35	(20)	57	43	(96)	40	60	(53)
Extensive	—	—	(*)	54	46	(28)	22	78	(51)

* Too few cases for statistical analysis.

It will be recalled that Labor vote also varied inversely with the degree of identification. Overall, the relationship between voting and friendship with non-Jews is maintained. What is significant is that belief by subjects that they have undergone only a moderate degree of identification (itself linked to a high Labor vote) clearly counteracts the expected impact of extensive friendship with non-Jews (associated with a high Liberal vote).

Table 9.18   Vote by Friendship with Non-Jews Holding Occupation Constant

Friendship with Non-Jews	Occupation											
	Professional			Admin.			Non-Manual			Manual		
	ALP %	LCP %		ALP %	LCP %		ALP %	LCP %		ALP %	LCP %	
None	52	48	(21)	52	48	(48)	60	40	(63)	84	16	(19)
Limited	30	70	(47)	53	47	(64)	63	37	(41)	86	14	(14)
Extensive	38	62	(29)	22	78	(18)	37	63	(27)	50	50	(10)

Table 9.18 suggests that overall the expected relationship between non-Jewish friendship and Labor voting is maintained. However, there is a different cut-off point for different occupations. Among Professional and High Managerial occupations where there is general lack of support for the Labor party, only those who maintain no non-Jewish friendships provide a majority supporting Labor. Any degree of socialising, however minimal, is sufficient to bring about a Liberal majority among this group. For the other occupational groups, where Labor support is higher, the cut-off point is below the next level, that of limited non-Jewish friendships. Thus among these groups it takes extensive non-Jewish friendships to break down the majority Labor support.

Identification

Here, too, when we held other variables constant, an increase in the degree of identification regularly brought with it a decline in the Labor vote. Two reinforcing exceptions stand out. While not detracting from the overall impact of degree of identification, moderately identified Australian-born Jews, and moderately identified professionals both produced exceptionally high ALP votes, 69 per cent (N = 13) and 53 per cent (N = 38) respectively. (We have already referred above to the high ALP vote of moderately identified Australian-born.) In the case of moderately identified professionals and high managerial class, the explanation probably lies in the status discrepancy. The phenomenon of lack of status consistency resulting in high Left voting as a protest vote and as an attempt to compensate for this situation has been well established in the United States by Lenski and others. A similar situation may exist here. Professionals and those in higher managerial occupations may be presumed to have a high expectation of degree of satisfaction, and cultural integration into Australian life. To the extent that they are disappointed in this, they manifest this in a high ALP vote. By way of contrast only 24 per cent of professionals with a high degree of identification vote ALP (N = 50).

CONCLUSION

The foregoing analysis has provided evidence in support of both the assimilation theory of ethnic voting propounded by Dahl, and the counter-theory of Parenti. (The mobilisation theory is probably less relevant to Australia because it depends crucially upon the existence of ethnic issues and ethnic candidates.) The major support for Dahl's theory comes in our findings that socio-economic and occupational mobility, increasing identification and structural assimilation do produce a decline in the strength of traditional Jewish Left-of-Centre voting patterns. On the other hand, major support for Parenti's theory is to be found in the continuing strength of perceptions of discrimination despite increasing identification and structural assimilation, in the maintenance of particular voting traditions among specific national groups (e.g. Eastern Europeans), as historical patterns handed down from generation to generation, and in the differing ways in which these patterns are eroded. Similarly, striking evidence is found for the strength of particular ethnic group values (e.g. political liberalism) and their influence upon voting behaviour. Nevertheless we could not establish any direct correlation between positive religio-ethnic involvement and voting. It seems that a two-step process is involved: group membership and involvement produces greater support for specific political values within the group than support for them among the rest of the population. These values then predispose the group, or those members espousing those values to vote in a particular way. These group political values, either derive from the general orientations of the group's cultural and religious value-systems, and are reinforced by historical circumstances, or may arise directly out of the group's historical experience. In the end, the two tend to merge; the group's experience, if repeated over a long enough period, will come to influence its values.

Thus the intensity of feelings of group membership and the forms of group belonging (e.g. strict religious observance), seem to have less effect on voting behaviour than the *fact* of group belonging, and the manner in which this exposes the group member to group traditions and values on the one hand, and discrimination and feelings of insecurity because of ethnicity on the other.

Relating this back to our specific data our analysis demonstrated the continued predominance of the traditional Left-of-Centre Jewish voting pattern among Melbourne Jewry, and isolated those factors that contributed to its decline in strength. Thus the fact that over 70 per cent of Melbourne Jews in 1947, over 60 per cent in 1961 and just over 50 per cent in 1966 voted ALP can be explained by the increase of Australian-born and of those well integrated; and of the upwardly socially mobile, during a record term in office by a Liberal party that publicly supported Jewish causes and interests, in an era of Australian history when anti-semitism and discrimination declined significantly.

Whether the ethnic preference for Left-of-Centre parties will decline further is a moot point. We have emphasised above that compared with Australians in equivalent occupations, Jews support the ALP more strongly. In the period under examination the ALP itself was at its lowest ebb in Australian political history. It is probable indeed that the marked improvement in its public support in 1969 was also felt among Jewry. In the future, ALP support could well increase if perceptions of discrimination were to become stronger, and in this context, it is significant that the perception of discrimination is not lower among Australian-born than among Polish-born (if anything it is a trifle higher). Nor will a mere numerical increase of Australian-born Jews necessarily lead to a radical decline in the ALP vote. For many years to come a large proportion of Australian-born Jews will be the children of Eastern European parents, and as we saw above they are significantly more ALP than the children of Australian-born parents. Political traditions of this kind once established often carry on long into the future. Moreover, there are limits to the upward social mobility of Jews: although never likely to reproduce the typical Australian occupational profile, it is not clear how much higher their occupational status will rise, if at all. Our figures also indicate that only 34 per cent of Australian-born Jews have more than a limited number of friendships with non-Jews, which suggests that here, too, there may be a ceiling, which will bar more far-reaching effects of close structural integration upon ethnic political preferences.

Given these conflicting pressures and the unpredictability of political life, it would be foolish to attempt to forecast the future voting patterns of Melbourne Jewry. But we can say with some degree of confidence that there will not be a steady, unilinear decline of ALP support until the Jewish voting pattern is identical with that of non-Jews in similar occupational groups.

REFERENCES

1. R. A. Dahl, *Who Governs?* (New Haven, 1961), pp. 23–5.

2. R. E. Wolfinger, 'The Development and Persistence of Ethnic Voting', *American Political Science Review*, Vol. 59 (December 1965), pp. 896–908.

3. For a statement of this theory in relation to politics see M. Parenti, 'Ethnic Politics and the Persistence of Ethnic Identification', *American Political Science Review*, Vol. 61 (September 1967), pp. 717–26.

4. Among others see L. Fuchs, *The Political Behaviour of American Jews* (Glencoe, 1956).

5. *Ibid.*

6. P. Y. Medding, *From Assimilation to Group Survival* (Melbourne, 1968), pp. 243, 256–7.

7. R. Taft, 'The Melbourne Jewish Community' (unpublished ms., 1947).

8. Medding, pp. 238–9.

9. Medding, pp. 241–3.

10. See Michael Kahan, 'Some Aspects of the Political Assimilation of Migrants in Australia', unpublished paper, Australian Political Studies Association, 1969 Conference, p. 3.

11. E. Litt, 'Status, Ethnicity and Patterns of Jewish Voting in Baltimore', *Jewish Social Studies*, Vol. 23 (1961), pp. 159–64. It should be noted that the findings of Maurice Guysenir, 'Jewish Vote in Chicago', *Jewish Social Studies*, Vol. 20 (1958), pp. 195–214, are similar to ours.

12. On this group see Medding, *passim.*

10

Party Preferences of Jewish Adolescents in Melbourne*

John Goldlust

Past studies of Jewish voting behaviour in a number of Western countries have consistently found that Jews tend to support a political party with more liberal economic, foreign and social policites.[1] In chapter nine Medding has analysed the voting behaviour of Melbourne Jewish adults. The aim of this article is to examine the party preferences of potential Jewish voters – a group of adolescents in Melbourne – with the hope of foreshadowing the direction of future Jewish voting trends. What are the major determinants of the adolescents' party choice? In a group of predominantly Australian-born youngsters, how persistent are the ethno-historical variables which strongly influence the voting preferences of many of their parents?

Party Preferences of Jewish Adolescents

The Sample

A self-administered questionnaire was distributed to 385 Jewish boys and girls in Melbourne, aged between thirteen and eighteen. The sample was drawn from nine government high schools spread through the metropolitan area (82 per cent) and three of the four Jewish private schools in Melbourne with secondary classes (18 per cent). Two groups are not represented – Jewish students at non-Jewish private schools and adolescents who left before completing high school. Combined, these two groups account for approximately 20 per cent of the Melbourne Jewish adolescents within the age group under study. 72 per cent of the subjects but only 17 per cent of the subjects' fathers were Australian-born; 52 per cent of the fathers were born in Eastern Europe and in Western or Central Europe.

* The paper is based on a chapter in the author's 'Jewish Adolescents in Melbourne', M.A. thesis (University of Melbourne, June 1969).

The questionnaire asked the adolescent subjects to identify the political party their parents usually supported and also which party they themselves would support if able to vote.

Family Influences

Studies of political socialisation in the USA have consistently found party identification to be one of the earliest learned political attitudes. Greenstein noted that some 60 per cent of his 8th grade (age twelve to thirteen) New Haven sample expressed a preference for a political party.[2] Another nation-wide study in the US reported that 84 per cent of the 8th graders gave a voting preference.[3] Moreover it appears that party identifications are adopted some time before issue differences between the parties can be discriminated.[4] Again, in a Melbourne study, Polis found that 68 per cent of his thirteen-year-olds nominated a party preference.[5]

In our survey of a somewhat older group of Jewish subjects 62 per cent had a party preference, which appears to be a significantly low figure, especially when compared with the 85 per cent of a predominantly non-Jewish sample of similar age who gave a party preference.[6] The comparison between the two groups (see Table 10.1) seems to suggest that the Jewish adolescents have less opportunity to ascertain and absorb parental political preferences.

Table 10.1   Comparison of Jewish and non-Jewish Adolescents on Selected Political Variables (in percentages)

	Jewish adolescents (N = 385)	non-Jewish adolescents (N = 124)
Hear most politics talk at home	40	47
Give parents' party preference	65	76
Give own party preference	62	85

This may be a cumulative function of two factors. Firstly, the Jewish parents seem less likely to discuss their voting preferences with their children. Table 10.1 shows that more of the non-Jewish children are likely to hear most talk about politics at home. Again, even when politics is talked at home, only 11 per cent of the Jewish subjects indicated that 'Australian politics' or 'political parties' were subjects 'usually talked about'.

A more subtle variable influencing the above results may be the internalisation by some of the Jewish respondents of the parental principle – based on European experience – that party preferences should not readily be divulged to strangers.[7] A high proportion of the parents of the Jewish subjects come from countries in which repression and terror were frequently employed against political

Table 10.2   Party Support of Jewish Adolescents and their Parents, as reported by the subjects ('no answer' and all other responses excluded)

	Party preference				
	ALP %	LCP %	DLP %	Other %	Split %
Parents (N = 230)	56·6	37·0	1·7	1·3	3·5
Adolescents (N = 219)	53·9	42·5	2·3	1·3	—

No significant difference between the two groups.

opponents and their supporters, and often remain, even in Australia, extremely cautious about divulging party support.

However, even when both parental and adolescent party preferences are given, there is a significantly lower level of parent-child consistency in party support amongst the Jewish group. Taking families where both parents vote either ALP or LCP, only 58 per cent of the Jewish adolescent respondents indicated that they would vote the same way as their parents, compared to 75 per cent of the non-Jewish adolescents who would follow their parents' preference.

This relatively high level of deviation from parental preference by the Jewish subjects favours the Liberals. While 42 per cent of both adolescents whose parents vote ALP, *and* those whose parents vote LCP deviate, because of the h avy pro-ALP preference of the parents[8], there is a slight overall gain by the LCP (Table 10.2).

Religious Values and Voting Preferences

Our adolescent study supplies further evidence against the Fuchs' thesis (discussed in chapter nine) that Jewish support for Left-of-Centre political parties represents the displacement of traditional

Table 10.3   Subjects' Party Preference by scores on 'Religious Practices' and 'Jewish Membership-Reference' Indices ('don't know' and 'no answer' excluded)

	Subject would vote:		
*Religious Practices Index**	ALP %	LCP %	Other %
Low (N = 31)	74·2	19·4	6·4
Medium (N = 102)	54·9	42·2	2·9
High (N = 86)	45·4	51·2	3·4
Jewish Membership-Reference Index†			
Low (N = 36)	69·4	25·0	4·6
Medium (N = 104)	51·0	46·2	2·8
High (N = 76)	46·1	50·0	3·9

Differences significant at ·05 level of confidence.

* The index is formed from the answers to five questions relating to adherence to Jewish religious rituals.

† The Jewish Membership-Reference index is formed from six questions relating to extent of subjects' social contact with non-Jews and attitude to limits of future contact (e.g. marriage to non-Jew). Scores from low to high indicate progressively greater social insulation, i.e. contact almost exclusively with other Jews.

religious values on to political policies. Table 10.3 indicates that the subjects who are least likely to support the ALP are those who are highest in their maintenance of Orthodox religious practices, and presumably are closest to the tenets and ethical values of traditional Judaism, and those who maintain the highest ethnic social identification, and therefore are the most likely to absorb 'Jewish values'. Thus, on both these variables the findings run directly counter to Fuchs' theory.

Class and Voting Preferences

Many of the previous Jewish voting studies have accentuated the minimal relationship of class to party preference. Indeed, for the parents of our subjects there is an extremely slight positive relationship between higher socio-economic position, as measured by father's occupation and tendency to vote for the LCP (Table 10.4). However, if we now look at the projected voting intentions of the adolescents in the same table, class appears to be a far more potent determinant of party choice.

Table 10.4 Adolescents' and Parents' Party Support by Father's Occupation ('don't know' and 'no answer' excluded)

Father's occupation:		Party supported:		
		ALP %	LCP %	Other %
unskilled	parents (N = 18)	55·6	44·4	0·0
	adolescents (N = 18)	66·7	33·3	0·0
skilled and white-collar	parents (N = 42)	64·2	35·8	0·0
	adolescents (N = 46)	56·5	39·1	4·4
smaller business	parents (N = 63)	62·5	32·8	4·7
	adolescents (N = 71)	52·1	40·8	7·1
larger business (4 + employees)	parents (N = 72)	47·6	48·2	4·2
	adolescents (N = 55)	42·1	56·1	1·8
professional	parents (N = 13)	77·0	23·0	0·0
	adolescents (N = 17)	65·0	29·5	5·5

It could be inferred that many of these youngsters are less influenced by European-based motives for supporting the party of the Left, and much more cognisant of the relationship between the policies of the parties and the socio-economic sector to which such policies have the greatest appeal.

While the children of professionals do tend to spoil the consistent trend in the table, it should be noted that despite the strong ALP preference of these adolescents, their support is still weaker than that of their parents.[9] With the exception of this group, the projected

ALP vote steadily declines in strength as we proceed up the socio-economic scale, from 66 per cent whose fathers are unskilled workers to 42 per cent whose fathers are proprietors/managers of larger businesses.

Again, when subjective class assessment is related to party support (Table 10.5), adolescents at the higher end of the scale strongly favour the LCP while their parents favour the ALP. Despite the dramatic economic rise of a large number of Melbourne Jews, especially those who arrived after the World War II, many still retain the voting preferences commensurate with their more modest origins. Their children's political attitudes, on the other hand, are more oriented to the family's current socio-economic position.

Table 10.5   Subjective Class Identification by Adolescents' and Parents' Party Preferences ('don't know' and 'no answer' excluded)

Subjective Class Identification		Party supported:		
		ALP %	LCP %	Other %
Upper/Upper-middle	parents (N = 66)	48·5	44·0	7·5
	adolescents (N = 66)	37·9	54·5	7·6
Middle	parents (N = 114)	54·4	40·3	5·3
	adolescents (N = 108)	54·6	42·6	2·8
Lower-middle/working	parents (N = 37)	81·1	16·2	2·7
	adolescents (N = 38)	79·0	21·0	0·0

However, the important difference between this pattern and that which we would expect amongst non-Jewish voters, is that the median point, at which Liberals and the ALP have equal support, is much higher up the socio-economic ladder for both the Jewish adults and their children. Only at the highest socio-economic levels do the Liberals receive greater support than the ALP.

A more indirect illustration of the effect of class emerges when adolescent party preferences are analysed by type of school attended. As the Jewish private schools charge quite considerable tuition fees, we would expect the family's economic position to bear some relationship to the type of school attended by the children. Indeed, an analysis indicates that 62 per cent of the private school subjects have fathers who are professionals or proprietors/managers of larger businesses, compared with 27 per cent of subjects from state high schools. Thus in Table 10.6, it is significant that while subjects at state schools maintain voting preferences almost identical to those of their parents, the children at Jewish private schools have switched from their parents' strong ALP preference to an even stronger LCP preference. It is in this predominantly upper-middle class, and generally more ethnically oriented group that the change away from parental voting preferences is most pronounced. In this context it is particularly interesting that the voting profile of parents with children at private schools is almost identical to that of the parents of the state high school pupils, despite the considerably higher socio-economic position of the former.

Table 10.6 School attended by Subject by Own and Parents' Party Preference ('don't know' and 'no answer' excluded)

| School attended | | Party supported: | | |
		ALP %	LCP %	Other %
Government High school	parents (N = 175)	58·9	38·9	2·2
	adolescents (N = 177)	58·2	38·4	3·4
Jewish Private school	parents (N = 47)	57·7	36·2	6·1
	adolescents (N = 42)	35·7	59·5	4·8

Differences within 'private school' group significant at ·05 level of confidence

Conclusions and Possible Implications of the Findings

1. The traditional Left-of-Centre voting pattern of Jews in other western communities is also present in Australia and appears to be the residue of the Jewish political experience of the past century rather than the natural political expression of traditional Jewish religious values.

2. The joint effect of long-term LCP government which has shown itself to be relatively friendly to Jews and supportive of Jewish communal and ethnic values (as well as maintaining a staunchly pro-Israel policy), together with a widespread socio-economic rise to middle and upper-middle class status have weakened the ALP plurality amongst older Jews and, both directly and indirectly, limited its appeal to the younger generation.

3. The Jewish youngster is less likely than his non-Jewish, non-immigrant counterpart to receive cues for partisanship in the home, and his party preference is thus frequently more consistent with other – often socio-economic – considerations. Consequently, there is an increase in support for the LCP and a complementary decline in identification with the ALP amongst the adolescents.

4. The heavy parental preference for the ALP, however, retains some influence and the youngsters projected support for this party is still disproportionately higher than we would expect from a predominantly middle-class group.

5. Under Australian conditions, the so-called ethnic voting pattern has only limited persistence after the first generation and, barring changes in Liberal Party policies adversely affecting the Jews as a group, we may expect a continued slide away from the ALP by Jewish voters and a closer approximation of the Jewish

voting distribution to that of other groups of similar socio-economic status. Whether it ever reaches this point depends on the strength of the residual factors in succeeding generations and any prediction requires future analysis of the extent of the persistence of the influence of these variables.

REFERENCES

1. Lawrence H. Fuchs, 'American Jews and the Presidential Vote', *American Political Science Review* 49 (1955), pp. 385–401. For Britain see, D. Snorman, 'The Jewish voter', *New Society*, 173, 20 January 1966, p. 13. Of the 44 Jewish members of the House of Commons in May 1970, 42 were on the Labour benches.

2. Fred I. Greenstein, *Children and Politics* (New Haven, 1965), p. 73.

3. Robert D. Hess and Judith V. Torney, *The Development of Political Attitudes in Children* (New York, 1967), p. 103.

4. See Herbert Hyman, *Political Socialisation* (Glencoe, 1959), p. 46; also Greenstein, p. 75.

5. T. Polis, 'Choices of Political Authority in Middle Childhood', B.A. thesis (University of Melbourne, 1962), p. 98.

6. The survey of 124 Melbourne secondary school children between the ages of twelve and seventeen was carried out in 1968 by the Political Science Department, University of Melbourne.

7. Of the adult Jews questioned in the 1967 Jewish Community Survey, 9 per cent refused to give their voting preference, while the Gallup Poll of February 1967 found that only 5 per cent of an Australia-wide sample refused to say how they voted in 1966.

8. An analysis of the 1967 Jewish Community Survey findings indicates that the thirty-five to fifty-four-year-old group from which almost all of the parents in our sample would come has a higher proportion of ALP voters than both older and younger groups.

9. The sample of professionals is probably extremely skewed as a large proportion probably send their children to non-Jewish private schools which are not represented in this study.

Part 4

On Being Jewish in Australian Society

11

Jewish Education in Australia

Geulah Solomon

THE INSTITUTIONAL STRUCTURE[1]

Jewish educational institutions in Australia span the whole range of education from the kindergarten to the tertiary level. At the stage of compulsory schooling, the most important institution is the Jewish day school, which is a post-war phenomenon. Most Jewish day schools are semi-autonomous, seeking to provide 'intensive' Jewish education for the societal function of promoting Jewish survival. The orientation of the majority is religious, ranging from ultra-Orthodox to the 'comprehensive religious approach' of those under the auspices of community-wide bodies like the Victorian Jewish Board of Deputies. The average time devoted to Jewish instruction is about 10 periods per week, with varying degrees of additional time drawn from 'leisure' hours. At the same time they emphasise academic success in public examinations, and tend to assume that their public status will be measured by this criterion.

These day schools are supplemented by various modes of part-time instruction: Yiddish schools;[2] right-of-entry classes in State schools; part-time Hebrew schools giving instruction on Sundays and week-day afternoons; and correspondence tuition. At its least the time schedule of the part-time student is the half-hour per week of the right-of-entry class; at its most it may equal or exceed that of the day school.

Tertiary education is available in Hebrew, Semitic and Middle Eastern Studies at Melbourne and Sydney Universities, and in Melbourne at the *Yeshiva Gedolah*, a Rabbinical Academy. The latter is an advanced rather than a tertiary institution. Its students range from those studying for at least four years and intent on rabbinical careers, to those studying for one year prior to tertiary education, or employment. Its curriculum is exclusively Jewish and concentrates on particular aspects of religious studies, mainly Talmud and Jewish Law (*Halacha*).

169

The Clientele of Jewish Education

In 1967, there were 12,128 Jewish children in Australia aged between six and seventeen years.[3] The largest proportion (54 per cent lived in Victoria, followed by 37 per cent in NSW and 9 per cent in the other states. Of these, 1876 were in all-day primary Jewish schools, and another 1101 in secondary day schools and departments, constituting 24.5 per cent of Jewish children in Australia.

In most Australian States, compulsory primary education extends from the age of six to eleven +. In 1967, therefore, only some 34 per cent of all Jewish primary schoolchildren attended day schools. Day school attendances decline on transfer from primary to secondary schooling. Only 17 per cent of all children in Victoria, New South Wales, and Western Australia between the ages of twelve and seventeen attended secondary day school classes, and in Victoria the dropout rate on transfer was 28 per cent. However, these statistics are somewhat misleading as conditions in the states are not strictly comparable. Victoria with seven day schools in 1967 was the only community with day schools up to Sixth Form standards. (In New South Wales, they included only Form 3, and in Western Australia, Form 2.)

Day school provision and utilisation was highest in Victoria. In 1967 83 per cent of those attending day schools were in Victoria. Among Jewish children in Victoria aged between six and eleven +, 50 per cent attended primary day schools, while 28 per cent of Victorian twelve- to seventeen-year-olds attended secondary day schools.

Western Australian primary day school utilisation compared favourably. Of 285 children in the six to eleven + age group, 42 per cent attended the sole day school, G. Korsunski-Carmel College. On the other hand, of the 2,005 children of primary school age in New South Wales, only 15 per cent attended Jewish day schools. In New South Wales, less than 2 per cent, and in Western Australia 6 per cent of children between twelve and seventeen attended secondary day schools. As further stages of secondary schooling are established, these proportions will probably increase.

Part-time Clientele in Australia

The corollary of a high ratio of day school enrolments is a correspondingly lower demand for part-time facilities. But a low ratio of day school enrolments does not necessarily involve higher part-time demand. It may merely mean that the community is indifferent or opposed to any Jewish education, or prefers informal home teaching. Part-time enrolments are, moreover, difficult to assess accurately. Current available statistics tend to be incomplete (some schools did not fully complete returns), others were not submitted and inaccurate (much duplication occurs in relation to part-time schools and right-of-entry classes, while some schools undoubtedly inflate their attendance figures). It is safe to say, however, that at least 80 per cent of the Jewish children in both Victoria and New South Wales who are not in day schools, receive at least some part-time Jewish education.

ATTITUDES TO JEWISH EDUCATION

The Education of the Adult Jewish Community

Those general factors which mould adult attitudes to Jewish education and influence the kind of education Jewish children receive may be inferred from data appearing elsewhere in this book. Especially important are the kind and level of education which the adults themselves received and how this affects their general religious and educational responses.

The conflict in the open society between the value systems of traditional Judaism and the host environment are particularly significant in this context. For Melbourne Jews, this is expressed as a conflict between two needs – the need to acquire Jewish knowledge for the maintenance of personal faith and group survival, and the need for secular knowledge as a source of livelihood, for citizenship, and for participation in the culture of the English-speaking world. Our study revealed that few Jews did not complete primary secular schooling, which suggests that secular schooling is widely valued. But it follows from the smaller number of adults who had obtained Jewish schooling, that Jewish schooling is held in lower esteem.

The level of Jewish education among adults confirmed the existence of a previous tradition of a 'sufficient' education culminating in the Barmitzvah ceremony. Moreover, the relationship between the education of adults and their synagogue attachment clearly indicated that tertiary secular education was strongly associated with a lessening of Orthodox commitment, while secondary (post-Barmitzvah) Jewish schooling was strongly associated with preservation of Orthodox commitment.

Overall the greater the amount of their Jewish schooling, the more likely were they to maintain personal faith and observance. This probably explains why many adults in our survey stressed Jewish knowledge as the objective of Jewish schooling, and why they desired a longer Jewish schooling for their children than they themselves received.

While philosophic considerations are of major concern to the educationist, the Survey had no direct questions concerning the nature, goals, and functions of Jewish education. Nevertheless attitudes towards the importance, desirability, and objectives of Jewish education can be deduced from other questions.

Is Jewish Education Important?

In listing the problems facing the community, education was ranked third in importance, after assimilation, inter-marriage and inner discord. That education was generally regarded as being important, and was something virtually all Jews thought about, was confirmed by the rarity of 'Don't know' replies to other specific questions about education. On the other hand, adults did not see education as the *sole* solution to communal survival, or as the community's most important single need. Thus in answering questions about fund-raising few adults (1.5 per cent) desired education to receive exclusive financial support, the majority (60 per cent) placed it on a par with communal and welfare needs. In general, therefore, education is regarded as one aspect of organised communal life, rather than as the chief activity and instrument of Jewish existence and survival.

What is Jewish Education?

Investigations of the nature, functions, desirability and objectives of Jewish education are fundamentally related not only to the nature of the Jewish community, but also to attitudes towards the nature and meaning of Judaism itself. As we saw in chapter 2, few of our subjects regarded being Jewish solely in terms of religion, nation or ethics. The majority defined their Jewishness as membership of a group defined in terms of common birth, culture, or destiny, or as a combination of a number of these various components.

The emphasis in defining Jewish education is therefore on its role in transmitting and preserving this 'common' basis of Jewishness, and suggests that Jewish education is seen as providing unity in the face of the diverse interpretations of Jewish identification found in the community. Since for adults being Jewish is principally their membership in a Jewish group, Jewish education, 'teaching and learning what it means to be a Jew' means group socialisation and group identification. At the same time, the preference for long-time Jewish continuity (expressed elsewhere in the desire for Jewish grandchildren [91 per cent], and in disapproval of inter-marriage [78 per cent]), suggests that future group survival is regarded as more important than individual development; that education is required to be future and adult-directed rather than immediate and child-centred; and that the community's social philosophy takes precedence over the educational philosophy of schools.

What is Jewish Education: Its Aims and Objectives

To specifically explore adult attitudes towards the aims and objectives of Jewish education, an opinion study of the stated aims and objectives of individual schools would have been required. In the ab ence of such an opinion study, the Survey found that the aims and objectives which the adults seek include:

1. Encouraging children to remain Jews when they become adults. Presumably this includes fostering pride and pleasure in being Jewish, ease with Jews, feelings of kinship with the community and Jews in other lands, a desire to aid and support Israel, and a willingness not to intermarry.

2. Developing understanding of what it means to be Jewish. To most adults, as we saw, being Jewish means sharing in a common origin, culture and destiny. Fostering understanding of this involves transmission of knowledge and information about the nature, development, and implications of the common origins, culture and destiny of all Jews. Principally, this is a cognitive objective, founded on the premise that there is an intellectual foundation to Jewish identification, to the acquisition of faith and values, and to practice and performance.

3. Promoting feelings of religiosity. Since about three-quarters of Melbourne Jews regard themselves as in some sense religious, this seems a logical educational objective. There is, however, a distinction between the adult Jew's rating of himself as religious, and his being religious by traditional criteria. Judged by 'deeds' such as adherence to Sabbath, to dietary laws, and to *tephillin,* the adult Melbourne community could hardly be called a religious society in the traditional sense, despite the 'last-ditch' persistence of religious rituals such as fasting on Yom Kippur or attending a Passover *Seder*, which are as much expressions of group identification as of religious ceremonial.

On the one hand, therefore, it would appear that adults desire to foster *knowledge* of traditional Jewish norms, rather than to create the normative Jew who *lives* by these norms. On the other hand, adults appear to be subscribing to a traditional concept of the function of education – that of fostering the 'normal' Jew rather than perpetuating the average one. The dichotomy bedevils many Jewish schools, faced with a clientele only part of whom see education as a dynamic process in transforming the community, whilst others want their children to 'know' but not necessarily either to 'believe' or to 'do'.

For Jewish schools, the practical implication of this dichotomy between religious principle and religious practice among adults is that Jewish subjects tend to be taught as a body of abstract knowledge, without the corollary that this knowledge is authoritative and its purpose is fulfilment in 'deeds'.

What is Jewish Education: The Content of Jewish Education

Traditionally, Jewish education is curriculum- rather than child-centred. The tendency for discussions about education to be correspondingly preoccupied with its content has been accentuated by the fact that the variety of 'modern' interpretations of Judaism has tended to fragment the traditional unity of the curriculum.

The traditional curriculum of Jewish studies was textbook- and subject-centred, divided into stages based on the study of the Pentateuch, the Mishna, and the Talmud. Whereas intellectual knowledge was the basis of the curriculum, the goals of education included both cognitive and affective objectives, meaning knowledge, behaviour, the acquisition of values, and the training of character.

In general, it is a curriculum derived from the traditional model which most Melbourne adults favour. About one-tenth of all adults believe the content of Jewish education should consist solely of classic Torah knowledge, as represented by study of Bible, Talmud, Law and Festivals, and another 40 per cent felt that these subjects should provide the core of the curriculum supplemented by other subjects.

Other adults felt that the curriculum should be primarily concerned with presenting Judaism to children as an ongoing civilisation with national connotations, by teaching subjects like Jewish history, modern Zionism and Israel, and contemporary Jewish life and affairs. About one-tenth would hav approved these subjects as he sole curriculum, and another 43 per cent would have liked them supplemented with either classical Jewish knowledge, or with Jewish (Hebrew or Yiddish) language instruction, or both.

Still others (11 per cent) felt that the curriculum should be exclusively devoted to transmitting a shared 'common culture', by the study of Hebrew and Yiddish literature in original or translation, and another 39 per cent felt that the common core of Jewish culture should be supplemented by either classical Torah knowledge (12 per cent) or ancient and modern Jewish history (15 per cent), or both (12 per cent).

The kind of curriculum which appealed to an adult was largely the product of his *Jewish personality* – of his educational background, his age and country of origin, his feelings about being Jewish, about Israel and about religion. The more sophisticated an adult's secular schooling, for example, the greater his approval of 'thoughtful' dialogue in education through subjects like Jewish history and contemporary Jewish life; the lower the level of his secular schooling, the more highly he rated the sole importance of classical Torah knowledge and skills, that is, the transmission of a fixed body of dogmatic knowledge.

The younger the adult, the more likely his desire for Jewish education to impart a broad and general Jewish education rather than concentrate on a number of distinct subject-specialities. Western European Jews laid greater stress on the importance of contemporary Jewish knowledge, while Eastern European Jews were more concerned with preserving a past-oriented curriculum. Australian-born Jews tended to lay greater stress on contemporary Judaism, including Israel, followed by language skills and literature; and Hungarian-born Jews attached equal importance to classical and contemporary Jewish knowledge.

Those who felt antagonistic to their own Jewishness presumably regarded classical knowledge as a form of religious indoctrination, and language skills as a barrier to integration, since they were totally opposed to these content-areas, favouring instead an historical and topical curriculum. In contrast, those who wanted their children to settle in Israel sought a curriculum primarily directed towards this goal, emphasising Hebrew language skills, Jewish (national?) history, and knowledge about Israel and Zionism.

The major factor in determining educational content, however, was the adult's attitude towards religion itself. Religious orientation clearly affects adult attitudes towards the content of Jewish education. Those who participated in institutionalised religion by attending synagogue placed greater emphasis on the knowledge and skills needed for such participation – language skills, knowledge of literature, and familiarity with prayers. Greatest emphasis for teaching classical Torah knowledge – the Torah-true way of life – was to be found among those who attended Orthodox synagogues, while those who never attended synagogue emphasised Jewish history and contemporary life.

Liberal Judaism, neutralism or negativism (secularism) in adult religious life were, in increasing degrees, negatively related to the inclusion of classical Torah knowledge in the curriculum, and positively related to knowledge about contemporary Jewry. History seems to be regarded as a 'religiously neutral' area of knowledge, fostering the common basis of collective existence without demanding action.

Adult attitudes towards the ideal curriculum did not include suggestions for subjects which might specifically foster objectives of personality-development, practical observance, or active participation in community life. The general emphasis was on 'what a Jew should know' rather than on 'what a Jew should be' or 'how a Jew should live'. Even among Orthodox adults, there was an

unconscious assumption that being a Jew and living as a Jew
followed automatically from acquiring intellectual knowledge.
However, the adults' assumption that intellectual knowledge is the
foundation of all Jewish identification, belief and behaviour cannot
be acted upon by the schools themselves without further examination of the uncertain relationship between cognitive and affective
objectives in teaching.

Is there an Australian Jewish Education?

In the United States, Jewish education takes cognisance, at least in
theory, of its American context by including subjects and goals
which are dictated as much by the 'American way of life' as by Jewish
needs.[4] In a general sense, all Jewish education in Australia is
also modified by the Australian environment; the Jewish school
is itself testimony to the religious plurality of the Australian society.

In Australia, however, the chief concession made to the local
context is through secular education and the English vernacular.
Although Jewish schools operate in Australia for life in Australia,
their role is seen as being less concerned with developing *Australian
Jews* as with developing *Jews*. The history of Jews in Australia,
the relations between Australian Jews and other Australians, the
administrative organisation of communities in Australia, are completely ignored in the curriculum of Australian Jewish schools.

This does not mean that preparation for life as Jews in Australia
is ignored. But it is not regarded as the function of the Jewish
school. It is transmitted rather through secular subjects and its
'social' reinforcement left to informal agencies. To some extent,
the lack of integration between the Australian and the Jewish
aspects of the Jewish child's formal education reflects the compart-
mentalisation of the Australian and Jewish areas of life. Many Jews
tend to see the Jewish aspects of their lives as quite distinct and
autonomous from the Australian aspects.

Has Jewish Education a Social Function?

Jewish adults emphatically do not desire Jewish education to create
a future 'social ghetto'. But they are ambivalent about the 'social
functions' of Jewish schools. On the one hand about 85 per cent
want their children to have some non-Jewish friends; on the other,
by supporting Jewish education, they preserve a separatist form
of schooling which fosters Jewish distinctiveness. Although it has
elsewhere been suggested that the social functions of Jewish education account for its high pupil clientele, only 6 per cent of Jews justify
Jewish schools solely in terms of Jewish socialisation.[5] Nevertheless
their concern with Jewish survival and continuity in general make it

more than likely that they are aware of, and strongly approve of the social consequences of Jewish schools, even if these are seen as subsidiary to the intellectual aspects.

The Subjects of Instruction

1. Hebrew:

Hebrew teaching in Jewish schools may be classified into three distinct but popularly-confused functions – as a modern 'living' language, as a tool for understanding Bible and Hebraic literature, and as preparation for reading prayers and liturgy. Over two-thirds of Melbourne Jews believe that Jewish schools should teach Hebrew. What, then, do they regard as its purpose?

Implicit in adult attitudes was the assumption that Hebrew is a technical tool with an instrumental value, to enable the study of other 'real' subjects like Bible and Hebraic and synagogue literature. Desire for Hebrew teaching accordingly declined, from 77 per cent among Orthodox synagogue attendants, to 62 per cent among Liberal attendants, 56 per cent among those who were 'neutral' in attendance and 43 per cent among those who never attended synagogue at all.

Less reliable information is available on the function of Hebrew as a modern language (largely due to ambiguity in the wording of the original Survey question). It may be assumed, however, that the majority of all adults indicated their desire for Hebrew to be taught as a living language. Generally, this proportion was lower among older age-groups. The apparently stronger desire by younger adults for Hebrew to be taught as a modern language may be ascribed to the greater influence of Israel in moulding the attitudes of younger people, direct contact with young Israelis, particularly teachers and emissaries, and visits to Israel. Apart from those who see education as preparing their children for migration to Israel, it can be claimed that most Jews want modern Hebrew teaching because it has more contemporary meaning for the Jew, both in terms of language and literature than any other language, it fosters kinship with Jews in Israel and elsewhere, and it provides contemporary and secular orientation to a curriculum that is heavily past and tradition-oriented.

2. Yiddish:

Melbourne Jewry is almost equally divided on the desirability of teaching Yiddish. Generally, more support for teaching Yiddish was found among women, among older age-groups, among East European Jews, and among those who attended Orthodox synagogues.

At the same time, support for Yiddish teaching was consistently lower among all categories of adults than support for Hebrew teaching. For example, two-thirds of Australian-born Jews thought Hebrew should be taught, but only one-third supported Yiddish teaching. More significantly, among Polish-born Jews, 75 per cent favoured teaching Hebrew and 67 per cent favoured teaching Yiddish.

In general, those who usually spoke Yiddish at home favoured Yiddish teaching (86 per cent). But the vast majority of those who spoke Yiddish also believed children should learn Hebrew (81 per cent), implying a general belief among Yiddish-speaking Jews that children should learn all languages which promote *Yiddishkeit* (Jewishness).

The majority of adults who advocated the learning of Yiddish regarded it as a home vernacular, not necessarily to be acquired in formal Jewish schools. Yiddish-culture schools have continued to exist because they provide a means of reinforcement; primarily, however, Yiddish is a language acquired in the home.

Hebrew, however, is a familial language only among the small proportion of Israeli-born adults, so that it *must* be 'artificially' acquired in formal schools. For this reason, the extent of adult demand for Hebrew education, and community concepts of its functions, are of vital interest to the Jewish school.

The Duration and Content of Adult Education

Jewish educational tradition regards study as obligatory for every Jew, 'whether he be rich or poor, whether he be in sound health or an invalid, whether he be young or very old.'[6] Study of the Bible and Talmud is itself the good life, to be pursued to the end of one's days.

What Melbourne Jewish adults believe should be the content of adult education bears little resemblance to the traditional model.[7] Although the core of the school curriculum was regarded as Torah-centred, very few adults thought adult education should be concerned with Biblical, or post-Biblical, religious knowledge. Most adults regard adult education ideally as a means of keeping abreast of contemporary events concerning Jewish life and Israel, or as a means of acquiring modern language skills (not formerly emphasised in their own education), or both.

Younger adults indicated a preference for adult education to concentrate on imparting modern Hebrew language skills, largely accounting in practice for the current success of modern Hebrew classes. Older adults expressed a preference for matters of historical, topical and Zionist interest. In any event, participation in adult education in Melbourne hardly accords with Jewish educational tradition. Only 4 per cent of adults actually attended existing adult education facilities. Almost half the community did not regard adult education as necessary, although proportionately more adults under thirty-five regarded it as desirable (69 per cent) than did their elders (55 per cent), and proportionately more synagogue attenders regarded it as desirable (52 per cent) than non-attenders (44 per cent). Even with a system of adult education whose content was more to their liking, only one-fifth of the adult community felt it would utilise such facilities. In short, for the majority of Melbourne Jewish adults Jewish education is the education of children. Thus, adults want for children an education whose continuation they reject for themselves.

Duration of Jewish Schooling for Children

In view of the fact that Jewish education is regarded as the education of children, what is its appropriate duration? More than three-quarters of the adult community felt that Jewish schooling should continue after the age of Barmitzvah, while only 17 per cent regarded education until the age of thirteen as 'sufficient'.

How do adult attitudes towards the duration of Jewish schooling compare with the level of Jewish education among adults? The vast majority of adults thought Jewish schooling should be of more than seven to eight years' duration. Among adults themselves, however, one-quarter had obtained less than six years of Jewish schooling, another one-quarter had obtained some seven to eight years, and about one-tenth had obtained no Jewish schooling. Generally, then, most adults believe a longer period of Jewish education is necessary for their children than they acquired themselves. At the same time, at least in principle, adults have become aware that mere elementary instruction is insufficient for the successful transmission of attachment to religious values. Accordingly, there seems to be a growing rejection of mere Barmitzvah preparation as a sufficient or satisfactory duration of Jewish schooling. Nevertheless, the duration of Jewish schooling which adults subscribe to in principle is not the duration which they obtain for their children in practice. In reality, some 25 per cent of all Jewish children in Melbourne in 1967 attended part-time schools for periods of seven to eight years or less.

What Kind of Jewish Education: Attitudes towards Educational Organisation

Most adults at least in principle preferred their children to be educated in institutions different from those which they themselves attended. The majority of adults had been educated in part-time institutions. But nearly half the adults thought children 'ought' to be educated in day schools, and only one-third favoured part-time. schools. Another 16 per cent were content with right-of-entry classes in State schools, and less than 3 per cent believed Jewish knowledge could best be acquired from parents or private tutors.

Underlying this change in organisational emphasis may have been a retrospective dissatisfaction with the type of education received by the adult and the institution at which it was imparted; a feeling that institutions appropriate in the period when an adult was educated are not the most adequate or most efficient in the present era; and the influence on the community of successful day schools. At the same time, increased support for the day school principle in Jewish education has been derived from progressive educational theories of the school's function in the socialisation, as well as intellectualising, process.

Some reasons for adult institutional preferences can be deduced from their statements of satisfaction or dissatisfaction with the education their children received. These suggest that adults are guided by the academic orientation of the school (the amount of knowledge it sets out to impart) and its academic efficiency; by the number of hours devoted to Jewish knowledge; by the extent to which children make friends; and by the degree to which affective objectives like feelings of pride and commitment have been successfully promoted. Thus, adults generally prefer the type of educational institution which they feel best fosters factual Jewish knowledge and promotes feelings for commitment and group survival.

In principle, since 'desire' is different from 'afford', socio-economic factors should bear little association to institutional preferences, as distinct from actual attendance at Jewish schools and classes. But there was a marked preference for day school education among those who could afford it, and for cheaper part-time schools among the less affluent. However, although right-of-entry classes and the State schools in which they are conducted are for practical purposes free, a larger proportion of Jews in higher status occupations preferred this form of education than did those in lower-status occupations. This links with the fact that strong associations with Jewishness appreciably affected institutional preferences. The more positive the adult's feelings about being Jewish, the stronger his preference for day school education, and conversely. Generally speaking, positive feelings about being Jewish were lower among those at higher occupational levels.

Those who wanted their children to settle in Israel strongly preferred day schools (63 per cent). There is here an implicit assumption that day school education fosters stronger feelings of Jewish identity and therefore encourages desire for emigration to Israel, as well as an overt assumption that day schools provide better preparation for Israel by modern language instruction and by employing Israeli teachers.

Irrespective of their level of secular education, adults preferred day schools to any other form of Jewish school. Similarly, day schools were the most popular in all age groups: among Jews of all origins except those born in Germany (perhaps because of its strong Liberal constituent) and among those who attended synagogue, especially the Orthodox-oriented (60 per cent in favour). However, preference for day schools declined progressively with Liberal (15 per cent in favour), neutral (37 per cent) and negative religious orientation (30 per cent), and with tertiary secular education.

Institutional Practice

The belief that day schools are directed towards religious objectives, and predominantly Orthodox religious objectives, accounts for the fact that those who attend a synagogue, and particularly those who attend Orthodox synagogues, are more likely to enrol their children in day schools. The corollary is that part-time schools enrol in rising proportions pupils from families whose orientation towards institutional religion is Liberal, neutral, or negative. This is not conclusive evidence, however, of objection on principle to day school education among Liberal Jews or neutrals. Such children might well be attracted to day schools whose orientation reflected their own views.

Among all 'ethnic groups' represented in day school enrolments, children of Hungarian, West European, Palestinian and Israeli, and Australian origin were best represented. Hungarian representation in day schools is marked high, largely as a result of the Adass Israel school, which provides virtually an ethnic religious school for the Orthodox Hungarian congregation. Australians and West Europeans have an historical tradition of denominational day schools similar to Mt Scopus College. Similarly, day schools are closest to the State religious or secular schools of Israel.

It should, however, be remembered that present (1967) enrolments in Jewish schools reflect the attitudes of *older* adults in the community. They represent no certain indication of where younger adults, aged 35 or less, will actually send their children, despite their present institutional preferences.

Evaluation of Jewish Education

From the viewpoint of the schools themselves, and of the community whose expectations may differ somewhat from those of schools, the community's assessment of educational objectives is crucial.

Unfortunately, meaningful data could not be obtained from the Survey because adults tended to confuse satisfactory achievement of their own goals with achievement by particular schools and particular children. Moreover, using an open-ended question to deal with assessment of values and goals provided inadequate criteria for adult evaluation. More than one-quarter of all parents were vague as to why they were satisfied with their children's Jewish education.

Some three-quarters of all parents claimed to be satisfied with their children's Jewish education. More than half attributed this to the child's level of achievement in factual knowledge, and to the development of positive feelings about being Jewish. Very few found the making of friendships with other children a principal reason for satisfaction, not because children had not made friends but because friendships were apparently regarded as a bonus and by-product of attendance at Jewish schools.

Less than one-quarter of adults expressed dissatisfaction with their children's education. Again the main cause of dissatisfaction was the small amount of knowledge imparted – conclusive evidence that the main objective of Jewish education is the acquisition of Jewish knowledge. Of other sources for dissatisfaction, the most frequently mentioned were poor teaching and poor organisation – in fact, impediments to the achievement of a satisfactory amount of knowledge.

It is apparent, however, from the number of parents who could not clearly express their reasons for satisfaction or dissatisfaction, that many Jews have no clear criteria by which to assess Jewish education, or leave it to the schools themselves (according to the type of school). The majority of those above who directly or indirectly emphasised knowledge as the prime aim of Jewish education preferred day schools, which suggests that their popularity derives in large part from their contribution in this sphere.

The younger the parent, the more likely was the child to attend a day school and the more likely the parent to be satisfied. Hungarian-born Jews had the highest proportion of satisfied members; the largest proportion of dissatisfied parents was found among those born in Germany and Israel; and Polish-born parents tended to be somwhat less satisfied than Australian-born parents.

Religious orientation provides a less meaningful association with educational assessment. Those who attended synagogue contained a larger proportion of both satisfied and dissatisfied parents than those who never attended synagogue at all. But exactly that achievement which satisfies an Orthodox attender provides dissatisfaction to a Liberal attender, and that which satisfies the traditionalist may be unsatisfactory to those who reject religious objectives.

The Future

This chapter has presented a brief outline of the salient features of the educational material contained in the 1967 Survey. A considerable quantity of material remains to be analysed and assessed. Much of what has been said about Jewish education in Australia, both by adults in the Survey and by communal 'experts' has been based in the past on hearsay and impression. In addition, therefore, to exploring the Survey data for its contribution to future Jewish educational planning and development, the menial task of collecting and up-dating statistical information is an urgent adjunct.

Another major task which faces Jewish educators is that of clarifying the 'philosophy' of Jewish education in Australia. Without clearly-formulated interpretations of the nature, function, and objectives of Jewish education in this country, educational reform operates in a vacuum. What schools achieve is directly related to what they see to be their role as schools, besides their function as community agencies. What they achieve is directly related to what they set out to achieve.

The Survey's success in illuminating the nature of Melbourne Jewry suggests that a survey of Jewish education would yield rewarding dividends to the community and to schools. Without information of the type which such a survey would yield, educational reform seems likely to remain the victim of individual whim and idiosyncrasy, implemented by hit-and-miss methods.

Finally, the acquisition of 'knowledge' about Jewish education through research must prove unavailing unless schools, administrators, teachers and parents are willing to adopt the traditional Jewish approach of applying such 'knowledge' in deeds, that is, to the process of learning and teaching which is, after all, the business of Jewish education.

REFERENCES

1. This section has appeared in greater detail in G. Solomon 'Jewish Education in Australia' in *Jewish Education*, Vol. 40, No. 2 (Summer 1970, New York).

2. See M. F. Klarberg, 'Yiddish in Melbourne', this volume, chapter 6.

3. Extrapolated from analyses of 1961 Census figures in Walter M. Lippmann, 'Demography of Australian Jewry', *The Jewish Journal of Sociology*, Vol. 8, No. 2 (December 1966).

4. A. M. Dushkin and U. Z. Engelman, *Jewish Education in the United States, Volume 1*, New York. American Association for Jewish Education, 1959.

5. G. Solomon, *op. cit.*

6. Joseph Caro, *Shulchan Aruch, Yore Deah*, 246:1.

7. *Ibid.*, 246:4.

12

The Impact of Jewish Education on Adolescents*

John Goldlust

A number of reported studies have examined the relationship between length and intensity of religious education, and religious or ethnic identification of Jewish children and adolescents. Unfortunately, large differences in methodological approaches, limited sampling and lack of uniformity in measures of Jewish identification adopted have resulted in few confirmed general trends amongst the findings.[1]

One unexpected finding is that while Jewish education, considered independently of other variables, promoted religious beliefs and practices, it had little generalised effect on Jewish identification.[2] Moreover, it was found that amongst the more traditional denominations there is no relationship between the amount of religious education and the respondents' general Jewish identification.[3]

Again, at the other end of the spectrum, investigators have noted that Jewish education has little impact upon children from less observant homes because the child has no parental example to reinforce the attitudes taught at school.

This chapter seeks to isolate intensity of Jewish education as an independent variable and examine its relationship to various measures of religious and social identification for a group of Jewish adolescents in Australia.

Measuring Intensity of Jewish Education

In differentiating between the subjects in terms of intensity of Jewish education received, two major criteria were applied. Those educated solely at Jewish day schools were separated from the others. Within this group we differentiated between the adolescents educated at strictly Orthodox day schools and those at the large communal non-Orthodox day school.

For those subjects whose Jewish education was obtained mostly, or entirely, in part-time classes, a scale of measurement was created

---

* This is based on material which first appeared in the author's 'Jewish Adolescents in Melbourne', M.A. thesis (University of Melbourne, 1969).

to enable them to be compared. Thus, the term 'one year' of part-time Jewish education refers to three hours per week of formal Jewish instruction per academic year.[4] On this basis, the part-time subjects were divided into three levels with regard to intensity of Jewish education, and together with the two day school groups a scale is formed. Table 12.1 summarises the division of the sample in terms of intensity of Jewish education.

Table 12.1 Division of the Sample in Terms of Intensity of Jewish Education

	Source of Jewish Education	N	%
Part-time classes	Low = weekly religious instruction period at a government school plus no more than 2 'years' of part-time classes	77	20·3
	Medium = 3–8 'years' of part-time classes	143	37·6
	High = more than 9 'years' of part-time classes	105	27·6
Day school only	Non-Orthodox day schools	39	10·3
	Orthodox day schools	17	4·2
	Total	381	100·0

Jewish Education and Religious Adherence

When the Melbourne adolescents' subjective religiosity is analysed (Table 12.2), the extreme position of the Orthodox day school subjects is immediately obvious. All of these youngsters consider themselves either 'very' or 'moderately' religious. The subjective religiosity of the part-time groups declines together with 'years' of Jewish education. On the other hand, a surprising 23 per cent of the non-Orthodox day school group see themselves as 'not at all religious' or 'opposed to religion'. This is higher than for all other groups, with the exception of the 'low' part-time subjects, who have received almost no Jewish education.

Looking at Table 12.2, there appears to be a number of subjects in the 'medium' and 'high' part-time groups from relatively observant homes. A comparison of the relative effectiveness of part-time

Table 12.2 Jewish Education by Subjective Religiosity (in percentages)

Subjective religiosity	Intensity of Jewish education				
	Part-time			Day school only	
	Low	Medium	High	Non-Orthodox	Orthodox
Very religious	0·0	4·2	4·8	0·0	58·8
Moderately religious	20·8	37·8	57·1	53·8	41·2
Slightly religious	45·5	37·1	21·8	23·0	0·0
Not at all religious	29·9	13·3	14·3	20·5	0·0
Opposed to religion	2·6	6·3	1·0	2·6	0·0
No answer	1·2	1·3	1·0	0·0	0·0

Table 12.3 Jewish Education by Scores on Jewish Practices and Jewish Beliefs Indices (in percentages) (Subjects who always keep the Dietary Laws are excluded*)

Scores on Jewish Practices		Part-time		Day school only
	Low (N = 74)	Medium (n = 119)	High (N = 83)	Non-Orthodox (N = 35)
Index				
High	9·4	24·3	44·6	37·1
Medium	63·5	58·0	48·2	54·3
Low	25·7	17·7	7·2	8·6
No index (insufficient questions answered)	1·4	0·0	0·0	0·0
Scores on Jewish Beliefs Index				
High	35·1	32·3	39·8	40·0
Medium	25·6	36·0	35·0	22·8
Low	35·2	32·0	22·9	37·2
No index	4·0	0·0	2·3	0·0

* Only four of the respondents from the *orthodox* day schools do not fully observe the dietary laws. This group is too small to allow a meaningful analysis and so is not included in the table.

classes and day schools in promoting religious adherence is more compelling if the subjects' home environment is controlled. Thus, in Table 12.3, those adolescents whose home environment is over-whelmingly positive to traditional Jewish practices and beliefs are not included. The level of dietary observance is a reliable way to assess the orthodoxy of the home, and thus subjects who observe the *Kashrut* laws both inside and outside the home are not included in the Table which compares intensity of Jewish education with scores on Jewish Practices and Jewish Beliefs Indices.[5]

We find the 'high' part-time and the non-Orthodox day school subjects hardly differ at all on religious observance. In fact, the 'high' group is slightly more observant on all the practices surveyed. Furthermore, there is little difference between *all* the groups in affirmation of a number of traditional Jewish beliefs, but interestingly enough, the day school attendants have the highest proportion who reject all or most of them.

These findings lend some support to those of Sanua[6] who noted that the synagogue attendance of Jewish adolescents reflects the frequency of their parents' attendance more than any other influence. He also found no relationship between Hebrew education and the number of Jewish holidays and festivals celebrated in the home.

The Melbourne data indicate that full-time education at a Jewish day school has little effect on the child's religious attitudes unless the home environment promotes the acceptance of the norms taught. It is likely that parents who desire their children to continue to observe traditional Jewish customs will make sure that the children obtain some formal instruction, but it appears to make little difference if the instruction is received in part-time classes or in

Jewish day schools. If the child is sent to part-time classes, the greater the parents' emphasis on traditional Jewish values, the longer the child will be encouraged to attend such classes.

The Jewish day school, unless it is a purely ultra-orthodox institution attracting only students from highly traditionalistic homes, appears to have little independent effect upon the adolescent's religious identification as measured by adherence to traditional practices and beliefs. It may, however, play a more important role in social identification and this will now be examined.

Jewish Education and Social Relations with Non-Jews

During adolescence, the social aspect of minority group membership becomes increasingly salient. The ethnic elements in the adolescent's identity resolution may be reinforced by the composition of the membership-reference group during this period. Adolescents with a positive evaluation of their ethnic identity will tend to be committed to a Jewish reference group and will thus mix socially and seek personal friendships mainly with other Jews.

The parent who is concerned with perpetuating Jewish group values and opposed to the disintegration of the ethnic group – its absorption into the general community – begins to discourage close non-Jewish friendships and interdating when children reach mid-teenage years. The youngster's activities are deliberately channelled into formal Jewish organisations that cater to recreational and social needs. The Jewish day school is considered by many to be the most efficient institution in this field, the general environment of such a school encouraging the development of a predominantly Jewish social peer group. This assumption finds support in the data of Sanua (1969) who reports that 73 per cent of his young subjects who attended a Jewish day school noted that all their friends are Jewish, compared with only 33 per cent of those whose Jewish education was received at afternoon school.

In our study, whereas little difference in religious adherence was found between the children educated at a non-Orthodox day school and some of the others, this is not the case when the close friendship patterns of the ubjects are compared (Table 12.4). Looking at the part-time groups only, the percentage of subjects with 'only Jews' as close friends increases with the intensity of Jewish education received. However, both the day school groups score significantly higher on this measure than any of the part-time groups $(p < .001)$.

Thus, the school environment appears to be a crucial variable determining the ratio of non-Jewish to Jewish friends, while outside the day schools, length of Jewish education bears some relationship to the ethnic exclusivity of close friendship patterns.

Table 12.4   Jewish Education by Number of Four Closest Friends who are Jewish
(in percentages)

| Number of four closest friends who are Jewish | | Intensity of Jewish Education | | | |
| | | Part-time | | Day school only | |
	Low	Medium	High	Non-Orthodox	Orthodox
All four	32·4	46·2	59·1	89·8	100·0
Three	19·5	20·3	20·9	7·7	0·0
Two	23·4	17·5	11·4	0·0	0·0
One	13·0	14·0	5·7	2·5	0·0
None	7·8	2·1	1·9	0·0	0·0
No answer	3·9	0·0	0·9	0·0	0·0

Looking beyond close friendship patterns to wider peer group relations, the subjects were asked how frequently they attend social functions at which non-Jews are present. Here again, the preference for Jewish company appears to be related to the level of Jewish education received by the respondent (Table 12.5). However, the subjects educated at an Orthodox day school are significantly more ethnically isolated than the other day school group ($p < .05$).

Although the proportion of the non-Orthodox day school respondents attending 'ethnically mixed' functions is small (and the question does not make it clear if non-Jews are necessarily in the majority at such functions), the distribution on this question does not differ significantly from that of the 'high' part-time group. While we noted above that the latter are likely to have more Gentile friends, for many the friendships are probably limited to school hours, or perhaps to informal sporting and recreational activities, but are not extended to more intimate social activities.

The pattern observed in Table 12.5 continues for the five groups when answers are compared on predicted parental attitude to interdating, actual dating behaviour, and attitudes towards a Jewish marriage partner (Table 12.6). Amongst the part-time groups, longer periods of Jewish education are related to a stronger orientation towards a Jewish social reference group. While the children educated at the Orthodox day schools favour minimal social contact

Table 12.5   Jewish Education by Attendance at Social Functions with non-Jews
(in percentages)

| Attendance at social functions at which non-Jews are present | | Intensity of Jewish education | | | |
| | | Part-time | | Day school only | |
	Low	Medium	High	Non-Orthodox	Orthodox
Never	3·9	14·0	19·0	25·6	58·8
Rarely/sometimes	83·2	75·6	70·5	71·7	41·2
Mostly/always	11·7	10·5	8·6	2·6	0·0
No answer	1·2	0·0	1·9	0·0	0·0

with non-Jews, the respondents from the non-Orthodox day school group consistently exhibit a similar distribution of attitudes to that of the 'high' part-time subjects. Indeed, Table 12.6 shows the former to be, if anything, less committed to endogamy than the 'part-timers', a finding that would undoubtedly undermine the implicit reasons of many parents for educating their children at Jewish day schools rather than Government schools.

The subjects were asked if 'Jews in Melbourne should mix more with non-Jews' and Table 12.7 summarises the answers. Interestingly enough the non-Orthodox day school subjects are strongly in favour of mixing 'more' with Gentiles. On this question, their replies distribute almost identically to those of the 'low' part-time group – adolescents who have had a minimal amount of Jewish education and have shown themselves to be little committed to a Jewish social reference group.

Table 12.6   Jewish Education by Parental Attitude to Dating non-Jews, Subjects' Frequency of Dating non-Jews, and Subjects' Attitude Towards a Jewish Marriage Partner (in percentages)

Predicted parents' reaction to dates with non-Jews	Intensity of Jewish Education				
	Part-time			Day school only	
	Low	Medium	High	Non-Orthodox	Orthodox
	(N=77)	(N=143)	(N=105)	(N=39)	(N=17)
Would forbid it	22·1	37·8	42·8	46·1	88·2
Would object	44·2	45·5	43·8	46·1	11·8
Wouldn't care/in favour	31·2	9·1	9·5	5·1	0·0
No answer	2·6	7·7	3·8	2·6	0·0
Dates with non-Jews. (Subjects who do not yet date excluded)	(N=58)	(N=93)	(N=75)	(N=30)	(N=8)
Never	44·8	49·4	68·0	60·0	100·0
Rarely/sometimes	43·1	44·1	22·7	30·0	0·0
Mostly/always	12·1	6·5	9·3	10·0	0·0
Attitude towards a Jewish marriage partner	(N=77)	(N=143)	(N=105)	(N=39)	(N=17)
Definitely Jewish	36·4	56·7	71·4	61·5	100·0
Probably Jewish	27·3	28·7	19·0	23·1	0·0
Will marry without regard to religion/prefer non-Jew	20·8	6·3	4·8	10·3	0·0
Don't know/no answer	15·6	8·4	4·8	5·1	0·0

However, while many of the latter group appear to be minimally concerned with Jewish survival and probably wish to see Jews mixing more in order to hasten 'assimilation', the motivations of the day school subjects are a little more complex. The previous Tables have shown them to be quite strongly committed to a Jewish reference group, but the cloister-type environment of a Jewish day school may engender some guilt about the extent of their

Table 12.7   Jewish Education by Attitude Towards Mixing with non-Jews (in percentages)

Jews in Melbourne should:	Low	Part-time Medium	High	Day school only Non-Orthodox	Orthodox
			Intensity of Jewish Education		
Mix less with non-Jews	5·2	3·5	12·4	5·1	23·6
Mix as much as they do at present	22·1	38·5	42·0	28·2	23·6
Mix more with non-Jews	52·0	39·9	28·6	51·2	11·8
Don't know/no answer	20·8	18·2	17·1	15·4	41·0

social segregation. They wish to remain Jewish but are not sure if it is necessary to go to such lengths in order to do so. On the other hand, the Orthodox day school students are more convinced of the necessity for educational and social segregation in order to maintain the integrity of the Jewish group, and a number consider that too many of the less observant Jews already mix too much with Gentiles.

Jewish Education and Future Group Survival

In an attempt to gauge the intensity of the adolescents' attitudes towards the survival of the Jewish group, they were asked: 'Would you like your children to bring up *their* children as Jews?' As shown in Table 12.8, the non-Orthodox day school respondents are no stronger in their desire for group survival than the 'medium' part-time group, and somewhat weaker than the 'high' group.

Table 12.8   Jewish Education by Desire for Grandchildren to be Brought up as Jews (in percentages) ('don't knows' included)

Children bringing up *their children* as Jews?	Low (N = 66)	Part-time Medium (N = 134)	High (N = 104)	Day school only Non-Orthodox (N = 39)	Orthodox (N = 17)
			Intensity of Jewish Education		
Desire it strongly	51·7	61·1	74·9	56·3	100·0
Prefer it	30·3	32·2	23·2	35·8	0·0
Wouldn't care/prefer not	18·0	6·7	1·9	7·9	0·0

Despite these findings, Table 12.9 indicates that *both* the day school groups contain a significantly higher proportion of subjects proposing to educate their children at Jewish day schools than any of the part-time groups. Amongst the latter, support for Jewish day school education increases with the intensity of Jewish education received by the subjects. It would appear from these figures that the day schools can expect a net gain in enrolment over the next generation, and, if not too many of the youngsters change their attitudes, an increasing proportion of Melbourne Jewish children will be educated at Jewish day schools. Some 20 per cent of the 'medium' and 'low' part-time groups propose educating

Table 12.9 Jewish Education by Proposed Jewish Education for Children (in percentages) ('don't knows' excluded)

Desired Jewish Education for subjects' children	Intensity of Jewish Education				
	Part-time			Day school only	
	Low	Medium	High	Non-Orthodox	Orthodox
	(N=58)	(N=125)	(N=94)	(N=39)	(N=17)
Jewish day school	19·0	21·6	51·0	89·7	88·2
Part-time classes	53·4	68·8	45·9	7·7	0·0
None/religious instruction at Government schools only	27·6	9·6	3·2	2·6	11·8

their children at day schools. As no length of time was stipulated, it is possible that some of the subjects anticipate only a few years of day school for their children (perhaps elementary school only), so they should obtain a minimal grounding in Jewish customs and traditions, in the hope that this will be sufficient to 'keep them Jewish'.

The day school appears to have won general support amongst adults, and apparently also amongst adolescents, as the institution most likely to promote maximum ethnic identification in the young. However we have observed in our study that when family attitudes to traditional observance and group survival is held constant attendance at a Jewish day school is in itself no more effective in inducing the subjects to be religiously observant or ethnically committed than five or six years of Jewish instruction in part-time classes.

Conclusions

1. Amongst Melbourne Jewish adolescents educated outside the Jewish day schools, increasing time spent in part-time religious classes is related to (i) stronger adherence to traditional religious rituals and beliefs; (ii) a more exclusively Jewish friendship group and social orientation; (iii) a firmer commitment to a future Jewish marriage partner; (iv) stronger feelings in favour of future Jewish group survival; and (v) increasing support for their children receiving a Jewish day school education.

2. Amongst those adolescents educated solely at Jewish day schools, the subjects from Orthodox day schools are consistently more ethnically oriented than the respondents from non-Orthodox day schools. There are only two issues surveyed on which the two groups do *not* differ significantly, and these are (i) the number of close friends who are Jewish and (ii) the desire to give their children a day school education.

3. It is also only on the above two attitudes that the non-Orthodox day school group is more ethnically oriented than the 'high' part-time group. Indeed, on a number of other variables the day school

group shows itself to be less committed to traditional Jewish values and the maintenance of a distinctive Jewish identity than one or more of the part-time groups.

4. From our results, there would seem to exist an optimum point above which greater concentration on Jewish studies and a Jewish educational atmosphere have little effect on ethnic commitment, and this point is below spending the total school life at a Jewish day school. Sending a child to one of the day schools may be a gesture of parents, hoping that the school will instil in the child a knowledge and love of Judaism and its values that the home is unable to do. When this is the case, the school appears to have little effect on the child's attitudes. From the curren analysis it would appear that the day school is attributed with a far stronger socialising power than it actually possesses. But in order to obtain a more reliable assessment of the institution's effectiveness, longitudinal studies comparing day school and non-day school subjects on aspects of Jewish identification some years after leaving school are required.

These results indicate that while both full-time and part-time Jewish educational institutions may play a part in reinforcing existing religious and social group values, without the support of a home environment favourable to these values, formal Jewish education appears to have a minimal influence on ethnic socialisation.

REFERENCES

1. They are reviewed in V. Sanua, 'The Jewish Adolescent; a review of empirical research', *Jewish Education*, Vol. 38 (1968), pp. 36–52.

2. See B. C. Rosen, *Adolescence and Religion* (Cambridge, Mass.), 1965.

3. V. D. Sanua, 'The Relationship between Jewish Education and Jewish Identification', *Jewish Education*, Vol. 35 (1964), pp. 37–50.

4. Thus, for example, a subject who reported eight years at a Hebrew Sunday School, was placed in the same category as another who concurrently attended both Sunday school and afternoon classes for four years. In the case of subjects who had spent some time at day schools, each year at a day school is counted as equivalent to two years of part-time study.

5. The Jewish Practices Index consists of items relating to fasting on the Day of Atonement, keeping the Jewish dietary laws, attendance at synagogue, observance of Sabbath restrictions and attendance at a Passover 'seder'. The Jewish Beliefs Index asked the subjects to affirm or deny five traditional Jewish beliefs taken from Maimonides' 'Thirteen Principles of Faith'. These are: the belief in the God of the Torah, the belief in the Jews as a 'Chosen People', a belief in the historical existence of Moses and his bringing down the Torah from Mt Sinai, the belief in the necessity of the good Jew to carry out all the laws as written in the Torah, and the belief in the future coming of the Messiah.

6. V. D. Sanua, 'A Comparative Study of the Religious Attitudes and Practices of Different Groups of Jewish Students', *Jewish Education*, Vol. 39 (1969), pp. 27–36.

7. *Ibid.*

13

Beyond the Third Generation: The Ethnic Identification of Jewish Youth*

Ronald Taft

In chapter 5 it was reported that the degree and type of ethnic identification of the adult Jews of Melbourne are a function largely of national and ethnic background. Thus the Jews who had been assimilated to the Western and Central European middle class were the least identified with Jewishness, followed very closely by the third, and later, generations of British- and Australian-born Jews. The Jewish identification of these groups was particularly low with respect to the ethno-national areas of identification such as Yiddish language and culture, and Israel. On the other hand, involvement in Jewish communal institutions remained fairly strong and moderate observance of religious rituals was maintained, as were positive feelings about Jewishness and the desirability of its continuation. However, there was some 'drift' in these respects between the first, second and third generations, and the question was asked at the end of the chapter whether the Jewish involvement of the third generation adults would be maintained by their children.

In order to investigate this question, a study was conducted on a sample of the children of the original respondents, where the children were still either in their late adolescence or early adulthood. In order to keep the population within limits, it was decided not to use families where the original adult respondent was married to a non-Jew, unless the latter had become converted to Judaism. Thus the population for the Youth Study from which the sample was drawn was defined as all of the children of the original respondents, whether living at home or not, aged between sixteen and twenty-five years, who had two Jewish parents and who still lived in Melbourne.

The method of selecting the sample was as follows. The demographic material on the 504 families was scanned at random, and all names of young persons who fitted the foregoing population conditions were chosen for interview. These were approached in their

* Thanks are extended to Mr and Mrs Leo Fink of Melbourne for financial assistance in the preparation of this chapter.

parental home by the interviewers, and where the child was living elsewhere, the parents were asked for their present address. An unexpected difficulty arose in some of the cases when a parent – usually the father – refused to co-operate by supplying the address, or by refusing permission for his child to be interviewed. This resulted in a loss of 10 per cent of the possible sample, but on every occasion that the interviewer was able to speak to the target person directly, a successful interview took place. It is difficult to estimate what bias may have been caused by the interference of the parents; the families tended to be less strongly identified with Judaism than did the others. It is possible therefore that the refusals biased the results a little by reducing the number of youth who had low Jewish identification. However, this possible bias is partly overcome in the analysis by comparing the youth respondents' attitudes with their actual parents.

The 115 respondents constituting the youth sample came from 89 families, and all but 22 of them were living with their parents (83 per cent). With the limitations mentioned above, they may be taken as an approximately representative sample of Jewish youth of their age, living in Melbourne. In interpreting the findings, however, it should be borne in mind that their parents were not a representative sample of Jewish adults in Melbourne. The parents differ from those interviewed in the Adult Survey in a number of respects: they had been married to another Jew, they had at least one child between sixteen and twenty-five years of age, and they had not refused to allow their child to be interviewed. Compared with the respondents in the Adult Survey, they included a greater number of immigrants from Eastern Europe and fewer from Central and Western Europe, and they tended to be older.

The data were gathered by interview, using a schedule consisting both of open-ended questions, such as 'What does your being Jewish mean to you?' and multiple-choice ratings such as 'How would you describe yourself with respect to religion? (Very religious, moderately religious, somewhat religious, not religious at all, opposed to religion, not sure).'

The interviews were conducted during January and February 1968 in the respondents' homes by interviewers who were all young graduates in the social sciences and who had all participated in the interviewing programme in the Adult Survey. In the interests of standardised rapport, all of the interviewers were Jewish.

CHARACTERISTICS OF THE SAMPLE

There were 69 females and 66 males in the sample. The age distribution was as follows: sixteen to eighteen years, 42 respondents; nineteen to twenty years, 31 respondents; twenty-one to twenty-five years, 42 respondents. One in six was married (nearly all females).

Occupation and Education

54 per cent of the respondents were still full-time students at the time of the interview, although they were all well above the minimum school-leaving age. 8 per cent of them were housewives, and 16 per cent were already working in professions or as business executives. The other 22 per cent were in white collar and skilled occupations.

The respondents were asked to indicate what type of occupation they expected to take up. The results are presented for the males in Table 13.1, together with some comparative data taken from the Adult Survey. The young Jews were very ambitious, and 56 per cent of them expected to attain a higher occupational level than that of their fathers. A comparison with the actual levels of Australian-born Jews in Melbourne (Table 13.1) suggests that their expectations are not unreasonable.

Table 13.1   Occupational Levels of Males (in percentages)

	Youth Sample Aspiration	Australian-born Jews in General	Fathers of Youth Respondents	Grandfathers of Youth Respondents*
Managerial & Professional	76	72	47	39
White Collar	2	14	28	31
Skilled Manual	21	10	22	28
Other	1	4	3	2
Total	100	100	100	100

* The father of the respondent in the Adult Survey.

The most popular choice by the young males was commerce, economics and business management (27 per cent), medicine-dentistry (16 per cent), science (14 per cent), law (15 per cent) and engineering and trades (20 per cent). One-third of the females chose teaching as their expected occupation.

All of the youth had completed at least 9th grade education and 69 per cent expected to enter, or had already entered, a tertiary level institution; 47 per cent of the entire sample expected to obtain a university degree. Only 7 per cent of their mothers and fathers had a comparable degree.

School Attended

The secondary education of 15 per cent of the respondents was obtained mainly or entirely in a Jewish day school, and another 15 per cent in other independent schools. The remaining 70 per

cent were educated in state high schools. Altogether, 37 per cent
of the sample had at some stage attended a Jewish day school.

Place of Birth

The country of birth of the youth respondents and of their parents
is presented in Table 13.2. Just over a half of the youth were actually
born in Australia, but almost all of the rest attended Australian
schools for all or part of their education. Few of the parents of
the respondents were born in Australia; nearly one-third came
from Central or Western Europe (including Britain), and the
remainder were mainly from Poland.

Table 13.2   Birthplace of the Youth and their Parents
(in percentages)

	Youth	Parents
Australia/New Zealand	58	11
Other British	2	6
Poland	9	47
Other Eastern Europe	5	8
Germany/Austria	9	11
Hungary/Czechoslovakia	5	9
Other (mainly Holland/France)	10	5
Israel	2	3
Total	100	100

Strength of Jewish Background

One in six of the youth respondents came from a strictly religiously-
observant home, while one in ten of the homes was completely
unobservant. Nearly half of the homes, however, observed most
of the dietary laws, and two-thirds were associated with an Orthodox
congregation – although they were often only nominally orthodox.

28 per cent of the parents usually spoke Yiddish at home, and
58 per cent of the youth sample claimed to be able to understand at least some Yiddish speech. Only 20 per cent of the youth
were fully conversant with both the written and spoken language.
All of the youth respondents claimed that they had been given
some special Jewish education, and 19 per cent claimed that they
could speak and understand Hebrew (not necessarily fluently).

'Ethnic' Background

In the analysis of the Adult Study, the respondents were catego-
rised according to country of birth, and the number of generations
from *shtetl* or ghetto-living. This distance was estimated from the

Table 13.3 Ethnic Background of the Youth

Background	No. of Generations*	Percentage
1. Yiddish-speaking parents†		
(a) Fully traditional home	1st	2
(b) Moderately traditional home	2nd	22
(c) Virtually no religious observance in home	2nd	6
2. European (non-British) Yiddish-speaking grandparents		
(a) Parents born Eastern Europe (mainly Polish)	3rd (possibly 2nd)	18
(b) Parents born Central & Western Europe & Israel (mainly German/Austrian, Hungarian/Slovakian)	3rd (possibly 2nd)	12
3. Australian/British parents,‡ Yiddish-speaking grandparents	3rd	10
4. European (non-British), remote or no Yiddish background (mainly German, Austrian, Hungarian, & Czech.)	4th (or more)	19
5. Australian/British, remote or no Yiddish background	4th (or more)	11

  * Generations defined in terms of distance from the traditional, Yiddish-speaking *shtetl* or ghetto. In this table the number of generations refers to the youth respondents.

  † Yiddish-speaking means that Yiddish was the normal language used in the home by the parents. Data regarding grandparents are based only on the one parent who was interviewed in the Adult Survey.

  ‡ Where at least one parent was Australian/British-born, the background is classified as Australian/British.

use of Yiddish by the respondent, by his parents and by his grandparents.

Table 13.2 sets out the distribution of the youth respondents according to this system of analysis.

In Table 13.3 some additional differentiations are made of the Yiddish-speaking homes according to the degree of religious observance. Thus only 2 per cent of the youth respondents come from a home which was both fully observant and used Yiddish as the normal language. At the other end of the spectrum, 30 per cent of the youth were at least four generations removed from Eastern European ghetto life, and, possibly, their ancestors had never lived in a ghetto during the past 150 years.

ETHNIC IDENTIFICATION OF THE YOUTH

The Measurement of Ethnic Identification

The identification of the respondents was measured by inference from two types of material: their expressed attitudes and feelings; and their actual behaviour with respect to Jewish institutions. Each respondent was given a score on six standardised scales each representing a different facet of Jewish identification. (For further details see Appendix III.) The scales were as follows: *Defence of Jewish Identity; Social Relations; Jewish Community Involvement; Positive Emotional Involvement; Religious Involvement and Observance; Identification with Israel.* In addition, the scale of *Identification with Australia* was also applied.

As far as possible the same items were scored in the Adult and the Youth Surveys, but there were certain difficulties in maintaining equivalence. For example, if the parents do not observe the dietary laws in the home, it is unlikely that the child will do so. In order to loosen the nexus between the parents' and the children's scores on the scale, the respondents were asked whether they 'intend to buy Kosher meat' for their own home when they establish one.

In the Adult Survey a scale of identification with the 'Yiddish language' was also used, but it was not possible to produce comparable items in the Youth Survey. On suitable occasions, however, the data have been analysed in connection with one particular item on the Yiddish scale, 'Do you favour teaching Yiddish as a living language to Jewish children?'

Scores on Ethnic Identification Scales

The scores obtained by the youth respondents are presented in Table 13.4 separately for boys and girls, and, according to age, for adolescents and young adults. The standard deviations of the scores are not repeated for each group as they differ little from those for the total sample. There are no sex differences in identification on any of the scales; the greatest difference occurred on Social Relations, but this is not significant. Age also has only a limited effect; the older respondents are more identified communally and the younger ones more identified with Israel. In both cases the differences are significant only at the .10 level and will not be interpreted as having any significance.

Table 13.4 also presents the results for the respondent's parent who was interviewed in the Adult Survey. The parents have higher Jewish identification on all dimensions excepting with respect to Israel. All of the differences are statistically significant.[1] The parents also score higher on identification, which suggests that identification with national and ethnic groups may be less typical of youth than of adults. In fact there is evidence that this is the case in other national groups.[2] However, the difference between the Jewish youth and parent respondents on the identification index was not significant.

If we use the parents' scores on the indices as a guide to standards, the youth are particularly low on Defence and Social, and are comparatively high on Israel and Religion. The scores on Religion

Table 13.4 Means on Identification Indices by Age and Sex

Index	Youth (115)	Male (57)	Female (58)	16–19 yrs. (55)	20–25 yrs. (60)	Parents (89)
Defence	2·2 (1·3)*	2·3	2·1	2·1	2·3	3·6 (1·4)*
Social	2·4 (1·8)	2·6	2·3	2·4	2·4	3·9 (1·5)
Community	2·5 (1·3)	2·6	2·5	2·3	2·7	3·5 (1·4)
Positive Emotion	2·5 (1·2)	2·5	2·6	2·5	2·6	3·5 (1·5)
Religion	2·8 (1·5)	2·8	2·8	2·8	2·8	3·3 (1·5)
Israel	3·6 (1·9)	3·6	3·4	3·9	3·3	3·5 (1·7)
Total Identi-fication	16·0 (6·3)	16·3	15·8	16·0	16·1	21·1 (5·4)
Identification with Australia	6·1 (2·0)	6·1	6·0	6·0	6·1	6·5 (1·8)

* Standard deviation

seem to indicate that there is less decline in identification in this respect between parent and child, and this might be due to the fact that the parents have already departed considerably from traditional observance. The comparatively high scores of the youth respondents on Israel must be considered in the light of the Six-Day War that occurred between the conclusion of the Adult Survey and the commencement of the Youth Survey. However, the higher scores on Israel obtained by the younger group of youth respondents when compared with the young adults (see Table 13.4), seem to indicate that there is a real age increase in the attachment of Jews to Israel, that is not due merely to the effects of the War. Further discussion on these results will be postponed until we have looked at more details of the comparison between the children and their parents on the individual indices and some of the items that constitute the scales for measuring the indices. These are presented in Table 13.5 which also includes results for the 116 Australian-educated respondents in the Adult Survey. These latter respondents constitute those who lived in Australia before their eleventh birthday and represent a group of adults who resemble the youth sample in that both groups received most or all of their education in Australia. The Australian-educated adults were all heads of households and were at least one generation earlier than the youth, and they constituted a rather different group than the youth respondents' own parents.

In Table 13.5 the respondents are classified as 'low' or 'high' (or in-between) on each identification index. The category 'low' means that the respondent has virtually no identification in that area, and 'high' means very strong identification to the extent perhaps of its playing an important part in the respondent's self-concept. The categories are used in an extreme sense in order to provide elaboration on the mean scores presented in Table 13.4.

Most of the data in Table 13.5 are self-explanatory and require little comment. Support is given to the impression already gained from the means on the indices that there is a great gulf between the parents and the children on items concerned with social identi-

Table 13.5   Percentage of Respondents Scoring High and Low on the Indices and giving Certain Responses (all Responses are Expressed in the Direction of Higher Identification)

	Youth (115)	Parents (89)	Australian-Educated Jews (116)
1. Defence:			
Low	10	1	4
High	18	54	39
Jewish teenagers should deliberately choose Jewish friends (not necessarily exclusively)	25	72	55
Is opposed to Jews marrying non-Jews	60	88	82
Is strongly opposed to Jews marrying non-Jews	15	48	34
Considers it unlikely that he would marry a non-Jew (this includes those already married to a non-Jew)	73	*	*
Strong desire that his grandchildren should be Jewish	48	80	69
2. Social:			
Low	40	9	29
High	20	39	26
Most of his friends are Jewish	65	91	74
Feels more at ease with Jews than non-Jews	32	65	51
3. Community:			
Low	22	10	5
High	6	22	22
Is an active member of a Jewish organisation	25	38	46
Probably will join a congregation when he is an adult	78	(78)	(80)
Reads Jewish newspapers	94	93	95
Knows the functions of the Jewish Welfare Society	74	92	92
Has a definite (either positive or negative) opinion about the Melbourne Jewish community	76	*	*
Has a clearly favourable attitude towards the Melbourne Jewish community	35	*	*
4. Positive emotional involvement:			
Low	22	14	11
High	19	54	44
Has strong positive feelings about being Jewish	70	83	76
Being Jewish plays a very important part in his life	24	45	36
If given choice would prefer to be born Jewish	84	*	*
5. Religion:			
Low	26	20	11
High	17	24	22
Describes self as:			
'Very or moderately religious'	34	55	57
'Not at all religious'	24	18	9
Attends religious services	90	84	94
Attends religious services several times a year	41	48	60
Prefers Liberal to Orthodox congregation for self	31	19	29
Full fast on Yom Kippur	67	67	70
Intends to keep Kosher household	32	(33)	(27)

Table 13.5   (continued)

	Youth (115)	Parents (89)	Australian-Educated Jews (116)
Intends to observe strict dietary laws (including outside of the home)	11	(17)	(9)
6. Israel:			
Low	25	20	37
High	45	36	21
If he didn't live in Australia would like to live in Israel	65	72	41
Describes self as very strongly ego-involved in Israel	19	*	*
How involved did you feel in the Six-Day War?			
At least some involvement	97	(96)†	*
Very much involved	58	(45)†	*
7. Total Jewish Identification:			
Low	15	1	6
High	7	21	14
8. Identification with Australia:			
Low	10	7	1
High	30	39	73
Would like to spend rest of life as a resident of Australia	55	80	85
Satisfied (i.e., not dissatisfied) with life in Australia	88	97	98
'Completely' satisfied with life in Australia	33	43	63
Has strong positive feelings about being Australian	66	61	75
Active member of non-ethnic organisations	14	15	30
9. Additional Items:			
Favours teaching Jewish children Hebrew as a living language	65	72	45
Favours teaching Jewish children Yiddish as a living language	39	53	35
Frequently speaks Yiddish	21	50	‡
Can understand spoken Yiddish	58	70	52
Can understand and speak Hebrew	19	*	*
Favours Jewish day schools for Jewish children	37	45	*
Thinks that the average Australian is quite friendly to Jews	42	47	47
Considers that there is 'a fair amount' (or more) of anti-semitism in Australia	32	40	32
Feels 'personally involved' in the treatment of the Jews by the Nazis	83	*	*
Feels strongly, 'personally involved' in the treatment of the Jews by the Nazis	55	*	*
Thinks that the same thing could happen in Australia in his lifetime	4	*	*
Supports the Australian Labor Party	55	55	38
Rates own social class as 'upper' or 'upper middle'	20	17	25

* No comparable information was obtained in the Adult Survey.

† This rating was made of a sample of adult Jews immediately after the Six-Day War, but they were not necessarily the parents of the Youth Sample (See Chapter Eight for details of this study).

‡ Not known, but almost certainly below 10 per cent, and then mainly with their own parents.

fication with Jews and with the preservation of Jewishness for future generations. Whereas 80 per cent of the parents strongly desired their grandchildren to be Jewish, this declines to less than 50 per cent in their children. Unless the children change their

views in the course of raising their own families many of their
parents are going to be disappointed in this area. While the children
are not lacking in positive feelings about being Jewish themselves
(Table 13.5, scale 4), they do not feel that the perpetuation of
Jewishness is of sufficient importance for them to restrict their
own social contacts with non-Jews or those of Jewish teenagers
in general. Only 15 per cent of the youth are strongly opposed to
Jews marrying non-Jews, even though such marriages usually mean
that any children will not be Jewish. Only 25 per cent of the Jewish
youth play an active role in Jewish organisations – that is, attend
meetings regularly or belong to committees – compared with 38 per
cent of their parents and nearly 50 per cent of Australian-educated
adults.

Nevertheless, most of the Jewish youth know something about
the formal Jewish community; three-quarters say that they probably
will join a Jewish religious congregation when they are adults, and
two-thirds of them have more Jewish friends than non-Jewish.
Despite their lukewarm opposition to Jews marrying non-Jews,
73 per cent of them think that it is unlikely that they will do so.

The fact that the older generation of Australian-educated adults
are more positive about their Jewish identification and their loyalty
to Jewishness than the youth, suggests that the latter may change
when they too become adults. The adults are almost as 'assimilated' socially as the youth, but they still maintain a high level
of Jewish loyalty and involvement in Jewish communal institutions.
In the Adult Study (chapter 5) it was found that the level of Jewish
identification of the respondents was partly influenced by position
in the family life cycle, so that those with adolescent children were
the highest, and those without children were the lowest. Thus, it
is possib e that the youth sample may increase their Jewish identification as their life cycle moves on. However, there is no strong
proof that the present youth will ever develop as much Jewish
loyalty and communal involvement as the earlier generation of
Australian-educated Jews. There may have been a significant change
in these attitudes due to life conditions and prevailing values in
present-day Australia, and our data cannot really sort out the
forces that will determine the future.

The data on religion in Table 13.5 indicate a slow erosion among
the youth of traditional religious observance and religious feelings,
but the decline is not nearly as marked on this scale as on the four
previous ones. The youth are about as likely as their parents to
attend religious services, to fast on Yom Kippur and to keep a
Kosher household, i.e. retain separate dishes for milk and meat.
There is a move towards membership of a Liberal congregation
in the future intentions of the youth, and it is probable that at

least one-quarter of them will actually join such congregations. (This estimate is based both on the responses given by the youth and by the actual memberships of the Australian-educated Jews.) Only one-quarter of the youth seem to be almost completely lacking in religious involvement, and even most of these appear to attend synagogue at least once a year, probably under family pressure. Again, looking at the responses of the Australian-educated adults, it seems likely that, when they are older, the youth will develop more religious feelings and will maintain at least their present level of synagogue attendance and religious observance.

One-quarter of the youth respondents show little or no involvement in Israel, while nearly one-half (45 per cent) are highly involved. This involvement takes the form of concern for the fate of Israel, and an interest in living there if Australia is no longer to be their home. More of the youth were highly identified with Israel than were their parents, and many more than the Australian-educated adults. It is difficult to attribute such a difference entirely to long-lasting effects of the Six-Day War, as was suggested earlier, but the possibility cannot be excluded. A follow-up interview study of Jews in Melbourne which was made just after the War (chapter 7) indicated that there was a substantial increase in identification with Israel as a result of it. However, even during the War, there was evidence that the youth were even more involved in Israel's fate than their parents. The contrast between the attitudes of youth toward Israel and those of the previous generation of Australian-educated Jews suggests that the Jewish youth do have an attitude towards Israel that is unique to the present generation. It is possible, however, that this special attitude may disappear as they, too, grow into adulthood.

The Total Identification scores represent the sum of identification with Jewishness in all areas, and these show a considerable decline from parents to children. Only 1 per cent of the parents could be described as being virtually without any Jewish ethnic identification, but 15 per cent of the youth fell into that category. At the high end, over one-quarter of the parents, but only one-eighth of the youth, were very highly identified with their Jewishness. The Jewish youth also scored much lower on this total than did the Australian-educated adult.

The results for Identification with Australia support strongly the suggestion already made that the youth are much lower on national identification than are the adults. It was already noted that the youth respondents scored lower on this index than did their parents, even though the former were mainly born in Australia. This difference becomes even more noteworthy when it is recalled that the youth respondents are less strongly identified with

Australia than the Australian-educated adult. The apparent drift from Jewish identification on the part of the youth needs to be viewed in the light of a general drift in loyalty, and, in that light, the identification of the Jewish youth with Israel is an even more notable phenomenon. If we compare the numbers of the respondents who are highly identified with Israel with those who are highly identified with Australia the figure is 45 per cent versus 30 per cent for the youth, 36 per cent versus 39 per cent for their parents and 21 per cent versus 73 per cent for the Australian-educated adult (Table 13.5). The corresponding figures for 'strong positive feelings about being Jewish' versus 'strong positive feelings about being Australian' also showed that the identification of the youth is comparatively as high on the former as on the latter. The figures for the youth are 70 versus 66 per cent, and for the Australian-educated adult 76 versus 75. Thus, when we take into account the general national alienation of the youth, their level of identification with their Jewishness is not as low as it appears to be at first.

In the study of the attitudes of Jewish adults it was found that the strength of the attitudes held by any respondent was often a function of his distance from the Jewish ghetto or *shtetl*. It was also noted that Jewish identification in the third generation was maintained more on the indices of 'Loyalty' (Defence and Positive Emotion) and 'Formal Identification' indices (Religion and Community) than on the 'Ethnic' ones (Social, Yiddish, and Israel). By classifying the youth respondents also according to their generational distance from the ghetto, it is possible to check whether these same trends occur.

The scores on the indices are presented in Table 13.6 for the youth respondents and their parents grouped according to the number of generations that the parents have been separated from the ghetto. When the two parents differed in their generation, the respondent in the Adult Survey was used as the basis for the child's generation. As explained in connection with Table 13.3, the use of Yiddish language by the parents or grandparents provided an estimate of the generational – rather than chronological – distance from the ghetto. The parents who still used Yiddish as their normal language at home, were called 'first' generation in the sense that they have carried at least one central aspect of the European ghetto with them (they were all born in Eastern Europe). Their children then are 'second' generation, and they are comparable, in that respect, to the 'second' generation adults. Many of the parents described as 'third' generation were actually more than three generations separated from ghetto or *shtetl* life, and so the children of second generation parents are not really comparable to them.

Table 13.6 Means and High and Low Scores on the Indices as a Function of Generational Distance from the Ghetto

Index	Parent's Generation								
	First (34) Youth		Parent	Second (46) Youth		Parent	Third (or more) (35) Youth		Parent
1. Defence									
Mean	2·6	1·3*	3·9	2·3	1·3	3·6	1·7	1·5	3·1
Low	3		0	11		0	17		3
High	21		68	24		48	8		51
2. Social									
Mean	3·0	1·4	4·4	2·6	1·2	3·8	1·6	1·8	3·5
Low	27		6	39		9	67		14
High	32		50	22		30	6		43
3. Community									
Mean	2·7	0·9	3·6	2·6	0·6	3·2	2·4	1·4	3·8
Low	18		3	20		17	28		9
High	6		15	6		22	6		31
4. Positive Emotion									
Mean	2·9	0·8	3·7	2·4	1·1	3·5	2·3	0·9	3·2
Low	9		6	26		13	29		23
High	29		59	22		55	9		46
5. Religion									
Mean	3·1	0·1	3·2	2·8	0·5	3·3	2·5	0·7	3·2
Low	20		27	17		22	29		11
High	24		23	28		30	11		17
6. Israel									
Mean	4·0	0·3	4·3	3·6	−0·3	3·3	3·1	−0·2	2·9
Low	15		9	24		20	37		31
High	53		59	43		30	40		23
7. Total Identification									
Mean	18·3	4·8	23·2	16·2	4·4	20·6	13·6	6·2	19·7
Low	9		0	13		0	23		3
High	6		32	13		11	0		23
8. Identification with Australia									
Mean	5·2	0·4	5·6	6·4	0·5	6·9	6·5	0·4	6·9
Low	21		12	4		2	6		6
High	21		18	35		48	40		51
9. Favours teaching Yiddish to Jewish children (percentage)†	71		77	33		60	17		20

* Figures in italics represent the decline in identification between the parents and their children. A negative entry indicates an increase. The decimal is rounded off from two decimal places.
† This item is included as a replacement for the Index of Identification with Yiddish which could not be computed for the youth.

Nevertheless, as we shall see, the children of the second generation parents are much lower on Jewish identification in most areas than are the third (and more) generation parents.

If we compare the scores on the indices for the three generations of youth, there is a steady drift in degree of Jewish identification in all respects. The greatest drift occurs on Social, Defence, Israel and Yiddish (the latter by implication from Item 9); there is a moderate drift on Positive Emotion and Religion and only a small one in Community. Thus the three Ethnic scales (Social, Israel and Yiddish) show the greatest drift with each generation, while the two Formal ones (Religion and Community) show little. This is consistent with the intergenerational trends found in adults, with the exception that in the latter group scores on Community increase in the third generation of Australian-born.

It has already been pointed out that the youth as a whole show the greatest divergences from the parents in their Jewish identification in the Social and Defence areas. We can now see that this applies also to each of the three generations, although the pattern of drift between parents and their children is not consistent in all areas. Thus, the children of the first generation parents have a high drift from their parents in Defence and Social, a moderate one in Community and Positive Emotion and very little in Religion, Israel and Yiddish. The children of the second generation parents have the highest drift on the two Loyalty scales (Defence and Positive Emotion) and on Social and Yiddish; there is only a moderate drift in the Formal areas (Community and Religion); and an actual gain on Israel. It is this generation of youth – strictly speaking, third generation Jews – that will represent the bulk of the Australian-educated Jewish adults of the Jewish community.

The children of the third generation adults show a similar pattern to the children of the second generation, but there are some additional noteworthy features: on Social, there is a tremendous drop from their parents' scores to the extent that two-thirds of the youth score low and there are also very few who have any strong feelings of Jewishness. In this latter respect they also represent a considerable drift in comparison with the children of second generation parents. In total, one-quarter of the children of the third generation Jews had virtually no Jewish identification, and none of them had a high identification – whereas, the distribution of their parents' attributes was just the opposite. The only area in which the children of the third generation parents were more identified with Jewishness than were their parents is Israel. 40 per cent of the youth are highly identified in this area, but, on the other hand, 37 per cent of his generation are not at all identified with Israel. It seems that involvement in Israel is an area where a real polarisation is taking place in the Jewish identification of Australian Jewish youth, so that some care very little about Israel and others care a lot.

It has noteworthy implications for the future of the Jewish Community of Melbourne that the children of the generation that has the least overall identification with Jewishness, is also the one whose own identification has drifted furthest from that of their parents. This will be discussed further in the Conclusion.

A Note on Intermarriage

It has been shown in chapter 2 that the rate of marriages between Jews and non-Jews increases according to generation. Consequently, it may be expected that there will be a substantial mixed marriage rate among the present Jewish youth of Melbourne, and especially among the children of third generation parents. Few of the youth respondents were already married, but the likely intermarriage rate may be inferred from the opinions of the youth concerning mixed marriages. 89 per cent of the parents of the youth respondents were opposed to these marriages, and, by definition of the sample, none of them were themselves married to non-Jews. The opposition to mixed marriages was much less among the youth: 74 per cent of the children of first generation parents, 61 per cent of second generation and only 37 per cent of third were opposed. Six of the latter group were already married, two of them to non-Jews.

The respondents were also asked to estimate how likely it is that they would marry a non-Jew. In the third generation, 11 per cent either had already married a non-Jew or considered it 'probable' that they would do so. An additional 38 per cent thought that it is 'quite possible' that they would intermarry. If one-half of the latter group and all of the former actually did intermarry this would mean that 30 per cent of the third generation Jews would be married to non-Jews. A calculation made on the same basis indicates a figure of 12 per cent for the first and second generations combined, and 19 per cent for the full youth sample. When we recall that the parents of each respondent were both Jewish, and that there might have been a sampling bias against respondents who have drifted away from Judaism (see above), this figure of 19 per cent is probably an underestimate of the true figure. In that case, it can be expected that there will be a rapid increase in the present figure of one Jew in twenty who is married to a non-Jew in Victoria (see chapter 2).

DETERMINANTS OF THE ETHNIC IDENTIFICATION

From Table 13.6 it appears that there is the expected positive relationship between the attitudes of the parents and those of the children. This can be further investigated by looking at the correlations between the scores of the youth and those of their parents on the indices.

The Total Identification scores of the youth correlate .44 with those of the parents. Only one of the parents' single indices, Social, was not significantly correlated with the child's total. Whether the parents preferred the company of Jews or not had little effect on the Jewish identification of their children in any respect other than whether they too preferred the company of Jews (correlation .22). The children's own scores on the Social index were correlated almost equally with all areas of his parents' Jewish involvement and, as has been pointed out in the section on generations, it appears to be largely a result of the respondent's distance from the full ethnicity of the ghetto.

Table 13.7   Correlations between Parent's and Children's Scores on the Indices*

| | | Parent's indices | | | | | | | Degree of close- |
		1	2	3	4	5	6	7	ness to Yiddish
	1. Defence	19†	07	17	28	32	23	35	33
	2. Social	25	22	16	28	23	21	37	36
	3. Community	00	−09	35	02	10	06	12	06
Children's	4. Positive Emotion	01	−02	26	32	25	12	25	23
indices	5. Religion	21	08	31	29	54	16	44	13
	6. Israel	20	−01	00	20	13	38	26	22
	7. Total Jewish Identification	22	07	28	33	37	30	44	32

* The ·05 level of significance is ·18. Although there are 115 children, the *degrees of freedom* are treated as 88, since there are only 89 sets of parents.
† Decimal omitted.

The aspect of the parents' Jewish identification which correlated the most highly with their children's identification, and which could have been an important determinant of it, was Religion. Whether the parents were religiously observant or not was a strong determinant of the child's religious attitudes and behaviour, although we should remember that some of the child's religious observance could be a direct result of parental pressure. But the parent's religious identification also correlated significantly with the child's scores on Defence, Social and Positive Emotion, although not with Community or Israel. The parent's Positive Emotional involvement with Judaism seems to be similar to religion in its relationship with the child's attitudes on several aspects of his Jewish identity. Most importantly, it seems that where a parent had a positive feeling about being Jewish, his children tended to have a similar feeling (.32).

The effect of parents being involved in the formal Jewish Community is surprising. Not only did it tend to make the children more highly involved in the community but it also made them more religiously involved. Possibly this latter effect arises from the fact that those parents who are involved in the community also tend to be interested in religious observance, and thus they pass on to their children an interest in both. However, this effect does not work both ways; the interest shown by the children in the community seems to be related to the parent's communal involvement, and not his religious involvement.

The parent's involvement with Israel is related to the child's involvement in that area and also to his feelings on Jewish Defence, but little else. In the reverse direction, the child's involvement in Israel is also related to his parent's involvement in Israel and little else.

The relationships of the parents' scores on the Defence index are interesting. The attitudes expressed by the parents who score high on this index imply that they believe that an effort should be made by Jews to keep their children and their children's children Jewish. Yet the parents' scores on Defence bear a low relationship to their children's identification with Jewishness, and this relationship is no higher with the children's attitudes towards Defence of Jewish identity than it is with other areas. The child's attitude towards defence of Jewish identity, like his preference for Jewish social relations, seems to come more from his parents' religious observance, and positive emotional involvement in Jewishness than from his parents' specific attitudes towards its preservation.

The Defence scale includes seven items that measure the respondent's desire that Jewishness be preserved for future generations, including one expressing the hope that his own grandchildren be Jewish. In support of this latter attitude, a person scoring high on the Defence scale opposes mixed marriages, favours Jewish education for teenagers and favours the latter having a predominance of Jews among their friends. Unlike the other aspects of Jewish identification, the Defence attitudes involve the parents in attempting to manipulate their children. Perhaps this is the reason why the children's attitudes towards Defence are related more to the parents' Jewish identification as a whole than specifically to Defence. In further support of this, the youth respondents' scores on the Defence index were highly correlated (.55) with their positive feelings about being Jewish and highly negative (.52) with their positive feelings about being Australian.

Yiddish Background of the Home

While we are considering the familial determinants of the children's Jewish identification we should remind ourselves that we have already demonstrated that closeness to Yiddish-speaking ancestors has an important effect. This is demonstrated in another way by the correlations in Table 13.7 that are derived from the parents' Yiddish-speaking generation, where the latter has been treated as a continuum ranging from 'parents speak Yiddish at home' to 'no Yiddish-speaking grandparents'. The correlations with the children's identification indices are significant for all excepting the Formal ones, Community and Religion. Degree of Yiddish background is more highly related to the children's scores on Defence and Social than are any of the parents' identification scores.

The effect of coming from a Yiddish-speaking home on the youth respondents' attitudes could already be derived from Table 13.6 where the first and second generation homes can be compared. These homes differ in that, while all of the parents could speak Yiddish, only the first generation parents actually used it as their main language. The differences between them show up fairly strongly on nearly all scales, but most particularly on Positive Emotion, and on opinions concerning the teaching of Yiddish to children. In the first generation youth, 88 per cent felt positively about being Jewish, but only 47 per cent about being Australian. In the second generation the respective figures were 67 and 63 per cent. It seems then that when a Jewish youth comes from a Yiddish-speaking home, this has a particularly strong effect on his emotional identification with his 'nationality'. It has been argued in the introductory section (and in chapter 5) that Eastern European Jews have traditionally been members of an ethnic and national minority group, and where this tradition persists in Australia through the use in the home of the national language, the feelings of Jewish national identification tend to carry over also to the generation which has been raised in these homes. It is not argued that the speaking of Yiddish in the home has a direct effect on the children, but that the national attitude that accompanies it is passed on.

A Note on Arguments between Parents and Children

We have observed that, while the Jewish attitudes of Jewish youth are to some extent transmitted from those of their parents, there is obviously considerable degree of 'slippage' between what the parents want in their children, and what the children actually represent. The differences are seen best in connection with the Defence of Jewish Identity scales. If parents are high and their children low in their belief in the importance of preserving Jewishness, it might be expected that there would be arguments between them on matters of Jewish observance. To measure this, a series of eleven questions was included in the youth interview concerning the intensity and frequency of argument with their parents on such matters as observance of Sabbath and Kashrut, social contacts with non-Jews and attending Jewish schooling. As a control, the respondents were also asked to rate in similar terms the extent of arguments that they have with their parents on other, not specifically Jewish, matters.

There was a significant negative correlation (.22) between the number of moderate or serious arguments concerning mixing with non-Jews and the respondents' scores on Defence; that is, those who scored low on Defence had more arguments of this type. It is interesting that the low scorers on Defence also tended to have more arguments of a general nature with their parents (correlation .25). It seems, therefore, that there is a disturbing effect on parent-child relationship arising from the parents' desire to put pressure on their children to preserve Jewishness combined with the children's lack of harmony with their parents' desires on this matter. Incidentally, less than half of the youth respondents reported any arguments, even slight ones, on Jewish matters, and these were mainly over either Jewish schooling or dates with non-Jews. One-third of the respondents in each generation report at least 'slight' arguments concerning the latter. About half of the respondents in each of the generations reported having 'fairly serious' arguments with their parents on 'non-Jewish' matters. On the whole, there were about as many arguments between parents and children on general matters as on Jewish-oriented ones, although the general topics played a comparatively bigger role in the first generation (58 per cent versus 32 per cent) and a smaller one in the second and third (48 versus 46 per cent, and 46 versus 49 per cent, respectively). This suggests that rebellion, or at least non-conformity, against family modes on the part of Jewish youth might begin with general aspects of living before it reaches specifically Jewish areas. When the clashes between parents and their children on Jewish topics do occur, it is more likely that they will concern mixing with non-Jews, or, to a lesser extent, Jewish schooling, than matter connected with religious observances.

Type of Jewish Education

Parents who wish to transmit Jewish knowledge and feelings of identification to their children, usually arrange for their children to receive some type of Jewish education (see chapter 11 for further details of the facilities in Melbourne). In the youth sample, 37 per cent had received at least some of their education in a Jewish day chool, 51 per cent had attended Jewish schools part-time for weekend or late afternoon weekday classes, and the other 12 per cent had received a minimal Jewish education from their parents or from teachers visiting their secular school. The mean scores on the Indices are set out in Table 13.8 for the youth and their parents. Since it might be expected that one of the determinants of the type of schooling would be the parents' Jewish identification, the differences between the parents' and their children's scores are also given. The figures presented for the parents in Table 13.8 indicate that hose who sent their children to Jewish day schools had much higher Jewish identification than did the other two groups of parents. Strangely enough the only exception to this trend is Social on which the three groups of parents did not differ.

Since the generations vary markedly on this scale, it should be noted that there were no generational differences in the percentage of the youth respondents who have attended day schools – although it is probable that the choice of actual school, that is, whether traditional or secular, would show differences.

Table 13.8 Type of Jewish Education of the Youth Respondents and Mean Scores on Indices

Index	Some day school N = 42			Part-time Education N = 58			Minimal Education N = 15		
	Youth scores		Parents' scores	Youth scores		Parents' scores	Youth scores		Parents' scores
Defence	3·2	0·7*	3·9	1·9	1·5	3·3	0·7	2·6	3·3
Social	3·2	0·6	3·9	2·1	1·8	3·9	1·2	2·5	3·7
Community	2·7	1·1	3·8	2·4	0·9	3·3	2·5	0·9	3·4
Positive Emotion	3·1	0·9	4·0	2·4	0·8	3·2	1·4	1·5	2·9
Religion	3·7	0·2	3·9	2·4	0·5	2·9	1·7	0·8	2·5
Israel	4·4	−0·2	4·2	3·3	−0·1	3·2	2·2	0·6	2·8
Total	20·3	3·3	23·7	14·5	5·4	19·9	9·8	8·8	18·6
Indentification with Australia	6·0	0·4	6·4	6·1	0·4	6·5	6·1	0·8	6·9

* Figures in italics represent the decline in identification between the parents and their children. A negative entry indicates an increase. The decimal is rounded off from two decimal places.

The differences in Jewish identification between the three groups of youth respondents are much greater than those noted above in the parents. This can best be viewed by looking at the figures representing the 'drift' in total identification from the parents to the children. While the day school respondents dropped a total of 3.3 points from the level of their parents, the part-time Jewish schooling group dropped 5.4 and the minimal group 8.8. The type of Jewish education obtained by the you h appears to have had a considerable effect on their Jewish attitudes which goes far beyond the influence exerted by their parents' attitudes. Compared with the other two groups, the day school group showed notably (and significant statistically) less drift on Defence, and Social, and somewhat, but not significantly less on Religion. Compared even with the part-time group, the minimal Jewish education group have greater drift on Defence, Positive Emotion, Social and Israel; this group showed very little retention of their parents' Jewish identification in these areas representing the Loyalty and Ethnic clusters. The minimal education group was very low indeed on all aspects of Jewish identification other than Community, Israel and Religion. Unless their own children receive a more intensive Jewish education than they did, they will probably not retain any Jewish identification even in these latter areas.

To put the findings of this section in a positive form, Jewish education appears to stem the drift in identification in direct proportion to its intensity. It is interesting to note, incidentally, that the intensity of Jewish education had no effect on the respondent's identification with Australia, nor did the parents of the three education groups differ with respect to this index. Evidently the choice of type of Jewish schooling is made by the parents without regard to their own identification with Australia.

Parents who are high in their desire to preserve Jewishness are likely to try to impose the maximum possible degree of Jewish education on their children. It is not surprising then that 24 per cent of the youth report having had arguments with their parents concerning their Jewish schooling. It is interesting that there were some parents of Jewish day school pupils (five out of twenty-five) who were low on the Defence scale, and there were others (ten out of twenty-one) who were high on it but did not send their children to day school at any stage (see Table 13.9).

What was the effect of type of school on the child's Jewish identification in relation to the parent's stand on Defence of Jewish identity? The relevant data are presented in Table 13.9. As expected from the data presented previously, the drift is greater for all groups of youth who had no day school experience. The five respondents who went to day school but had 'low defence' parents actually developed higher Jewish identification than their parents, especially on Israel. Either they developed Jewish identification as a result of their day school experience and in spite of their parents, or they were sent to Jewish day school because they already had a strong identification. Assuming that the school was responsible for the changes, the major areas affected were Israel and Defence.

Day school attendance had a fairly substantial effect on the children of 'medium defence' parents in the areas of Defence and

Table 13.9   Effect of Day School on Jewish Identification of Youth in Relation to Parents' Score on' Defence of Jewish Identity'. (The Entries Represent the Degree of Drift from Parents to Children.)

| Index | Parents' Defence Scores | | | | | | | | |
| | Low | | | Medium | | | High | | |
	Day school N = 5	No DS 20	Differ- ence*	Day school 27	No DS 42	Differ- ence*	Day school 10	No DS 11	Differ- ence*
Defence	−1·2	0·3	1·5	0·2	1·9	1·7	3·0	3·7	0·7
Social	1·4	2·0	0·6	0·7	1·9	1·2	−0·1	1·8	1·9
Community	−0·4	0·7	1·1	1·3	1·0	−0·3	1·2	0·7	−0·5
Positive Emotion	−0·6	0·3	0·9	1·1	1·2	0·1	1·3	1·5	0·2
Religion	−0·6	0·7	1·3	0·2	0·6	0·4	0·8	0·1	−0·7
Israel	−3·0	−0·6	2·4	0·0	0·4	0·4	0·2	−0·2	−0·4
Total	−4·4	3·2	7·6	3·6	7·1	3·5	6·4	7·6	1·2

* This represents the algebraic difference in the amount of drift between the youth who attended and those who did not attend Jewish day school. The larger the difference, the greater the apparent effect of day school attendance.

Social, and in the case of the 'high defence' group, in Social. It seems clear that the greatest effect on Jewish children of attending a day school occurs in those whose parents are low or medium on Defence, rather than high. One curious effect is that day school attendance increased identification with the two Formal indices (Community and Religion) in the low defence group but decreased it in the high defence group. Perhaps the school provides a road back into the community and religion for the former, but a substitute for them in the latter.

General Level of Education

Is there any relationship between the youth respondent's ethnic identification and his parents' level of education or his own anticipated level of education? The level of education of the two parents of the respondents correlated .30 with each other and .28 with the respondents' own expected level. This means that a considerable number of young Jews whose parents received a low education will themselves have a high one, and it may be recalled that 69 per cent of the youth aspired to tertiary level studies. This makes it important to study the relationship between education and Jewish identification, since the rapidly increasing level reached by Jews may have significant consequence.

In chapter 5 it was reported for the Adult Sample that level of education had only a small effect on ethnic identification, although the more highly educated respondents did have lower scores on the Social and Defence indices and higher scores on Community. The relationship was complicated by the fact that most of those with elementary education only, that is, up to eight years' education, were Yiddish-speaking, and the relationships between educational level and ethnic identification already begins to operate by the 9th grade level.

The scores of the youth respondents on the indices are presented in Table 13.10 in accordance with their parents' level of education. In line with the above-mentioned relationships between the parents' education level and Jewish identification, the children of better educated parents are also lower on Defence and Social and higher on Community. These differences could be directly attributable to the influences in the home that tend to bring the identification attitudes of the children in line with those of the parents.

The eighteen homes in which the parents had reached tertiary level education are interesting. The children of these parents were higher on Total Identification than were those with nine to twelve years. The scales on which they were higher were Community, Positive Emotion and Israel, but they were lower on Religion. Very few (only two) of the children of tertiary level parents were

Table 13.10 Identification Scores of Youth in Relation to Parents' Education

Index		Parents' Education*		
		Less than 8 years	9–12 years	Some Tertiary
	N	25	72	18
Defence				
X̄		2·6	2·1	2·1
Low		4	11	17
High		28	15	17
Social				
X̄		2·8	2·3	2·1
Low		32	42	50
High		28	20	11
Community				
X̄		2·3	2·5	3·0
Low		24	22	17
High		0	7	11
Positive Emotion				
X̄		2·8	2·4	2·7
Low		12	22	33
High		30	22	38
Religion				
X̄		2·8	2·9	2·4
Low		40	21	28
High		28	14	17
Israel				
X̄		3·6	3·4	3·9
Low		28	28	11
High		48	43	50
Total				
X̄		16·9	15·7	16·2
Low		12	15	17
High		12	6	8
Identification with Australia				
X̄		5·8	6·1	5·9
Low		8	11	6
High		32	33	28

* Based on the respondents in the Adult Survey

low on identification with Israel, and half of them were high. This group of youth respondents were especially low on Social and half of them had no preference for Jews in this respect. On Positive Emotions, they were polarised; that is, they tended to be either low or high.

Putting together all of the findings on the effect of parents' educational level, we can conclude that this will play a minor role in the future of Jewish identification, since very few of the present generation of parents have less than ten years. A similar conclusion is reached if we consider the relationship between the youth respondents' ethnic identification and their educational expectation. The only statistically significant relationship with the identification measures was that those with higher anticipated education had less Positive Emotional Identification with being Jewish, but they also expressed less satisfaction with being Australian. Perhaps all we can conclude is that the more highly educated youth felt more alienated from national groups in general, but it should be noted that even this effect was really quite a weak one.

Socio-economic Class

Socio-economic class was measured in two ways: by the respondent's father's occupational level and by his self-rating of his class. Despite the fact that the first generation were lower on these class measures, there was virtually no relationship with the identification measures. This is consistent with the findings in the Adult Survey.

Parents' Congregation Membership

The parents' memberships fall into three groups: Orthodox congregation (52); Liberal congregation (15) and No Membership (48).

Table 13.11   High and Low Scores of Youth and Parents on the Indices in Relation to Congregational Membership (in percentages)

			Membership			
	Orthodox		Liberal		No Membership	
N	52		15		48	
	Youth	Parent	Youth	Parent	Youth	Parent
Defence						
Low	4	0	33	7	10	0
High	27	77	0	20	15	42
Social						
Low	25	6	80	27	45	8
High	27	36	7	20	17	50
Community						
Low	17	0	20	7	27	23
High	4	39	13	33	6	2
Positive Emotion						
Low	14	4	47	20	23	23
High	18	78	13	40	10	34
Religion						
Low	15	0	27	7	38	46
High	27	46	0	7	13	6
Israel						
Low	21	4	53	53	21	27
High	52	54	20	13	46	25
Total						
Low	10	0	33	7	15	0
High	10	34	0	7	6	6
Identification with Australia						
Low	8	4	0	7	15	8
High	35	48	40	73	27	21

The percentage of high and low scores on the scales are presented in Table 13.11 in relation to congregational membership. The picture is not a clearcut one for a number of reasons: firstly, there are only fifteen families that belong to Liberal congregations and secondly, memberships interact with nationality and generation, so that Liberal members tend to be at least third generation, while those who are not members at all are a combination of intensely ethnic but not religious Jews, religious immigrants recently arrived, and highly assimilated non-religious Jews. To deal with the No Membership group first, the parents tend to be low on most aspects of their Jewish identification. Naturally they were low on Religion, but they were also quite low on Community and Positive Emotion. Defence and Israel were also below the average for the parent group. Social was fairly high, presumably because of the immigrant status of the No Membership group, and, for the same reason, identification with Australia was low. The children of these parents have a similar pattern, allowing for the usual drift from Jewishness that occurs in all groups, particularly in the Social, Defence and Positive Emotion scales; however, the respondents in the No Membership group showed an actual gain over their parents on Religion and Israel.

As might have been expected from the generational status of the members of the Orthodox congregations, these parents were much higher than the Liberal on all of the Jewish identification scales, excepting Community. The greatest difference was on Israel, and this was matched in the opposite direction by the higher Identification with Australia scores of the Liberal Jews. The differences between the Orthodox and the Liberal youth largely match those of the parents, with the exception of Israel. The very large gap between the involvement of the two groups of parents on Israel is partially closed in the youth; that is, the Liberal youth tend to be more involved in Israel than their parents, whereas the Orthodox youth are less involved than their parents.

If we consider absolute levels of identification, it is notable that one-third of the Liberal group of youth have no desire to perpetuate Jewishness and half have little positive feeling for Jewishness. 80 per cent of them are low on the Social scale and it seems likely that a substantial proportion of the Liberal youth will marry non-Jews. (This likelihood is supported by the finding reported in chapter 2 that Liberal Jews have the highest rate of mixed marriages.) The relative lack of Jewish identification among the children of Liberal families becomes very important when it is recalled that 50 per cent of the British-Australian respondents in th Adult Survey were affiliated with Liberal congregations (see chapter 5), and that one-third of the youth prefer Liberal to

Orthodox services. However, before firm conclusions could be drawn about the effect of congregational membership on the attitudes of Jewish youth, account would have to be taken of generational and national differences, and also differences in the type of Jewish education obtained by the respondents. The rate of attendance at Jewish day schools is lower in Liberal families than in others and this might also have a considerable influence. The number of respondents available from this Survey does not allow an analysis of these interaction effects with congregational memberships but they are potentially important.

Effect of Anti-Semitism

Do the respondents who have experienced anti-semitism personally, have higher Jewish identification than others? It might be expected that being the object of anti-semitism could drive a young Jew into a closer tie with his ethnic community. In fact the only index that showed any such relationship was Defence; that is, there was a low, but significant, correlation (0.19) between reported experience of anti-semitism and a desire to preserve Jewishness.

Further questions were asked about the friendliness of Australians towards Jews and these also correlated significantly with only one of the indices – Religion. In this case the more religiously observant respondent perceived Australians as more friendly towards Jews.

There is thus little evidence that the ethnic identification of Jewish youth is influenced by the respondent's feelings of insecurity as Jews. There was not even a relationship between Identification with Australia and any of the questions concerning discrimination, anti-semitism and the unfriendliness of Australians. Ethnic identification seems to be a function of positive social and cultural influence and personal preferences rather than a response to feelings of rejection by the outside community. Thus the respondents should not be thought of as marginal persons who have moved out of their own ethnic group, and yet are rejected by the larger group and thus forced back into the ethnic group. In this connection it is interesting to note that there was a zero correlation between the Identification with Australia scores and the various measures of perceived discrimination against Jews, and against themselves as Jews.

CONCLUSION

The findings of the Youth Study suggest that a considerable drift in Jewish identification has occurred between the parents and thier children, and that its manifestation is greatest between the third generation parents and their children. The most drift occurs with respect to the two scales that concern Jewish social exclusiveness and the conscious attempt to preserve Jewishness as a characteristic that differentiates Jews from other people. The third generation of adults was characterised in chapter 5 as having 'sentiment without commitment' to Judaism; the same seems to be true of their children who still retain a good deal of positive feeling about being Jewish but with little commitment. This 'fourth' generation of youth do not have strong feelings against intermarriage, and it is probable that a substantial proportion will marry non-Jews. The 'tolerant' attitude towards mixed marriages stems from their disapproval of exclusive attitudes; typical comments on intermarriage made by the respondents were 'Each individual should be judged on his own merit'; 'I don't think that barriers and restrictions of religion should override personal feelings.'

These attitudes towards intermarriage are reflected in the Defence and Social scores which are particularly low in the fourth generation, and especially in those whose third generation parents were actualiy born in Australia. It is this generation that shows the greatest drift from Jewish identification between parents and children, despite the comparatively low level from which the parents themselves started. However, the lack of Jewish identification in the fourth generation should not be overstated. Less than a quarter of these youth could be described as virtually without any feeling of identification with some aspect of Jewishness and only a fifth would prefer to have a different identity if given their chances over again. Two-thirds of the fourth generation youth say that their being Jewish plays either 'an important' or 'a very important' part in their lives. This is not much less involvement than that of the third generation youth (the children of second generation parents), although the latter are much more opposed to intermarriage.

The factors that appear to influence the attitudes of the fourth generation particularly are their social assimilation into the general Australian youth community and their frequent attendance at private Protestant denominational schools. These factors are not just a matter of the social class and educational level of the homes or of the child's anticipated educational and occupational level: unlike the American experience, there are no differences between the generat ons in these respects. Where the groups do differ is in the *number* of generations during which the parents have had a good secular education and have pursued a middle-class way of life as members of general Western society. As a result of this assimilation over more than one generation, the parents have placed less stress on their children having exclusive and segregationalistic attitudes and consequently the latter have dropped, to a large degree, the defensive manoeuvres that are aimed at the preservation of Jewishness. These more assimilated generations of Jews also have dropped, to a larger extent than the less assimilated, some of the religious observances that, by their nature, provide serious obstacles to free intercourse between Jews and non-Jews. In particular these are the strict observance of dietary laws and the restrictions on activities during the Sabbath. Very few of the third and fourth generation adults and youth observe these strictly, whereas they do attend religious services, join congregations and describe themselves as 'religious' to the same degree as the other respondents.

The third generation appears to have a need to 'legitimise' its Judaism in terms of the norms of the larger society. This need makes them opposed to the parochialism and segregation behaviour of the generations that are closer to the ghetto style. This anti-exclusive attitude would explain the views expressed by some of the respondents in the Youth Study, but it carries weight only with some of them, and then only in certain respects. Consider some of the exclusiveness and segregationist views that were expressed by many of the fourth generation respondents. One-third of them favoured Jewish children attending Jewish day schools, and one-sixth actually attended one. 40 per cent were members of exclusively Jewish organisations; 30 per cent were definitely opposed to intermarriage, and 40 per cent were highly involved with Israel. With the exception of intermarriage, these percentages are not vastly different from those in the second and third generation groups of youth respondents.

What then do the results of this survey portend for the young Australianised respondents and their future children? The findings cannot be interpreted as supporting a simple and continuous dropping away of Jewish identification and Jewish self-identity in all of its aspects. It is true that there probably will be a continuous and substantial rise in the incidence of mixed marriages in the future, and it can be assumed that, as in the past, few of the children of these marriages will remain Jews. This trend could, however, change in the future as a result of the development of different attitudes in converts to Judaism and towards these converts by other Jews, but at the moment it would be difficult to predict that this will take place.

In the case of the majority of the respondents who will probably marry other Jews it can be expected that their Jewish identification will increase as they start to produce their own families. This increase is likely to affect their attitudes particularly in the areas related to the preservation and maintenance of Jewishness and informal social relations with other Jews; in other words they will probably become more exclusive in their attitudes and behaviour than they are at present. Nevertheless, it can be expected that their own children will hold similar anti-exclusive attitudes to heir own present ones, unless circumstances change.

What could bring about such a change? This has already been discussed to some extent in connection with the Adult Survey in chapter 5. Attitudes towards religion in Australia might change towards a greater respect for non-rational aspects of life. There might also be a greater acceptance of identification with ethnic communities than there has been in the past, as a result of the growing experience in Australia of cultural diversity arising from the broad immigration programme of the past twenty-five years, and from the mass communications emanating from the USA that promote positive ethnic identification for minority groups.

But the contingencies discussed above are purely speculative. The more substantially based factors that may effect the future are the development of Jewish day schools and the existence of the State of Israel. If most of the Jewish youth who favour Jewish day school education actually send their own children to such schools, this could have an important influence on their future ethnic identification. As we have seen above, this influence is especially strong in the critical Defence and Social areas, but it applies to all other areas also, with the possible exception of Communal involvement. On the other hand, attendance at Jewish day schools does not reduce Identification with Australia, and it must be considered to be a legitimate form of schooling in accordance with general Australian norms.

The case of Israel continues to be puzzling. Something about this country clearly appeals to a romantic streak in most Jewish youth in Australia (see chapter 7). It is startling to recall that over 70 per cent of the respondents reported that they thought of volunteering to assist Israel during the Six-Day War and that this included 60 per cent of the fourth generation youth. Nevertheless, there is no reason to believe that this intense and romantic involvement with Israel would survive should Israel enjoy a period of peace and comparative security a a nation. The number of the youth respondents who have little involvement with Israel is higher than the figure for their parents in each generation, as was the number who are more highly involved. In other words, despite the romantic attachment shown by many of the youth, there also is an increasing number for whom Israel provides no source of Jewish identification. This number could increase greatly if Israel's status as a nation becomes secure, and comparable to that of other nations.

To sum up, there is a considerable drift in Jewish identification in Jewish youth from the position of their parents. This is particularly marked in those who come from second and later generation Australian homes, especially where traditional religious observances are largely absent and where the Jewish education given to the child was not intensive. Whether this drift will continue to the point where a sense of Jewish identity is altogether lost is dependent on a number of intangibles, of which the future of Jewish day schools might well be the most important.

REFERENCES

1. Because the 115 youth respondents come from 89 different families, the number of degrees of freedom has been treated as 88 rather than 114.

2. R. Taft, *From Stranger to Citizen* (London, 1966), pp. 31ff.

14

The Personal Experiences and Views of Young Jewish Intellectuals

---

For me, being Jewish is intimately connected with 'Melbourne. Growing up in Hobart one of the highlights of my school life was the two weeks we would spend each year in Melbourne. For months I looked forward to the trip, reading and re-reading airline brochures that promised us the latest in luxurious air travel (for children in the fifties the Viscount was as glamorous as the 747). Melbourne was, after Hobart, the CITY, a huge, exciting promise of the zoo, train rides and a somewhat exotic family life.

We always stayed with my grandmother (my grandfather, Aaron Patkin, died when I was six: my memories are of a large and somewhat terrifying silver-haired man). Her flat, hard in the centre of the East St Kilda/Caulfield borscht belt, was strangely foreign after the double-fronted brick and weatherboard fences of Hobart: the samovar, the heavy blue curtains between lounge and dining room, the cooking smells of gefilte fish and chopped liver. (Who more than we Jews, define themselves by cuisine?) My mother's family and family friends would drop in and out while we were there, and I wondered at their ability to swap two or three languages unthinkingly.

Occasionally, we would be in Melbourne during Passover, and the family gathered to feast. In Hobart such holidays passed by unmarked. There is a synagogue there; in fifteen years' living in the city I never once entered it. My parents' friends were English and Australian, unredeemably Anglo-Protestant, except for a couple of middle-aged Jewish ladies who drifted in and out of our lives. But with the minute Jewish community we had no contact, and at school I avoided ever admitting being Jewish.

In Melbourne, however, being a Jew was different, for there one belonged and a part of this was one's Jewishness. Passover dinners were irritatingly slow in beginning – all that drama with the matzah, and those self-conscious songs – but they did offer a sense of family community we lacked in Hobart. Once or twice my sister and I went to the Alma Road Synagogue, but the service seemed disappointingly mundane: I remember the Cantor's voice and my shock at discovering one paid for seats during the holidays. And one time my mothers' cousin, Ben-Zion Patkin, took me to the Toorak Road Synagogue where prayers for the dead were being droned in Hebrew.

Yet, on looking back, there is no doubt that for those two weeks I did feel Jewish, and that has remained indelibly connected with my image of Melbourne. Mine was not a 1950s version of George Johnson's Melbourne. I never went to League matches and though I too travelled on the Brighton line it ended for me several stations earlier, at a shopping centre where only the butchers and chemists seemed to speak English. Melbourne for me was rich food, the *Jewish News* and a glimpse of a world far apart from the WASP gentility of my Hobart school.

*

In many ways this image persists. Melbourne is undoubtedly the chief Jewish city of Australia, just as it is the Italian (but not the Greek) centre. When I came back to Melbourne to teach at Monash in 1966, after two years in the US, I was very quickly made aware of its Jewish quality, and the dilemma, faintly perceived in my childhood, of my Jewishness was suddenly apparent.

That is: I consider myself Jewish yet I have no social, religious or cultural ties with the community. Few of my friends are Jewish (but more, it is worth noting, in Melbourne than in Sydney). Except for occasional visits to my grandmother when in Melbourne, I have now few family ties to reaffirm my Jewishness. And I am not a Zionist. It is not so much that I am hostile to Israel, it is rather that it doesn't impinge very much on my consciousness. I remember during the Six-Day War a Jewish professor at Monash, grasping me in the corridor and asking me had I heard the news. I was, for a moment, genuinely bewildered.

Indeed I remember my irritation at those Jews whose concern seemed so much for Israel, so little for what is of enormously greater consequence for me, namely the war in Vietnam. That, I felt, was their real obligation: were they not, after all, citizens of Australia? And if they felt their political allegiance to lie with Israel, rather than here, should they not emigrate? Indeed I often found during the 1967 crisis that non-Jewish friends were far more zealous than I in their support of Israel.

I am not yet able to resolve this problem. Cultural pluralism is increasingly a fashionable intellectual style (the title of Peter Medding's first book referred to much more than either Jews or Melbourne). In part this is due to a recognition that much so-called integration, whether of aboriginals in Australia or Negroes in the USA, is in fact a term that disguises the reality of Anglo-conformity. In the idea of the melting pot the one group that is never expected to melt is the dominant WASP elite, and in reaction to this, there is today the assertion by all sorts of ethnic groups, whether they be Welsh, Walloons, Québècois, Negroes, Italians or Jews, of their determination not to be melted into the prevailing cultural mould.

Undoubtedly this is a valid desire, and, in the way it gives individuals a sense of pride and societies a source of diversity, it can only contribute to the richness of human experience. Yet this desire has within it a certain unfortunate potential. The search to maintain the cultural and social identity of a group too easily disintegrates into a narrow and parochial ethnocentrism, of which the Melbourne Jewish community seems to display some of the nastier characteristics.

When I was lecturing at Monash University, a prominent professor invited all Jewish members of staff to lunch to meet a visiting American rabbi. (That this happened at Monash seems to be significant; it would probably be much less likely to occur in a Sydney University.) He was there to advocate the establishment of Hillel on campus, and in conversation admitted quite freely this would promote social segregation. When pressed he said this was necessary to discourage dating 'out' which leads in Jewish mythology to marrying 'out'. This in turn was undesirable because it weakened group identity. (Similar arguments used by black nationalists in America are often assailed as reverse racism.)

Now it is not easy to reconcile the demands of a group with that of the individual. But by and large this attitude represents to me a most unfortunate tendency among self-conscious Jews. It is unfortunate because any demand that restricts individual potential and choice in this way seems to me an artificial limitation of individual autonomy. Unfortunate too, because if Jews are to live in Australia we should both contribute to and gain from whatever cultural heterogeneity can be developed.

Cultures are not static, nor need they be perpetuated in their existing form. Certainly there are elements in Jewish culture that are attractive and that one would wish to see permeate society. Equally there are aspects that are not. Portnoy's complaint is not unknown in Australia and obsessive anxieties are very common among my Jewish students.

In a naïvely old-fashioned and romantic way I believe in some sort of melting pot, itself of course a Jewish invention. (The phrase comes from a turn of the century play written by Israel Zangwill; it has recently been restated in a broader sense by the Blue Mink.) Of course cultural diversity is a good thing, and something Australia sadly lacks. But true cultural diversity does not result from the zealous preservation of barriers, whether of class, religion or race. The tendency for Jews in Australia to imitate Catholics and seek a separate school system can only deprive children of the richness of meeting people of diverse backgrounds, and learning to live fully with them: Mt Scopus seems to me undesirable for similar reasons to Geelong Grammar or a local parochial school. Certainly I would like to see much greater diversity and experimentation in our school system But not, please, one stratified by the allegiance of parents which they seek to impose on their children.

*

Being Jewish must of necessity show itself at different levels, and it would be undesirable if we seek to impose any one version on our fellow Jews as the Jewish Board of Deputies seems at times to have attempted. For some – but, I suspect, a minority – it is essentially a religious commitment. For others it is related most closely to historical memory and community solidarity. For even more it seems linked with pride in and loyalty to Israel.

But for the first of these, Jewish identity was obviously dramatically reinforced by the experiences of Nazi Germany and World War II. Before that, my grandmother once said, I had lots of non-Jewish friends. Now I'm no longer sure I can trust them ... (My other grandmother, who lives in Vienna, has adopted the other sort of reaction: to make her life psychologically supportable she tries to deny all knowledge or memory of what happened.) Yet these memories fade: however horrendous they are, a new generation finds its atrocities in My Lai not in Auschwitz. Which adds a particular poignancy to the generation gap of Jews, for generation gap is essentially a product of the historical memories shared by particular age groups.

I have already said I consider myself Jewish. Yet by the same token being Jewish is, for me, intimately connected with being Australian and it helps define myself in relation to the rest of the community. For as a Jew, and hence a non-WASP, I am slightly marginal, standing outside the shared experience of the dominant groups with whom I come in contact. (Australia has perhaps far less of an Establishment than most societies: none the less there are certain mores and historical patterns that are not fully mine.)

For which I am now grateful. I was not always so: at school, as already related, being Jewish was a cause for embarrassment. Children find it very difficult to bear with being different, and the sheer ignorance of my peers was perhaps a greater cross than open anti-semitism would have been. But perhaps the most valuable part of being Jewish is that it offers some insight into the plight of other minority groups and the unending and unresolved tension between preserving one's cultural identity and 'making it' in the wider world. I am sure that my understanding of American blacks has been enhanced by being Jewish, though I am equally sure no black would appreciate this comment being made. More poignantly, it should be possible for Jews, just because of their own experiences, to understand and empathise with Arab anger and frustration, of which we have become the principal target.

Unfortunately though, for most people experience of persecution makes them no more likely to be tolerant themselves: indeed, if anything, persecution corrupts both persecutor and persecuted equally. One does not have to deny the dreadful realities of historical anti-semitism to regret the reaction it has created in many Jews. In America the most obvious manifestation of this is the New York Jewish Defence League. In Australia it lies perhaps in the very crude anti-communism that many Jews have adopted, and that leads them into strange support for right wing policies and politicians.

The Soviet Union, it is argued, persecutes Jews. (A fact hardly to be doubted.) Thus Communists are racists. Thus we should support all those who oppose Communism – and rally behind Thieu and Ky. A crude stereotype? No, the actual logic of an argument put to me as to why Jews should support the war in Vietnam. It is an argument helped by the fact that the right in Australia has by and large been less tainted with anti-semitism than in most countries, Eric Butler being perhaps the most notable exception. But it has had the sad political effect of placing Jews in a common cause with politicians, and this is true of many in the Liberal Party, who are sympathetic to other forms of racism, such as that of South Africa. And if Jews, through our historical experience, can teach Australians anything, it must be the horror and indignity of any form of racism.

And perhaps here my themes come together. I do not believe in assimilation, whether of Jews, aboriginals or anyone else. I do believe in integration. The first implies becoming the same: God knows we have too much of this in Australia anyway, where Tocqueville's tyranny of the majority is all too obvious. But the second implies the development of a richer, more diverse society by the free mixing of peoples who are aware of their own distinct cultural background, but who are also aware that cultures evolve a blend and strengthen each other through contact.

*

This is a cry for the humane and liberal Jew who too rarely seems found in contemporary Jewish society, particularly perhaps in Australia. Which is not to deny the undoubted contribution of

Jews to Australian cultural and artistic life (though perhaps, dare one suggest more as consumers than participants: our leading art dealers, not our artists, are Jews) and the almost unparalleled work of Jewish social service agencies. And yet one could wish for more. Perhaps our trouble is that in seeking to retain social cohesion we have taken on too many of the less attractive features of Australian society.

That is, Jews in Australia are often simultaneously great boosters of the Australian way of life while retaining almost total social (and in many cases political) isolation from it. There is a crudeness and a coarseness about Melbourne Jews that grates, albeit it is part of the whole *nouveau riche* pattern of the society. It shows itself in the $50 a head dinner for Gorton, or the loud henna-ed Jewish women who pack Chequers and have invaded the Gold Coast in antipodean imitation of Miami. It is revealed in the narrowness of the Jewish press, which is very much a version of the Australian suburban weeklies, with some Israel-boosting thrown in. In its way it lay behind the hounding of Senator Cohen, whose comments on the Soviet Union were naïve but no more so than most comments from his opponents.

It would be an irony if 'group survival', to refer back again to Peter Medding's terms, were so successful precisely because the group has so little that is really different culturally from the host society. Yet I suspect, in some muddled way, that this is the reality of the situation. Attempts to keep Jewish youth in the community are so frenetic precisely because there is so little to preserve.

Indeed were the community less concerned to maintain its solidarity and demand loyalty from its members, Jews in Australia might contribute more and not less. From the little I know of it, I suspect the intellectual vigour of the Jewish community has declined as its numbers have increased. There will soon, no doubt, be drive-in synagogues in the outer suburbs (Liberal only) and greater and greater funds will be raised there for Wizo, but this is hardly the essence of the Jewish tradition of which so much is made. Melbourne will remain an important Jewish centre, but because of schools built and trees planted, not because of cultural, intellectual or spiritual values.

Maybe I would be more sympathetic to the cries for cultural pluralism were this not the case. But I find the Jewish community in Melbourne can offer me very little, and I regret that it seems to be offering so little to Australia. A community that is as intensely self-preoccupied and insular as Melbourne Jewry has little in common with that part of the Jewish tradition that stressed its role in the world and its common community with all men.

DENNIS ALTMAN

II

In their perennial anxiety about the fate of Jewishness, Jews have, it seemed, always been clear about what they have sought to preserve. For me this question is not so clearcut. Nor am I clear as to how to describe, let alone define, my kind of Jewishness. In a way, this difficulty has been experienced by a growing proportion of Jews for over a century. The evolution of numerous forms of Jewishness and the ideologies and rationalisations to buttress them has been a great source of tension for many Jews. I am an heir of this proliferation and carry some of its inheritance, probably adding something to the increase in the modes of being Jewish.

Some personal background may help. I was born almost within earshot of the bombing of Warsaw. Our building was destroyed in one of the early air raids while we sheltered in the cellars. In 1940 we fled illegally across the Russian border and were interned in Archangelsk. From there, we made our way on foot and by raft, to Turkestan, in Central Asia. My first memories are of Uzbekistan and particularly of our month-long ride in cattle trucks out of Russia back to Poland after the war. I have, however, a vivid sense of the earlier period from the many stories, often fantastic and bizarre, frequently tragic, which I heard from my parents. But these experiences paled in significance when compared to what we heard in Lodz in 1945. For many years after, the conversation would turn to who had survived, who had not, the daily escapes from death, the horrors seen and endured, and these left their mark. Some years later after our arrival in Australia in the early fifties, after a Warsaw Ghetto Commemoration at the Kadimah, a night of fiery Yiddish speakers to a tense, pained audience, I remember being overcome with feelings of anguish and vengeance. Most of our family died in Panar, near Vilno. Several uncles survived; one as a guerilla, but he lost his wife and child, another in Lodz with only one of his three children alive. The images of those days in Poland are still with me, such as the bombed out courtyard which we looked out on in Lodz and the endless rows of rubble in Warsaw.

My parents are of that generation of Polish Jews which rebelled against the traditionalism of their elders. They were part of the attempt to modernise Jewish life and radically circumscribe the authority of tradition and religion. The family on both sides is a mosaic of the political movements that swept through Eastern European Jewry in the twenties and thirties. The ideological identifications seem as much familial as political. One side is descended

from a *Chassid** whose children became either Bundists or Communists (two of them spending over a decade in Soviet camps under
Stalin). On the other side the grandfather was a *Misnagid*† who produced mostly Zionists. The rationalism that guided my parents'
youth was handed down to me, and, as an agnostic once told me,
removed my ear for religion. The content of their rationalistic Jewishness included a mixture of mild Zionism and luke-warm Bundism.
They sent me to the Yiddish School and, more for social than political reasons, at first, I went to Skif, the Yiddish Socialist Youth
Organisation affiliated to the Bund.

The decade in Skif served as my formal education in Jewishness.
There was some ambivalence in it, reflecting an earlier ambiguity
within the Bund between nationalism and internationalism. However
there was little question where the real commitment lay. We were
instilled with the Bundist view of Jewish history and Bundist
memories. Of the parade of modern Jewish heroes which formed
the staple of our models, I do not recall one Zionist or, with the
exception of Anilevitch, any non-Bundist heroes. Yiddishism was the
main core of our beliefs. Almost all of us came from Yiddish-speaking homes and we had a sense of its richness and vitality which has
remained. Yet most of us felt that Yiddish was dying and was
unlikely to again become a mass living language. Occasionally we
would be lectured by a sad and wishful thinking elder about the unexpected possibilities, the currents under the surface, which would
pluck Yiddish from its inevitable end. And looking at us, he would
indicate the best source of his hopes. Yet we would mostly talk to
each other in English. Socialism tied to Yiddishism was to solve
'the Jewish problem'. There was a residue of anti-Zionism, mostly
expressed in the opposition to Israel's apparent discouragement
of Yiddish. For much of the time, however, Israel was simply
ignored.

This non-Zionist upbringing has left its imprint although we generally tended to be much less impassioned than some of our elders.
While I can sense aspects of a double identity, it is harder to believe
in a double loyalty which some Jewish spokesmen speak of. Doubt-
less I feel closer to Israel than to many other countries, yet it would
be dubious to define sympathy and concern for its survival as
loyalty. It has also made me more critical of Israeli policies,
particularly towards the Arab refugees.

---

* Chassid, is a follower of Chassidism, a more mystical approach to Orthodoxy
popular in Eastern Europe in the nineteenth and early twentieth centuries. There
were many Chassidic groups organised in personal followings of various dynastic
spiritual leaders known as Rebbes.

† Literally an opponent, those in Orthodoxy who specifically opposed Chassidism.

If much of what we acquired, and then as group leaders repro-
duced, was in its way ethnically narrow, it did create a concern, at
least at the ideological level, with the larger society in which we
lived. Socialism it was taught, was meant not only for the Jews, but
for everybody.

Perhaps out of a tendency to take such pronouncements too literally, I became, as an undergraduate, involved in radical student
politics. Somewhat to my surprise most of my Jewish friends took
a spectator role in these activities. In general very few Jews participated in the larger student community at that time – late fifties and
early sixties. It was then that I became to some extent uncomfortable with the separatism I had been brought up in. Not that I
acquired a sudden aversion to Jewish exclusiveness or cliqueishness.
It just became in a subtle and growing form, odd and personally
irrelevant. My friendships and socialising became roughly equally
divided among Jews and non-Jews, with the tendency for the latter
to predominate. The group I had grown up with in Skif, which had
formed a warm alternate family during my teens, became less involving. These days we still meet several times a year and while the
memories of our youthful community are strong, our relationships
have not, with some exceptions, developed beyond that stage. Yet
I greatly value what seems to me a permanent bond.

My sympathy for the kind of Jewishness which defined itself in
exclusivist terms declined. I was, for example, repelled by the debate
some years ago over who was a Jew. I acquired a strong dislike
for the everyday verbal denigrations of non-Jews – *goy, yok, shikse,
shaigets,* which seemed to me hardly different from the gentiles' use
of *yid.* Trying to live completely within the Jewish community was
increasingly less appealing, even though, I did, for a while, become
involved in some of its institutional work. Nor did I find the faults
of the Jewish community a significant reason to take a greater
interest in the general community.

What brought to the surface many of the questions about my
Jewishness was my intermarriage. The notion of intermarriage had
not occurred to me as a personal possibility and until then I would
probably have rationalised against it. Nor was it without personal
difficulties. The whole of my Jewish experience reappeared in full
force. Yet, at another level, to marry out seemed a natural thing
to do, just as it was and is at best dubious to weigh considerations
beyond the commitment of two people to each other. The idea of
conversion by either of us seemed quite ridiculous.

Some of the tensions and difficulties arose in part from the fact
that like all Jews, I had been brought up to consider Jewishness in
group and institutional terms only. What I had been moving to was
a more personal Jewishness outside these forms. A Jewishness that

accepts distinctiveness without seeking separation or segregation. The idea of pluralist ethnic co-existence often put forward by Jewish spokesmen contains in practice a narrow and limited notion of pluralism. While making the perfectly legitimate demand that Jews be politically and economically integrated into the larger society with the right to maintain distinctive attributes, they appear, at the same time, to be doing their best to keep the Jewish fold exclusive in the values they propagate and the institutional structure they have built to sustain them. While one can understand this reaction in terms of the Jewish historical experience and what some may regard as the implicit cultural imperialism of the majority, it is not for me a satisfying way of being a Jew. It seems a rigid and unnecessarily narrow way of overcoming the problem of double identity.

There does not appear to have been any significant changes in the intensity of my Jewishness. I do not feel marginal although I am distant from the institutional forms of the Jewish community. I identify with much of Jewish history and with that part of Jewish culture I know something about, which is mainly Yiddish and what has been strongly influenced by it. Yiddish has for me a strong nostalgic pull, but it is not a consuming interest, although my appreciation of some aspects of Jewish culture has probably increased.

Jewish continuity is to me not an absolute. It depends on what is carried on and how. If continuity means social insulation and exclusiveness it would be of little interest. If continuity means, for example, that, as one fairly prominent Orthodox Jew informed me, he could not let his children play with mine, then it arouses in me pity and hostility. Or that it may result in the experience of a schoolboy with a Jewish sounding name who was warmly greeted by the Jewish boys and unceremoniously ignored when it transpired that he was not Jewish.

It is very hard to imagine my friendships restricted only or even mostly to Jews. The idea seems very odd now. I do not feel any perceptible connection between Jewishness and degrees of intimacy among my friends. I would find it equally odd if told by a gentile that due to his ethnic background he or she could not feel as close to me in a personal sense, as to others. While I can understand the pull of ethnic ties, they are distinct from personal ties, even if, at times, these may overlap.

It is not clear to me how my political commitments have affected my conception of Jewishness. Just as my upbringing has given me a deep link to a parochialism, my politics have tended to give me a more universalistic outlook. I doubt however if the connection in the latter case is necessarily very strong. Clearly in the Australian context there are more significant political and social problems to worry about than the welfare of the Jews. More directly I am left with an uncomfortable, distasteful feeling when confronted by what appears to be the primary political question of ethnic vigilants – is it good for the Jews? No doubt the overall political conservatism of the community is a factor in my distance from it.

Our children will learn probably as much about Jewishness from my wife as from me. The Jewishness which I hope they will learn will be in terms of an appreciation of the more admirable values which emerged from the history of the Jews. They will, I expect at some stage face choices and problems arising from being children of a mixed marriage but I doubt that these will be the most difficult problems they will encounter. Their attitude to Jews and Jewishness will, in part, be influenced by what they think of me as a person, and how they are received by the Jews who follow the formal rules of Jewish identity.

I doubt whether Jewishness will disappear with the evaporation of anti-semitism or increasing intermarriage. While much of Jewish behaviour is a reaction to prejudice or persecution or the expectations of it, there are deeper feelings seeking expression. Jews do not appear to have evolved a means of coping with a society that is generally tolerant and the desire of their young to make individual choices about their life unencumbered by traditional ethnic laws, yet wishing to maintain some aspects of their parochial ties. Oversimplified dichotomies like continuity and assimilation do not help. There are and will continue to be many kinds of Jewishness, and many ways of being Jewish.

LEON GLEZER

III

When I was thirteen I sometimes went to a special Sunday morning class at one of the Melbourne synagogues, and one day a boy sitting next to me asked the Rabbi 'If Australia were at war with Israel, what should I do?' The question has always stayed with me because it represents perhaps the basic problems of being a Jew and of being a member of the Jewish community in Victoria.

As the son of Polish Jews, I was probably luckier than most of my Jewish friends because of the general liberalism of my parents. Like many Jews, the sum total of their religious belief consisted in the yearly visit to 'shule' on *Yom Kippur*, and two *Seders* every

Pesach. They sent me to a High School, and this is where I could first look at the Jewish community through the eyes of others. At our school there were about one hundred Jews *v* one thousand gentiles. Only on Friday mornings during Religious Instruction were the two groups separated officially, but somehow there was always a division. At lunchtimes, in classes, the Jewish students sat together, or if they did sit with other students the friendship could not continue past the end of school, for to my knowledge none of my friends even brought a non-Jew home. And the most important facet of this phenomenon is that the non-Jews *felt* this Jewish exclusiveness. Anti-semitism never existed at our school, but I can always remember my Jewish friends talking about it. I can always remember some degree of fear and of aloofness from the other students. It was as if the idea of the 'Chosen People' had really permeated the consciousness of my Jewish friends, and they showed a degree of distrust of non-Jews.

By the time I reached Matriculation this feeling had intensified. One of the greatest problems that Jewish students had in their Matriculation year was their high achievement motivation. More and more there was a gap between the Jewish student – alienated, sticking to themselves, not participating in general activities – and non-Jews. As political consciousness grew, it seemed that Jewish interests were focused on Israel and Jewish affairs, whereas other students were becoming involved in local politics. The issue of Vietnam is perhaps a perfect example of this. Many of my friends argued in support of the American role mainly on the grounds that to support America and its international prestige is to support Israel, for without USA aid Israel would be overrun by the Arabs. In the field of international politics perhaps such reasoning is justified, but the importance of it is that it served to further increase the feeling of alienation that my Jewish friends felt. The concern for Israel led to further difficulties in terms of the almost fanatical identification with Israel and the similarly fanatical dislike of the Arab states.

At University the position radically changes. Jewish students divide into two groups: those that maintain their purely Jewish contacts and set themselves almost completely apart from the rest of the students; and those who form an 'intellectual elite', and one hyper-active in politics, and take the lead in various fields such as student publications, student political groups and other societies. But almost a pre-requisite of university activism, is a severance from the bonds of religious identification. This is where the problem of Israel *v* Australia comes in; for as one's political identification shifts from Israel to Australia then one loses tolerance for the chauvinism of many Jews. For instance, a case can definitely be made out for considering Nasser as a great national leader, but to say so in front of a Jewish audience is to commit sacrilege. Similarly to sympathise with any of the ideas of the New Left is to invoke wrath from one's parents and their friends as being anti-Israel and anti-your-Jewish-heritage. One of the best examples of this is a cartoon I recently saw in the *Jewish News*. It showed a boy and a girl, two members of the New Left, holding a banner with 'Anti-Jewish Causes' written on it, and walking towards a cliff of perdition. This is an extremely important source of conflict, for the assumption of most Zionists is that any criticism of Israel is unjustified, and to object to, say, the military use of napalm by Israel, is to be anti-Jewish. This is a symptom of what one could call Jewish hyper-sensitivity, or more properly mild paranoia. I know that this may be an extreme statement to make, and I should point out that I do support Israel's continued existence and I do support a degree of Jewish cohesion in Australia. But the criticism I think that can quite justifiably be made is that there is too much unwillingness on the part of many Jews in Australia to assimilate, or at least to accept non-Jews into their circle of friends.

I suppose that many of the criticisms I have been making seem too severe, but this does not mean that one can't appreciate a Jewish background. Among the things to be thankful for are the interest that my parents and their friends have always had in theatre and other cultural endeavours. Similarly, there is a strong social life, and although limited in its scope, there is considerable interest in charity. I have also always been impressed by the amount of emphasis placed on education in Jewish families, and in the self-sacrifice which Jewish parents show to their children. As *Portnoy's Complaint* shows this can sometimes work in reverse and to the detriment of a child's full individual development. Nevertheless the contact between parent and child is very much closer, or at least appears to be closer, in Jewish than non-Jewish families. My parents, for instance, have shown an unusual amount of tolerance for my political affiliations.

However if one is to draw any general conclusions from the experience that I've had in regard to my Jewish background, I suppose that the characteristic of Jewish life in Melbourne is its self-consciousness and its identification with Israel which in turn influences many Jews' views in regard to world politics. The major source of conflict which I've experienced has been between the rigid adherence to the 'rightness' of Israel and the Jewish ethic, as opposed to a more liberal world-view that one encounters at a University.

JACK GRINBERG

IV

Like most Jews of my generation, who while not religious, cling without quite knowing why to the concept of being a 'cultural Jew', I also have somewhat ambivalent reactions to the Jewish community as such. Clearly certain features of that community mark it off from other minority ethnic groups, in particular its socio-economic status. By and large real poverty seems scarce – indeed at times it is the affluence which seems overwhelming. The bejewelled bosoms and hands at most Barmitzvahs and weddings are matched only by the extravagance of these affairs themselves. These spectacles indeed are generally considered safe only for Jewish eyes. The caricatured wedding scene in the film *Goodbye Columbus* and the opulence of Jewish life portrayed was greeted with reactions ranging from amused embarrassment to thinly-disguised fear. Several people told me that, although they laughed right through the film, 'it would have been better if the film had only been shown to Jews'. So it is not just a collection of affluent individuals but a highly self-conscious community – a community which does look after its underprivileged with a multitude of social and welfare organisations and which in 1967 raised $1,000,000 for Israel in an incredibly short time.

So self-absorbed does this community seem that one is tempted to think of it, in some respects as a ghetto, self-imposed in a social and geographic sense. The term itself is mockingly but commonly used by Jews and non-Jews alike. Caulfield for instance, is to many the 'heart of the ghetto'. Now the 'ghetto-community' was I'm sure tremendously important for the psychological adjustment of European refugees to an Australian society from which they were culturally and spiritually alienated. Critics often seem to lack sensitivity to this fact. On the other hand, we the post-war generation must detach ourselves, if only to see where we fit in. After all it is the post-war generation who have been the major beneficiaries of the community's affluence. Many have also imbibed the 'ghetto-mentality' intact. The combination is often unpleasant, combining a kind of local chauvinism with unthinking materialism. Jewish day schools espouse high ideals of learning, but an unthinking response to being a Jew in a non-Jewish society often typifies the end products.

Jewish parents, like others, maintain that they want only 'the best' for their children. But a definition of 'the best', and the life-style this usually implies, does, it seems to me, need some rethinking. At the very least the problem needs recognition. There is undoubtedly a tension between being a Jew, and a member of a small and exclusive community and being a member of the wider community – a tension which is largely ignored by the Jewish community. It has straightforward and simple solutions for the two interrelated problems of how far to mix with the outside community (the *goyim*) and how a Jew should determine interests and priorities. These solutions pervade community mentality and organisations, particularly youth groups, although they are offered at differing levels of sophistication. On the simplest level relations with the *goyim* should be as limited as possible (business is business, but friendship? who knows where it will lead?) and a Jew should naturally identify with Jewish causes. Communal ethos holds that it is not only emotionally understandable that Jews should behave this way, but that it is also morally correct for them to do so. How often for instance does the question of publishing the *amount* of donations to Israel with the *name* of the donor, arise, so that a form of social blackmail could operate? In my experience there is little questioning of this ordering of priorities and interests, even among people of my age.

The barrenness of these positions becomes clearest to me in the university environment, where it seemed that few Jewish students made social or even intellectual contact with non-Jewish students. It is important to go to University, but to get a degree, not because it's a growth-producing experience. And the degree? – it offers financial security, so that marriage and a home can follow. And there is nothing wrong with this as a life-style. It does of course offer little excitement, and it may have quite undesirable consequences. Where a barrier exists between the Jewish community and the outside community there is the danger of invoking self-fulfilling prophecies. It may be quite true to say 'there's always a barrier between them and us' but if we never give even a select number of 'them' a chance? My own experience, which I admit may be exceptional, has shown me that the 'us – them' axis can be broken and that valuable and I hope permanent friendships have resulted without a noticeable loss of identity on anyone's part. Although lip service is paid by many Jewish organisations to this ideal in such things as inter-faith services etc. few truly take advantage of the social benefits of a free society.

Those who do not fit easily into the mould which the community seems to value – the conformist, one might say, non-separating Jew – often find themselves completely alienated. A radical politics of concern, sometimes upheld as one aspect of the Jewish heritage, seems to command little allegiance from a community which holds dinners for Liberal Prime Ministers at $100 a couple. The extreme result of such alienation can already be seen in the United States. Seymour Lipset,[1] an American political scientist writes,

1. S. M. Lipset, 'The Left, the Jews and Israel', *Encounter* (December 1969), p. 32.

Many Jewish parents, unlike Gentile parents of equivalent high economic class background, live a schizophrenic existence. They sustain a high degree of tension between their ideology and their life-style. This is their hypocrisy, and it is indeed the contradiction which their children are rebelling against.

Haters of everything the community seems to stand for – exaggeratedly material values and indulgent self-interest – can also be found here. They too have resolved the tension between being a Jew and a member of an outside community in a simple and decisive manner. They cease to have in any real sense any Jewish identity. I recognise the sources of their disaffection but their solution leaves me uneasy. I can only recognise the tension and incorporate it into my general awareness of myself. On the other hand, the community, its values and organisations offers little that I can identify with. Yet being a 'community' drop-out does involve some feeling of loss. Like most people I feel the need to belong to something a little smaller than the human race. Perhaps therein lies the attraction of the concept 'cultural Jew'.

When I turn inwards my fairly clear 'objective' assessments tend to disintegrate. After all I find difficulty in rationalising my own position, even to my own satisfaction. Many people, and by and large I can see why, reject the concept of a 'cultural Jew'. What is Jewish culture after all? Don't we usually mean either European culture or Yiddish culture? And how can one be a Jew and practise nothing of Judaism? Answers to these questions elude me – I am left only with my emotional commitment. I have had no religious upbringing or training, and since my early teens no desire to experience any religious feeling. The Jewish God is only marginally more comprehensible to me than the Christian Trinity. And yet there is this feeling of identification. For instance, quite illogically, I was quite happy to get married in a synagogue rather than in the sterility of a registry office. And the wedding service seemed both charming and meaningful: largely I think because of its confident and warm assertion that the family unit under the *chupah* is one, and because of its long history and tradition.

This sense of historical perspective which Judaism has, recording its tragedies, victories, the triumphs of individuals for thousands of years, is something that particularly appeals to me. And while detesting extreme forms of nationalism I find something wonderful in the collective insanity of a people who refuse for thousands of years to disappear just because everyone else wants them to do so. I also find it somewhat terrifying. As with so many of my responses to being Jewish, I am ambivalent.

The experience of World War II has become for me the emotional touchstone of my identification with Judaism. For my parents' generation, despite their ways *en masse*, I experience at times a sense of total admiration and even awe. Because while it is easy to criticise, it is hard to feel. At a resort much-frequented by fairly wealthy Jews, I was struck by the smartness, the chic, of many of the women. Next I noticed that the faces were somehow hard and the impression was of a brittle fragility. And I thought how little really jewels or chic, or homes could compensate for what they had lost, and damn all the criticisms that can be made of these people. Because amongst them are people, incredible as it now seems, of incredible bravery and toughness, people who walked past the Germans with children in their arms and who lied and scavenged and hid to keep their children and themselves alive, and what if subsequently they turned out to be over-possessive Mamas and Papas? Do we, do I, have the right to accuse them of being neurotic. I am struck by the mirror of my own ambivalence in the argument between Portnoy and his sister:

I suppose the Nazis are an excuse for everything that happens in this house!
Oh, I don't know, says my sister, maybe they are.

I identify in a similar way with Israel. In 1967 I was stunned (like many people) to find out how much I care. In the first few days before the magnitude of the Israeli victories were known, only one thought really made sense to me – it can't happen again, two million Jews can't die again. Since then of course I have argued about Israel with people who have taken a pro-Arab stance and while I regard much of what they say as grossly unfair I do try to understand it, and the more I understand it the less hope I have inside that Israel will ever live in peace. All that doesn't affect my basic emotional response to Israel – regardless of technicalities I want Israel to exist – whether with this bit of territory added or that bit taken away is irrelevant.

There is something else of course – Israelis are dying for what they want, and therefore for what I want. So is it just an emotional luxury rather than a necessity? Another question I can't answer.

For me, being Jewish is almost entirely existential. That is the way it must be, the only way it can be. It leaves many problems unsolved, in particular I worry if any of this can be communicated to children. However, a formal pattern of observance of rituals and rites which I find strange is certainly not the answer. Of course I am not alone in trying to articulate this feeling of being an existential Jew, some of my best friends are ...

SUE HEARST

V

Being a Jew means being different. There should be no equivocation about the fact — calling oneself a Jew equals claiming some separation from the rest of the world, whether one is devoutly Orthodox, devoutly Liberal or devoutly atheist. Most people would agree. But many are reluctant to admit that holding on to Judaism implies belief in its superiority, at least in response to one's own needs.

Let me first avoid the obvious misunderstanding. By 'superiority' I mean that Judaism feels it has certain unique teachings to communicate to the world, which a Jew feels he can propagate through the example of his actions.

What are these teachings according to an Orthodox Jew? To do proper justice to this question would take an enormous literature spanning 3,000 years, and a detailed account of an equally vast history. However, if it can be summed up at all, it is in this simple doctrine: the definition of man (as of any one man) is in his actions. In case this should appear a trite statement, let me elaborate on what it involves.

It involves for example, restraint from eating certain kinds of foods. These laws were not intended as a hygiene measure, or only incidentally so. No one can stipulate the reason for such laws. But it is possible to describe, with great wonder, what their observance achieves for an individual. Food is to be enjoyed; the Talmud itself states that there is no celebration without meat and wine. But in avoiding certain meats, a Jew proclaims to himself, to the world and to God that he can control at will his instinct to eat. And this is so precisely because there is no discernible reason for spurning just these foods.

Celibacy, if not totally forbidden, is severely censured. Once again, this is only partly to ensure survival of the species. The Song of Songs may indeed be symbolic of the relationship between God and Israel. But the fact that the author chose sexual imagery to communicate the loftiest of all ideas speaks eloquently of the attitude of the public for whom the work was meant. In Judaism, the strict laws confining sex to marriage are not inspired by prudery or shame. So much the contrary, that sex is considered important enough to be reserved for man's highest expression of love, directly analogous to his love for God.

In all this, there seems to emerge the deliberate celebration of man's physicality. And this is a large part of the truth. Man is a being composed in the first instance of physical drives. It is in their fulfilment, not their debasement or denial, that his greatest achievements begin. And the definition of their fulfilment in Judaism, lies in two interdependent things. Firstly, their satisfaction and enjoyment, and secondly, the constant ability to control them.

Self-control of course is not itself the principal goal. It is a factor which helps man to live with himself, to maintain his standing with others, and in the end to define his relationship with the entire universe. Finding his place in the universe has always been a deep-rooted yearning in man. To the Jew, self-control forms part of the satisfaction of this yearning. Among the animals, man alone stands upright. To Judaism this is symbolic in that the head is placed above the viscera and sexual organs – symbolic of man's striving to go beyond mere dependence on and living for his instincts and passions. In prayer, the Chassidic Jew ties around his waist a black cloth belt, the *gartel*, which effects a temporary separation of the upper and lower regions of his body. Once again it must be stressed that this does not mean a renunciation of his physical self, but an assurance that he is master over it.

To some degree, this mastery is represented by the intellect. In traditional Judaism, learning is venerated above every other virtue. The heroes of Jewish history are nearly always the scholars: Rabbi Akiva, Rabban Jochanan ben Zakkai, Rashi, Maimonides, Hillel, the Baal Shem Tov, not to mention Moses, are a few of the more famous names in a vast gallery of countless sages.

But the intellect itself is not respected above all else. The head covering worn by all Orthodox Jewish males is a constant reminder that to place ultimate faith in reason is a narrow and arrogant attitude, and that one must separate between the power of one's own intelligence and the intelligence 'above' it.

It has been mentioned that the reasons for certain Jewish laws are not fathomable, and yet the effect of their observance on the individual is profound. We are indeed required to reason out the laws to the full capacity of our intellect. But the beauty and serene wisdom behind them can never, never be communicated to someone who has not experienced them for himself. A perfect example is the Sabbath. It is a day designed to be physically and psychologically distinguished from all others. By not working or travelling, by enjoying special meals eaten amidst joyful family singing, and by learning and prayer, the Jew refreshes his body and his mind. To those multitudes who scorn without experience let me categorically state that not driving, not writing and not turning on a light *are* spiritually beneficial. And this is true because this particular style of sabbath observance shuns the ordinary weekday activity and proclaims that man is holy.

How? 'Remember the Sabbath day to keep it holy'. The sacredness of Sabbath is its commemoration of the creation of the world. God, who is infinite and eternal, must exist in everything he created, including every single human being. By his actions more than his beliefs, man is able to reach towards God simply by developing that part of himself which *is* God. The principles of the Torah define how this may be done. In fact, ideally every single function of the Jew's life is self-regulated in accordance with the Torah; and every law emphasises man's dignity and unity with God.

For many, the most striking feature of Jewish law is its unfailing practical wisdom. Life is valued above almost everything else. Therefore we are not merely permitted but strictly commanded to transgress even fundamental laws in order to attempt to save life. In fact, the importance of this life is so strongly emphasised that no dogma exists concerning life after death. Heaven and hell are not mentioned in the entire Old Testament. The practicality of Judaism is likewise seen in its constant avoidance of extremes. Jews are not teetotallers but they seem usually to remain sober. Marriage is hallowed and celebrated exultantly, but divorce is not stigmatised if partners are incompatible. Abortion is forbidden, but not if the mother's life is involved.

Certain of the laws of course are clearly rational; for example, the abundance of social laws defining the Jewish concept of justice. It is by now commonplace that the Jewish nation was founded on the principle of freedom: 'And proclaim freedom throughout the earth unto all the inhabitants thereof', the slaves leaving Egypt were told. That this is true in material reality is commendable in itself. But there is a far more profound purpose in this than is apparent. In ancient Israel a man had to free any slaves he had every seven years, and a slave wishing to remain with his master had to have his ear pierced as a mark of shame. Slaves were not permitted to be returned if they escaped, and if injured by their master, had to be set free.

The Hebrew term *tzedakah* includes the duty of giving to the poor – compulsory for every Orthodox Jew. But it does not mean the same thing as 'charity' and in fact has no equivalent in English. It comes from the root *tzedek*, meaning something like 'justice', 'righteousness'. It implies that social equality is the natural, righteous state, and is totally free of the self-congratulating connotations of the world 'charity', which if anything tends to perpetuate an unequal system. Always, Judaism upholds justice, but why? It seems a superfluous question: equality is now considered its own justification. But in Judaism, it speaks not only for itself. Mosaic law has often been criticised for its high number of capital crimes, from murder to defiance of parents, adultery and incest. But what is overlooked is the list of unbelievable conditions to be met before the Jewish courts could bring a conviction. The commission of the crime needed at least two eye-witnesses who had warned the accused beforehand that his proposed action was an offence, and of the punishment for it. Confessions and circumstantial evidence were not admissible. Witnesses could not be related to any of the parties involved, and had to be of irreproachable character (people who gambled money on 'card games or pigeon-races' were considered unfit). Even after sentence had been passed, the court was obliged to reopen the case up to five times if the accused had something substantial to add. If these conditions were not all met, no conviction could be reached, and it is difficult to imagine how a verdict of guilty could ever be brought. In fact according to one Talmudic sage, a court which passed a death sentence once in seventy years was regarded as 'murderous'. This, it will be remembered, was taking place at a time when every other nation was throwing its children into the fiery bowels of stone gods. 'He who saves one life', a Talmudic saying reads, 'is regarded as if he had saved the whole world'.

One could say that the ancient sages who so fervently guarded the lives of even the criminals, were deeply humanitarian. But this would be to see only half the point, and none of it at all. If we had the chance to ask any of them why they strove to establish the sanctity of life, I strongly suspect that they would have said, 'because God commands it'. Oddly enough, if we ask an Orthodox Jew today why he observes the dietary laws or the marriage laws or the Sabbath, he will probably answer, 'because God commands'.

I believe that this common attitude to two different kinds of law provides an enlightening indication about the Jewish way of thinking. It may be noticed that exactly half the Ten Commandments concern laws regulating the behaviour of man towards his fellow-man. The first five deal with the relationship between man and God. ('Honour thy father and thy mother' falls in this group because God is regarded as an equal partner in the creation of each individual. Therefore to honour one's parents is to honour God.) To be humanitarian is a sacred duty, and to forsake this duty is to express contempt for God, who exists in every human being. But it is not the whole answer to man's struggles, and if treated as such it can become a false god, just as materialism did in the minds of people a generation ago. What then is the way in which an Orthodox Jew sets out to solve these questions?

Let us return to those aspects of Judaism which occupy man in his dialogue with his God, for example, the Sabbath and dietary laws. In the mind of a Jew, they are identical in importance and purpose to the social laws and principles of justice. When he says that God created man in his own image, the Jew does not mean that he thinks the Creator has human features. He means that man is capable of the highest elevation his soul can yearn for and his imagination embrace; but to achieve this he must be both a lover of humanity and a lover of God. And the two are not at all different. The commandment in Leviticus which instructs the Jewish people to proclaim freedom throughout the earth is certainly spoken in condemnation of slavery. But the enslavement of one man by another is no less terrible than a man's enslavement to his instincts. The social and personal laws are not only of equal importance, but of common aim. In achieving personal freedom through the control of his actions and in serving mankind through actions, the Jew sees an identical purpose — the affirmation of the dignity of man and the realisation of that part of him which, by his share in creation, is God.

'Hear O Israel, the Lord our God, the Lord is One' is the definitive statement of Jewish faith. It is said three times every day, and uttered immediately before death. Man is defined by his actions, and every last action regulated by Jewish law reaffirms the unity of God, which speaks in part the unity of the universe, and the rightfulness of man's place in it.

CHAIM MEHLMAN

VI

In reflecting on being Jewish in the Australian Jewish community I do so not as a detached observer, if there ever was such an animal, but as a young Jew, committed almost in the gut, to Judaism, but in the manner which I will define. As I understand it (and my understanding of Judaism is born of a solid 'Talmud Torah' education built upon by Zionist youth movement work and synthesised by studies in Israel), Judaism, its theological component aside, has two basic features. Firstly, a social philosophy, and secondly, a cultural history.

The social philosophy is the Jewish view of humanity and the Jewish role therein. It is a prescriptive code of ethics that in the history of morality was revolutionary at the outset and has yet to be superseded in its principle tenets. This can be illustrated in the following examples. First, in the festival of Passover where Jewry defined the notion of slavery by discovering the only meaningful alternative – Liberation. Moreover the Jews first revealed to the world that a people subjugated can only *collectively* be liberated, that liberation is a social and not an individual action. Finally (predating the New Left by 3000 years), the Jews affirmed that national self-determination is a people's right. It is for other peoples, if they so wish, either to learn this lesson or otherwise, but it was the Jews and no others who taught it to mankind.

Second, the notion of the Sabbath (Shabbat). Consider a world where time was measured in Days and Months. Man only knew how to work, to slave, it was a world of superstition. Yet the Shabbat introduced a new concept of time, a new dimension into human existence. It preserves the one dimensional Master-slave relationship in theory, but abolishes it in practice. For on Shabbat the Jew was commanded to cease his daily routine, to reflect on his human condition and to attempt to transcend it. On the Shabbat, the Master-slave relationship was dissolved and the truly human relationship instituted. The Jew was commanded, once a week, every week at least, to treat his fellow man as he would have him treat himself.

The Shabbat is the highest holiday in the Jewish calendar (apart from the Day of Atonement) and it occurs once a week to remind man of what he is, *and he is what he is to others*. The Shabbat is the most rudimentary form of humanist praxis, its role being to heighten human social consciousness, by regularly suspending the economic relationships which routinise and then debase human consciousness. In an era of the ideological absolutism of the ancients or the dictatorships of the moderns, nothing can be more revolutionary than the systematic demand that man not only think and believe good of others but also treat them accordingly.

The 'cultural history' referred to above, is the history of the modalities of Jewish liberation together with the various attempts to suppress and repress the Jewish people and their Jewishness. What seems clear to me is that the ethos of Judaism is intrinsically a corporate one. On the national level this means that Israel is the only place where a Jewish life can be lived to the fullest. Everywhere else can only be ancillary.

Judaism is opposed then to the individualism of Christianity. Judaism teaches that humanity is a social experience and that only a social life is humane. Praxis is a Jewish concept because Jewish action *can only be* social action, while in the world we live in the morality and ethos of Judaism combined with this social imperative means that Judaism can truly only be a revolutionary praxis intolerant of social inequity, inhumanity and the moral bankruptcy of the Western Christian world. It is no accident that the Kibbutz is what it is in Israel, while the monastery is the Christian form of collectivism. The former is naturally human and the latter unnatural and anti-social.

We do not live today in a Judaeo-Christian civilisation – there is nothing much Jewish about it at all. In fact it is the 'cardinal sin' of Jews who wish to be accepted as part of the modern world that they accept this false definition of this culture as a Judaeo-Christian one. The only connection it has with Judaism is negative. In its hodge-podge attempt to universalise itself, Christianity lost the humanity of Judaism and substituted Divinity, lost the emphasis on social action on praxis or deed and substituted rather faith – blind faith in a pantheon of gods and its worldly attendants, relating very uneasily to this world and human conduct.

While Judaism asserts that even God or faith in him, cannot pardon a sin committed between men, the Christian god and his human servants can and do dispense this and that sin with monotonous and predictable regularity. No wonder at the attraction for some of Catholicism. No wonder that Marxists committed to changing the world must be committed to overcoming Catholicism as it is traditionally understood. The crucial difference between Judaism and Christianity is that the latter is a mythology, while the former is a history – a human history, the history of the Jews.

*

Looking at the contemporary Jewish community in Melbourne my feelings are ambivalent. For on the one hand we have developed a super network of Jewish communal organisations with few parallels in the world today. This is coupled with a powerful community identification with Judaism that lacks nothing in its sincerity and solidarity with world Jewry in general and Israel in particular. Much of this is explained by the large proportion of Melbourne Jews who are refugees from the Holocaust.

But somehow, in the surge to be strongly re-identified with Judaism, its content has been instrumentalised, made barren. Its social values have been neglected. The prevailing *day to day* ethos of the Jewish community today is not of the prophets but of the profits, though this is not a consequence of Judaism but evidence of its abandonment.

This is often most clearly seen in the content of Jewish education. Instead of emphasising the dynamic and revolutionary heritage of the Hebrew prophets like Yechezkiel, Yeshiahu, Yermiahu, Yoab and so on, in order to capture the young Jewish heart and mind through their ethical rationality and critical faculty, we have Judaism presented as primarily a theology.

When the Rabbi declares that Judaism is a 'Faith' he makes his first tragic concession to non-Jewish values. He is then partly to blame when the young Jew at University rejects religion in general and Judaism in particular, as irrelevant. This rejection is a direct consequence of a narrow education that emphasises formal rules and mores, paranoically fixed on a rigid observance of ritual, avoiding the historical, the national, the poetic, the transcending and the liberating.

Even in community work we witness the selfishness of organisational 'benkel-chapping' or leadership and power seeking. The pre-war socialists have been bourgeoisified, idealism is equated with naïvete, and realism with materialism. Instead of a strong idealistic community leadership, Melbourne Jewry is bedevilled by a consortium of 'roof bodies'. It seems that in the Melbourne Jewish community everyone wants to be a fiddler on the roof, a cock of the coop, no one wants to build a house, a grass roots tradition. One can't help feeling that there is a giant masquerade going on. The community is led by an undemocratic Board of Deputies, content in believing that they are the true leaders of the community. And why not? They are all presidents elsewhere. In fact we have a whole class of gentlemen who wander from one executive to another, always leading, never following.

But where are the led? Where is the grass roots community following? What sort of participation in running the community does the ordinary Jew have? Very little, for the community structure is a network of closed interlocking elites with a circulating but rather limited personnel. Most members of the community are represented a number of times on the Board – once as members of synagogues, the Zionist movement, as Yiddish speakers, and so on. What is more, these divisions and sectional interests are products of the past and often largely irrelevant to the new generation.

*

At this stage I wish to touch briefly on a few of the responses by organised Judaism to the condition of the Diaspora. First, Orthodox Judaism, which as I have earlier intimated, has ossified the form of Judaism and thereby lost its content. It has become a religion of the status quo, its legitimacy depending heavily on its acceptance by non-Jews as a religion per se. What is very sad is that the small Chassidic movement which is the *only* transcendant element of Diaspora Orthodoxy, tends to dissipate the revolutionary force of its ideology. Chassidism, on its own account, focuses on transforming the individual and not his society; thus from the standpoint of the Zionist imperative it tacitly bestows legitimacy on the Diaspora as such.

Second, Liberal Judaism, which has made a fetish of religion. Here Judaism is *formally* reduced to the absurdity of a faith – to a religion like all others. The reference point of liberal Judaism is Christianity – its philosophical negation and historical oppressor, consequently, it is unintelligible *except* in a Christian environment and is *therefore* redundant in Israel and retrograde in the Diaspora.

Third, the anachronistic Bund, which has, in its turn made a fetish of secularism. This numerically insignificant group offers a clear denial by Jews for Jews, what they freely and without question grant others, namely, the right to national self-determination. Why should only Jews be denied this right?

The reference point of the Bund is also the non-Jew just as it is for Liberal Jews. They are the last of the internationalists. Even after the Yugoslavs, the Cubans, Vietnamese, Chinese, Blacks have all forgotten the internationale, these pathetic Jews deny their own history and their own future in a final attempt to convince the goyish socialist that the Jews, too, can contribute to the socialist movement, but all that they would have us contribute is our self-denial.

Finally, I come to my own position, socialist-Zionism. That is to say, an understanding of Judaism that is not only compatible with socialist humanism but that also predates it. A radical Zionist or socialist-Zionist can but declare that in this world of nation states and power blocs, the Jewish people in order not only to survive but also to flourish must realise that *Zionism is nothing but the political expression of Judaism.*

Not an end in itself, socialist-Zionism is the apparatus by which the Jewish people can be truly liberated from both overt oppression such as in the Soviet Union, and Arab countries, and from the covert oppression as in the marginal status in Christian capitalist society. Moreover, this first step to liberation is not contingent on a world revolution but on self-help. Freedom is something a people create. It is not something handed to them on a platter.

What is crucial here, is that Zionism *is the necessary precondition* for the realisation of the whole constellation of Jewish values, some of which were discussed at the outset. It is the *only* context in which Jewish self-determination can make any sense, for Judaism in the Diaspora (read Christian world) is reduced either to a theology in a secular society or a subcultural minority, forever caught between the vicissitudes of opposing economic classes in that society. A minority sub-culture beholden to the powerful social interests in order just to survive. Consequently, Diaspora Jews may tend to adopt a conservative role, making Judaism a rationale for the status quo. And is this, after all, what Judaism is all about?

NO. There is a positive contribution the Jews have to make to this world. The vision of the Jewish prophets is not a metaphysical utopia but a political programme derived from moral imperatives that deny the subjugation of means to ends. And if we look at the history of the Left in the last sixty years, can we not say that it is in need of a firmer moral foundation?

For the Jews at least, and for others if they so desire, there is a way to socialist society without secret police, dictatorships of the proletariat, concentration camps, cultural revolutions, murderous terrorism. The kibbutz is the last chance of voluntarism, democratic collectivism, of communism in the real sense of the word.

The kibbutz is not just an experiment in Israel, it is the brain-child of Jewish idealists and Jewish idealism. It is the direct conse-quence of a small and scattered people's demand, after 2,000 years of exile, to take charge of its own destiny.

The kibbutz demonstrates to the world, that society is only a human product, and if it is made by men, then it can be remade by them – if they will only will it. If this experiment should be extinguished by outside forces then mankind may be torn between two hegemonies – the one that will want to maintain society by force and the other that will want to liberate it by force.

Both alternatives are inhuman, both are intolerable.

As for the Jews, we can only seek to rebuild our social world as we understand it, by the principles that our progressive heritage has bequeathed us. We must trust that the world will either some day learn that all peoples have a collective right to choose their own destiny or discover that the denial of this right may lead to a holocaust out of which human life itself may never recover.

DAVID MITTELBERG

VII

The following is a personal perspective, based on a selective view-point. The claims I'm about to make will not be representative of the whole Jewish community (although they do at least seem to me to be true for the Eastern European Jewry I've encountered). Despite my limited experience, however, I *believe* my claims to be broadly accurate; and if I'm wrong, that may signify just as much about the public profile of the Jewish community as it does about me.

*

To grow up as a post-war Jew in Australia is to grow up absurd. The country is free, and we carry terror in our veins; we are sexually uninhibited and without guilt, and suffering becomes us; we talk and write endlessly, and there are no words for what we know.

Presences contort us: our parents' generation are shells, wrecks, fragments – nerves gone, future gone, enslaved and obsessed by the past. They sweat to wrench security from an alien society, and distrust anything they cannot touch. Their flesh is all the world has left them.

What can we do? They are good people, warm and loving, without malice, selfless at best, and proud of their sons' progress in the Gentile world. But they are such little, narrow people. Two-thirds of them are self-employed, or are themselves employers: their work absorbs their lives; it is their grip on reality. For entertainment, they visit compulsively, play cards, or watch films. They support a solitary bilingual community newspaper – a scrappy, dull, conservative rag, read for its social column, its social notices, its front page Israel news – which is distinguished only by its complacent mediocrity.

Their spokesmen are untiring, as they should be, in their concern for Russian Jewry, or Israel, or local anti-semitic outbursts. But beyond that – nothing. No Vietnam, no conscription, no education crisis, no party politics.

As burghers, our parents' generation are simple, loud, earnest, common, orthodox, sad citizens. They live on a cultural island. For most purposes, the world 'out there' does not exist. Intensely and almost exclusively ethnocentric – preoccupied with internal feuds and squabbles; claiming their own, even amongst rebels, when distinction is achieved; shrilling judging criticism for its effect on the community image, and not on its accuracy – they are intellectual peasants, rustic philosophers, in a complex society they refuse to confront.

Even domestically, they give us a double-binding love. They create stability and security at the cost of maturity and growth. The warmth they bestow upon us can have a claustrophobic intensity, demanding that we fulfil their hopes, answer their dreams, abjure their fears, and live the life they were denied.

But, finally, we cannot blame them. They have endured. We cannot ask for more. They offer few guiding strengths and insights, but they compel us to comfort and remember them. We are irretrievably *of* them.

If we are to grow, however, we cannot always give in to their implicit emotional demand that we defer to them. We cannot live their lives, nor should we. But some of us try. Among my generation, the situation is complex, and depressing.

The worst of my generation are very bad: wasteful, coarse, stupid, materialistic, unthinkingly conservative, prematurely middle-aged. They reinforce the very worst features of their parents, for a crucial different reason: they are too well off. They've grown up in affluence and security, and thrived in the wrong directions. A car at matric, a trip at graduation, a house on marrying, a law firm to enter, a medical partnership to join, a parent's business to manage – the world is made bright and easy, theirs if only they *achieve*.

They are the future cream of private enterprise Liberals: he who wants, gets; he who gets, ought to; he who doesn't, shouldn't.

Like their parents, they are invisible men, non-joiners and non-sayers. From a position of unprecedented educational advantage, they do nothing. University is merely a vocational training centre. Uninterested in throwing off parental values, or modifying those wishes, they're happy as they are, clannish and quiet. Too clever to fail in their ambitions, and not intelligent enough to change them, they prepare for their own particular professional ghettoes.

Above all, they are content. They are 'making it' – making it in the eyes of both communities – which is all that they desire, and all that they deserve.

Among the active Jews of my age, there is the traditional left-radical-revolutionary spectrum, combining the typical Jewish qualities of moral righteousness, utopianism, minority attitudes, and self-mesmerising rhetoric. The best of my contemporaries, however, get beyond this. They seem more open to experience, more sceptical of slogans and dogmas, more committed to *discovering* the truth. They are still idealists, but in a more tough-minded way: people have to be convinced of the necessity for change, but change can be worthwhile only if it comes through the operation of intelligence informing passion. They will, therefore, argue intelligently *because* they care so much.

They have a sense of mission, I suspect, but it issues in earnestness rather than righteousness. Gradualists, not revolutionary utopians, they still emerge as distinct individuals – partly because they are very scrupulous about their liberal or radical stances. They reach no position lightly. When they make statements, they are almost consciously honest and free of elaborate or conventional rhetoric. Their minds seem supple; unlike their revolutionary friends, they reveal intellectual stamina as well.

However, these men are still their parents' sons. In a strange way, they are materialists. Often brilliant students, they specialise in the 'hard' Arts disciplines. They become, characteristically, Political Scientists, Sociologists, Psychologists, and rarely English teachers or Modern Linguists. If they're creative, they write reportage, sociology, or prose – but almost never any poetry. Like their parents, although in a more complex way, they prefer what they can measure, and watch, and judge, to what they can sense or guess at. Although they want to do something, ultimately their world is physical: they want to see patterns and links and shifts. Although they may be sensitive and subtle privately, although they may be aware of the contours of the soul, they don't find it possible or necessary to handle such realms professionally.

This phenomenon, of a very intelligent and sensitive non-poetic sensibility, seems to me quintessentially Jewish, although I don't know why it is. However, I do know what it's like to grow and develop in this environment. As a young Jew, and as an uncharacteristic Jewish literary intellectual, I feel both witness and victim of two alien cultures.

Firstly, as a young Jew, I feel alienated from the community which created my identity. There is little in that community which I find nourishing or inspiring. Apart from their basic goodness, idealism, and warmth – which are all double-edged qualities – few Jews, old or young, offer me less pain than joy, or more strength than weakness. They are either yesterday's martyrs or tomorrow's sellouts.

At the same time, I am undeniably of them. I understand them better, I can see them more clearly, than any of my Australian friends. If I criticise or attack them, it is because I want them to deny history – I want them to be better than they've become, and as good as they could be. It may be a secularisation of the 'chosen people' myth on my part: nevertheless, I believe that Jews have the capacity and responsibility – because of their terrible heritage, and not despite it – to be better people than most of those around them.

'Capacity and responsibility': these become large problems for the Jewish intellectual. As an observer of an alien culture, the intelligent Jew has at least two problems. In the first place, as I feel it, he is vulnerable and ignorant before that culture. He has a terrifying appreciation of man's capacity for evil, and he has a deep knowledge of human intimacy and spontaneity. But between these polarities, nothing prepares him for an understanding of the harsh dull banalities, the groupings of power and influence, the mechanisms of religious ties and rivalries, the competing social styles – nothing prepares him, in short, for an authentic appreciation of the processes of his society, the processes by which that society grows, changes, or regresses.

It's not simply that the Gentile world is strange to him: it's more that his specifically fine Jewish qualities, of awe, wonder, idealism, earnestness, intimacy, are somehow irrelevant to the texture of the larger society he lives in. And this, surely, is one reason for the heavy Jewish investment in the Social Sciences – this is the most obvious way in which intelligent Jews can come to see their invisible society.

Secondly, an intelligent Jew is alienated from Australian society in the way that any marginal man experiences. The society he knows best – the one he thinks and works and lives in – is not his own. He belongs in Australia, but Australia does not belong to him. He is a cultural tenant to an unyielding landlord. This is not a painful experience, but it is a bemusing one. It forces him more on to his own resources, a tendency which may now be instinctive for Jews.

At the same time, this cultural marginality places the intelligent Jew in a unique position. He knows the best and worst that men can do, he can observe institutions and styles without completely internalising their values, and he can bring to bear a European consciousness upon an insular and insulated society.

These are rare abilities, and they create the capacity and responsibility I mentioned before. It seems to me that the best Jews of my generation are in this privileged position, a position which may never be equalled. We are the heirs of tragedy, and the children of sorrow; but we know at what cost our parents have arisen from these ruins, and we know how much of living they sacrificed. Unlike those who will follow, the past is not just history to us, and the future is not assured.

We have to make health in our own time, and by ourselves. And, to grow and flourish as human beings, we may have to become less Jewish in the traditional sense. This may not be avoidable, but it also seems to me to be worth it.

HENRY ROSENBLOOM

15

Conclusion: Jews in Australia — Continuity and Adaptation*

Peter Y. Medding

The evidence presented in this book suggests that Jews in Australia in the 1960s positively affirmed their Jewish identity, and accepted it with pride and satisfaction. Very few reacted negatively by exhibiting self-hatred, Jewish anti-semitism, and rejecting that part of their identity. Similarly, there were few who had a passive or neutral approach to being Jewish, for whom it was merely a formal part of their existence with little meaning for them. For the rest, as Ronald Taft demonstrated in chapter 5, Jewishness was positively valued and expressed with varying degrees of intensity, ranging from moderate affirmation to a vital and all-embracing identification. But it was also apparent at many places throughout the book that being Jewish was expressed in many diverse ways, in varied and multiple patterns of cultural, religious, and emotional involvement, and social and institutional affiliation and participation. Nevertheless, these different patterns of expressing, feeling and identifying with Jewishness did not result in a sundering of the group. Despite internal differences and tensions, Jews who were Jewish in so many different ways, were also linked together by common commitments, feelings of belonging together, and common destiny and interdependence of fate, accentuated by two major events in Jewish history: the attempted Final Solution, and the establishment of the State of Israel. These were closely linked not only in 1948, but in 1967, too, when for a few short days its survival was thought by many Jews to be in doubt, and which, as Taft has shown in chapter 7, brought back to them the traumatic memories of the period 1933–45.

Of particular interest in this context is the extent and degree of formal religious connection with synagogues (only 15 per cent never attending), combined with the belief held by four-fifths of the sample that they were in some way religious. On the other hand, the same religious commitment was not apparent in our subjects' views of the meaning to them of their Jewishness, as seen in chapter 2, where

---

* This should be read in conjunction with chapter 1.

for only 6 per cent was Jewishness expressed solely in terms of religion. These two findings are not contradictory; rather they accord with the fact that for the contemporary Jew, Jewishness is multifaceted. Religion while no longer the all-embracing component, is still of considerable importance in terms of behaviour, if not definition. Religious performance constitutes one of the main ways in which the other definitions are fulfilled; through it belonging, pride, shared fate, culture and tradition, ancestry, birth, and upbringing are expressed.

It might also be noted again that synagogue attendance seems to be more important to Australian-born Jews than to those from Europe. It was pointed out in chapter 4 that this was because of its increasing importance *vis-à-vis* other expressions of Jewish commitment which were stronger in Europe, such as Yiddish culture, and the various forms of Zionist ideology. More broadly, formal religious identification and commitment have become the clearest and most convenient defining criteria of the place of Jews in pluralist societies such as Britain, the United States and Australia. A group achieves greater legitimacy under democratic and egalitarian norms when defined in terms of religion with clearly recognised and accepted rights of freedom of conscience, rather than as a national group, a separate culture, or an ethnic group. This is a prime example of the way in which Jewish self-definition and self-expression in Australia have been influenced by the prevailing pattern of the surrounding society.[1]

One must also place Jewish religious definition and performance in more direct comparison with the behaviour of other religious groups in Australia. The Australian Census for 1966 revealed that about 90 per cent of the population identified with a religious denomination, even though response was not compulsory. Only 0.8 per cent gave no religion, whilst about 10 per cent gave no reply. On the other hand in a Gallup Poll Survey 25 per cent said that they never went to church, 48 per cent went occasionally and only 27 per cent went every week. (Here the differences between Catholics and most Protestants should be noted: 54 per cent Catholics went weekly compared with 31 per cent for Methodists, 14 per cent for Presbyterians and 13 per cent for Anglicans.) Similarly, over 88 per cent of Australians who married in 1961 did so in a church rather than in a Registry Office.[2]

For Australians, formal religious affiliation seems both to be a matter of habit, and becoming more secular in character. The similarity with Australian Jewry is marked, although the impact is most certainly different. The mere fact of similar rates of attendance at services and marriage in religious surroundings should not mask the very different internal meaning. More generally, going to church represents an affirmation of belonging to, and unity with, a Christian majority; going to synagogue affirms basic differences with, and separation from, the rest of society, whether it goes to church or not. Whereas for nominal Australian Christians, religious affiliation is a habit and a label produced for the Census taker, for Australian Jews even those who attend synagogue only once or twice yearly (albeit on a regular basis), it represents an important aspect of personal identity.

There is another important aspect of the close connection between Jews and their religious institutions and practices. These create awareness of being part of a great religious and cultural tradition of universal historical significance. Even if they reject its particularistic and national aspects, they may still feel pride in its ethical and humanitarian aspects, and in its universally significant goals and humanitarian aspects, and in its universally significant goals and aspirations. In terms of the cultural pressure referred to in chapter 1 as often constituting the lot of immigrant, religious and ethnic minorities, Jews in Australia may feel that they have less reason to regard themselves as inferior, and under pressure to reject their own values and replace them with the dominant ones. On the contrary, in the context of an Australia that has no clear sense of national identity, that is not the scene of historical events of universal importance, that has not been a standard setter for human goals and aspirations (however decent a place it may be to live in), they may believe that their own culture and tradition have greater universal significance.

The degree of religious connection with the ethnic community and its patterns of close socialisation, residential concentration, organisational involvements, primary and secondary group affiliations, and deep-rooted cultural, emotional and national (Zionist) commitments do not seem to have prevented the simultaneous development and maintenance of marked satisfaction with life in Australia and positive emotional feelings about being Australia. The two loyalties are maintained side by side rather than held to be mutually exclusive or in conflict, and provide the basis for plural cultural identities. Thus only about 5 per cent of our respondents felt dissatisfied with life in Australia, which compares very favourably with responses for other immigrants.[3] Similarly, many more Jews intended to remain in Australia than other migrant groups; only 11 per cent of Jews did not intend to remain, and as we found in chapter 2 over 85 per cent exhibited positive feelings about being Australian. In this context it is instructive to recall that three-quarters of this group were not in Australia at the age of ten. And, as we saw, while the degree of positive feeling about being Jewish was slightly more intense than positive feeling about being Australian, the amount was about the same. In our view this remarkable degree of positive Australian feeling among this predominantly immigrant group probably stems from the situation of Jews in their countries of origin, combined with their economic success and upward social mobility in Australia, of which more below.

This identification with Australia has developed within, and perhaps despite, the social network of the Jewish community itself, where according to our findings, most of its members feel more at ease with Jews (though simultaneously neither believing Australians to be unfriendly, nor concerned much about discrimination in Australia), mix more with Jews, have closer friendships with Jews, participate more in Jewish organisations than in non-Jewish organisations, live in areas of Jewish residential concentration, and send a large proportion of their children to Jewish day schools. The Jewish community undoubtedly caters for many if not most, of the primary and secondary social needs of its members, and for some of their literary, dramatic, and Yiddish cultural demands. On the other hand, it does not cater to their general cultural needs; music, films, art, drama, and literature amongst others, are, from impressionistic evidence, well patronised by Jews.

A number of conclusions can be drawn from this pattern. Whilst social life and interaction is mainly confined within ethnic boundaries, this does not seem to differ greatly from national norms; Mol reports that amongst Catholics generally about four in ten had three of their five closest friends in the local congregation, with the proportion being greater among those educated in Catholic schools; among Protestants the equivalent figure was between 24 per cent and 30 per cent.[4] (These figures were for the local congregation; had the question been asked about Catholics or Protestants in general, the proportion would certainly have been higher.) Similarly, Jupp found among national groups of immigrants (including the British) that friendship tended to be carried on mainly within the group of ethnic origin.[5] Second there is a marked degree of reciprocity of feeling between Jews and non-Jews. In Mol's sample of Protestants and Catholics about 60 per cent said they would feel friendly and at ease with a Jew (compared with between 10 per cent and 23 per cent with a Communist, 31 per cent and 49 per cent with an atheist, and about 60 per cent with an Italian).[6] Among Jews about 60 per cent felt more at ease among Jews, and 35 per cent equally at ease among Jews and non-Jews. In analysing the non-Jewish response one can note a number of divergent elements: Australians seem more ready to accept Jews than vice versa, and Australian acceptance of Jews has greatly increased in the past twenty years. Thus a survey in 1947 found that 60 per cent did not want Jews as migrants, in 1971 this had fallen to only 13 per cent.[7]

Conversely 40 per cent of the population still do not feel friendly and at ease among Jews (which might partly explain Jewish hesitation at the prospect of friendship with non-Jews), yet at the same time Jews are more acceptable than atheists or communists.

The ethnic community and its network of primary groups and secondary associations are usually conceived of as the channel within which ethnic differences and distinctiveness are maintained and perpetuated. It is, however, not often recognised that paradoxically many of these same ethnic institutions promote and further the general cultural values and behaviour patterns of Australian society. To function satisfactorily these ethnic institutions must conform to the general patterns of associational behaviour that prevail within Australian society, particularly if they come in contact with, or aspire to play any role in the outside community. Similarly if their leaders are to be successful in achieving group goals they will have to operate within the rules set by the outside society. In this way the leadership acts as a conveyor belt of general values. It is for this reason that ethnic leaders are generally those who have already learned the workings of the wider community and attained a degree of acceptance within it. In short, we might say that immigrants may come to learn the rules of participation, and the workings of the wider society through participating in ethnic organisations and institutions, and that consequently, these serve to induct them into the larger community while cushioning them with social support. Rather than being antagonistic to the larger community they are complementary to it, and perform essential tasks and functions for it. Rather than draw the immigrant away from the wider society they bring him closer to it.

The Jewish day school plays an especially significant role in this context. Initially established to create awareness among Jewish youth of their religion, heritage and tradition, and to ensure that they receive a concurrent Jewish and secular education, the day schools have, of necessity, involved a degree of social separateness. But these need not be considered a ghetto that further separates and segregates young Jews from the rest of society and inevitably breeds an antagonistic and negative attitude towards society, or leads later to difficulties in adjustment when the students go out into the world. One might regard the Jewish day school set-up in a completely different light, as vehicles and channels of socialisation into Australian society, where the pupils receive the same insights into, and understandings of the wider society, as pupils in other educational systems. This is partly due to their existence within a uniform state-controlled syllabus structure. What each of the school systems does is to add its own independent ethos and viewpoint to the common core. Thus the Jewish day school should be viewed as the conveyor of two cultures, rather than solely as the promoter of a particularistic ghetto Jewish culture. Further evidence of the role of the day schools as socialisers into the general community can be found in the fact that students at the largest day school, when surveyed by Goldlust, in chapter 12, expressed a desire for more extensive friendships with non-Jews, which their school situation by and large prevented them from attaining. This desire indicates a broad and outgoing attitude to the outside world, rather than a narrow, negative, rejecting 'ghetto' outlook.

Further impressionistic evidence in the same direction can be gained from observing the behaviour of Jewish students from various school types at universities. Jewish students from day schools participate at least as actively, if not more actively, in general university affairs as those from other systems. Overall, then, the basis of the criticism of the day schools as the creator of social segregation needs to be re-examined. Even in the non-Jewish schools the Jewish students tend to establish informal networks of close friendship consisting mainly of Jewish students with whom they share common values, organisational affiliations and pre-existing long-term friendships outside school. Friendships with non-Jews while more common than among day school students generally tend to be less intimate and more peripheral than Jewish relationships, a condition which becomes accentuated as dating evolves and marriage comes closer.[8]

The major social difference between the day school and non-day school environment is that in the non-Jewish schools the Jewish students are a minority. Minority situations engender many consequences, but the one that lies at the basis of the criticism of day schools is the characteristic insecurity of minority membership – the fear of distinctiveness. Day schools with their majority situation tend to create pride and loyalty, which enable many of their graduates to participate in general university activities on the basis of a frank recognition of the cultural differences that exist, and even their accentuation, as a means of having them accepted. The day schools and their products can thus be regarded as cultural pluralism in microcosm; participation in the norms of the general society, whilst maintaining and emphasising particularistic ethnic group distinctiveness.

There is, of course, another common outcome of both types of school environment: rejection of the Jewish element as too particularistic and parochial, in contrast to and often triggered by a preference for what are felt to be general, universal, fundamental and significant world problems. We shall return to this concern below when we examine the situation of young Jewish intellectuals.

Attention should also be paid to the importance of the Jewish community's socio-economic structure – its concentration at middle class and upper middle class levels, the rapid socio-economic mobility of the former refugees and immigrants, and the marked degree of overall economic security achieved by the community, currently being consolidated in the tremendous concentration upon tertiary education among the youth. Clearly, economic integration in terms of economic success has taken place; Jewish immigrants, by and large, have 'made it', and have established themselves in their new country of adoption.

Such economic integration, and the achievement of middle class status affects the behaviour and operation of the Jewish community itself in many ways. Firstly at the value level there is a much closer degree of congruity between Jewish values and class values than would have been the case had Jews been concentrated in the working class. Even poverty-stricken and working class Jews, as Lionel Sharpe points out in chapter 3, accept and believe in the middle class goals and aspirations of the rest of the Jewish community. In point of fact the gap between the reality of their situation, and their aspirations constitutes part of their problem. But on the other hand their middle class values, and the capacity of the charitable and economically secure middle class community in which they live, together provide a means to the solution of their problems. It is the community which enables the younger generation to gain the education which the parents wish for their children that will lift the family out of poverty and break the vicious circle of economic distress. So too it is the shared Jewish and middle class value of sobriety which further facilitates this process by preventing family disintegration. Indeed, the strong Jewish value emphasis upon family stability and concern is also important in this context. Similarly, that Jewish immigrants and refugees have been able to rise economically is in no small measure due to the capacity of the middle class and economically stable community to assist, motivated in the main by the value of charity deeply ingrained in Jewish communal institutions for many centuries. As Lipset has pointed out, among Jews and non-Jews of equivalent socio-economic status, the former are more charitable.[9]

This socio-economic success and security have enabled the community to establish a network of communal institutions catering for a wide range of undertakings and concerns in all fields of Jewish endeavour, as has been made clear in many chapters of this book. Thus, far from being the enemy of Jewish survival, as has often been asserted, in this sense, at least, economic success has been the condition of Jewish survival.

A further consequence of Jewish economic concentration in the middle class so far has been a lessening of discrimination and anti-semitism, which has occurred in a number of ways. Firstly, there has not been a scarcity of jobs and no direct competition for them; on the contrary there has been a shortage of labour so that the Australian working classes, in the past antipathetic to foreigners, have had their fears of unemployment assuaged, and can afford to be slightly more tolerant of the immigrant who is different. Moreover Jews are, by and large, not in competition for jobs at this level. Secondly, there have been greatly expanded opportunities in the middle sectors of the economy, where Jews have become comfortably integrated without arousing fear and mistrust. Overall, there is little evidence of discrimination against Jews in white collar and professional occupations. But this is not to deny the very real continuation of elite anti-semitic prejudice and the continued exclusion from prestigious social and recreational clubs, which sometimes spills over into occupational discrimination. Jews who cannot join clubs are not employable in those executive positions in business which are closely tied to club life.

But while these represent some of the advantages of economic success, the pursuit of economic gain and material security by the middle class community arouse the critical ire of two very disparate groups in the Jewish community: the rabbinate, on the one hand, and young intellectuals, on the other. From very different vantage points both take the Jewish community to task. For the rabbinate the pursuit of material success and material gain are the enemy of the spiritual life, and lead to neglect of sacred traditions and cherished values. They distract man from the superior pursuit: the pursuit of the good life as enshrined in the holy writings, the search for inner religious fulfillment, the life devoted to serving God and one's fellow man, and not in indulging the self. For the young intellectuals, several of whom are represented in this book, the problem is that material success has become everything; rather than being a condition of the good life it has become the good life itself. It stifles the creative intelligence, dulls the senses and diverts the mind from very pressing problems. It is marked by ostentation, by the insecurity and grossness of the *nouveau riche*, by over-indulgence in children, by over-emphasis on comfort and luxury, by attempts to bribe, punish, threaten, cajole, restrict, smother, and subject the younger generation by the use of material deprivation or lavish inducements. These tactics produce conformity, security, and stability, at the cost of intellectual achievement, creativity, truth, beauty, freedom and 'doing one's own thing'.

The young Jewish intellectuals represented here grapple with the meaning of Jewishness and Jewish loyalty in the context of the wider society and world. It is first and foremost interesting to note that they do *not* attempt to deny their Jewishness or their connections with the Jewish community, or the way in which they themselves have been moulded by it. On the contrary, they affirm their membership of this community, and in doing so lambaste it in the name of something higher – a secularised version of what is best in the Jewish tradition and Jewish values. What worries them about the Jewish community is that in many ways it does not live up to its own highest hopes and aspirations, does not achieve its own highest goals, and does not contribute to the wider society on the basis of these commitments. They want the Jewish community to be better than it is in order to make the world a better place. In its stead they find, as we saw above, a stifling intimacy, warmth, conformity, and parochialism, and a grating and jarring materialism. At the same time they are, by and large, forgiving, and understanding; being the sons and daughters of the generation that went through the horrors of Europe they somehow understand the motivations that have inevitably created these responses, despite the fact that they are not those which they choose to affirm. For their part they believe that to be Jewish has meant to be discriminated against and persecuted; and therefore the Jewish response should not be to smother the pain and suffering in material security, possessions and consumption, but to dedicate themselves to trying to make the world a better place for all. And what is more they refuse to judge.

But here lies the problem. How does a distinctive ethnic minority participate in the world at large to make it a better place? On the basis of its own tradition? Is this not parochialism? Or on the basis of conformity and a complete throwing in of one's lot with the outside world? Yet is this universalism or is it defection from a grand tradition that should be maintained because so many others, brethren, have died in its name, and in order to keep it alive? This is indeed a dilemma: cultural uniformity seems too closely akin to forced assimilation, as well as entailing the loss of what is affirmed to be good, desirable and warm about Jewishness; cultural pluralism seems to be too much like parochialism, and too close to the things about the Jewish community that are criticised. What, indeed, is the mid-point?

Israel, too, plays an important role for the intellectuals. The threat of its destruction conjures up the history of the attempted destruction of Jewry in the past, and engenders emotional commitment to its survival and to the notion that *never* again shall Jews be led like lambs to the slaughter, and a sense of common destiny with its inhabitants and with all Jews throughout the world. The question, however, remains, does the commitment go any further? Are there other meaningful expressions of Jewish commitment? What is to be passed on to the next generation? And without the formal Jewish parochial institutions and individuals, how is the universal in Jewish life to be transmitted? Thus while affirming

Jewishness, our intellectuals remain, at the end, somewhat ambivalent. While mostly alienated in the formal sense from the community and its institutions and predominant organisational and social concerns, they are not alienated emotionally from the Jewish People as a whole, nor from major aspects of its tradition, heritage, culture and group identity. In this they are far removed from the self-hating alienated Jewish intellectuals of past generations.

Our discussion to date has concentrated more upon the structural aspects of pluralism and ethnic separation and distinctiveness, and less upon the cultural aspects and value differences. A word about these now will set the picture in proper perspective. Despite all the shared Australian national and middle class cultural values, Jews remain separated from the rest of society first and foremost by the religious distinction, by the historical and value differences that sharply divide Christians and Jews. This difference amounts not only to a negative separation from other religious groups, but also entails a positive connection with a different value system and world-view that affects its adherent's way of life and thinking over a wide range of issues; in family matters, social relationships, politics, economics, education, in fact, across the whole gamut of human existence. The chapters of this book revealed a number of such aspects of value difference, which represent Jewish ethnic cultural continuity. Particularly striking were their patterns of political liberalism, and their tendency to maintain Left voting preferences, despite upward socioeconomic mobility. Their strong traditions of charity and self-help, family stability, and sobriety, referred to above, also bear repeating in this context. Perhaps most striking of all was their high valuation of formal education and their remarkable level of educational aspiration and achievement, compared with the general population, which Walter Lippmann pointed out in chapter 2.

Jewish cultural continuity and value differences are predictably strongest in relation to the national cultural tradition taken as a whole: its languages, literature, folklore, its history and its contemporary concerns and interests. Yiddish, Hebrew, Zionism, the culture of Jewry in the past, the culture of modern Israel, the vast literature in these and other languages emanating from the many places where Jewry have lived, but particularly from Eastern Europe, and later the United States and Israel, embody values and experiences, understandings and nuances that set Jews off from the rest of society. While many non-Jews have come to share the experiences of leading American and British Jewish writers who loom large on the world literary scene, the same literature carries different messages for its Jewish readers, reinforcing as it does different meanings and connotations. In the contemporary world Jews everywhere are able to share in the Jewish cultures of Israel and the United States, in particular. Thus for small communities like Australia to maintain cultural continuity to match their structural separation there is no longer a need to produce cultures of their own. They can simply import them.

This process sets into relief the intermittent waxing and waning of Jewish cultural expression, identification, commitment and loyalty. While for some these are, in the main, emotional in nature, for most the stronger the cultural and value aspects, the stronger the emotional commitment. In particular, this generation has witnessed the decline of a major aspect of Jewish culture, the Yiddish language as a vernacular (though some of its ethos and literature live on in translation) and the demise of the self-contained cultural world that it represented. On the other hand, Israel currently exercises a magnetic attraction for Jewry throughout the world; and part of its attraction is that it has come to mean so many different things to different people. For the religious it is the return to Zion, the chance once again to fulfill fully Divine commandments, and the centre of traditional scholarship and religious leadership. For the Zionist it is the culmination and fulfilment of the political hopes of ages, and the establishment of national sovereignty. For the culturally inclined it is the reborn centre of a resurgent national culture. For the politically and sociologically oriented and for the ideologists it represents a unique social laboratory, an experiment in communal and co-operative living, and a democratic society guided by the best ideals of humanitarian concern, justice, and equality. For those living amongst non-Jewish majorities as insecure minorities it represents psychological normalisation that can come only from living in a majority society. For those concerned about the common destiny of the Jewish people, and about the community of fate, it stands for a secure haven and refuge, and the focal point of Jewish existence, not to speak of the fact that two and a half million Jews live within its borders. Zionism and interest in Israel, support for it and commitment to it, in each and every one of these ways has increased in recent years, as was most evident in the Jewish response to the Six-Day War in 1967. This represents, of course, the major heightening of Jewish commitment and identification in recent years, and it is one that appeals especially to many idealistic youth. (It does not appeal to all idealistic Jewish youth; some see it as the epitome of undesirable Jewish particularism.) But the vast majority of Jewish youth support Israel, and many have visited it.

This situation is likely to have far-reaching effects upon their Jewish commitments and loyalties and sense of self-identification. It will constitue a key dimension of their self-image not possessed by many of their parents, and one reinforced positively by the surrounding society. It will, for the thinking ones, involve problems extending beyond mere emotional involvement, itself not to be dismissed lightly. It will give rise to questions about the whole heritage and its transmission, and the meaning of being Jewish. Such concerns may lead to a later decision to send children to Jewish day schools where they will be exposed to a broader range and variety of Jewish commitments. Here as elsewhere, Jewish commitments engendered in one aspect of Jewish life generally tend to spill over into others.

But this is the nature of the Jewish commitment, with its many facets. Not only does it have a vast range of internal sources and variations upon which to draw and with which to provide nourishment, and a wide variety of forms of expression – cultural, social, economic, as well as religious – these are, in addition, often reinforced, played upon and put under pressure by their existence within a majority, which however liberal, pluralist, and democratic, is nevertheless not Jewish. In short, being a minority, with the attendant possibilities if not realities of prejudice and anti-semitism, may serve also to reinforce these commitments, although as we pointed out above they may also lead to pressure to cut loose from the commitment that creates such tension. But this interaction of the internal and the external and their combined effects upon Jews, are not new in Jewish history; they are its very stuff. Jews in Australian society play out a contemporary version of the ancient and continuous drama; the differences between their version and others represent a unique Australian Jewish response to the pressures of continuity and adaptation.

REFERENCES

1. On the influence of the societies within which Jews live upon the internal patterns of Jewish life see S. M. Lipset, 'The Study of Jewish Communities in a Comparative Context', *The Jewish Journal of Sociology*, Vol. 5 (December 1963), pp. 157–66.

2. For an extremely interesting analysis of the place of religion in society, and for further analysis of the figures quoted see K. S. Inglis, 'Religious Behaviour', in A. F. Davies and S. Encel (eds), *Australian Society: A Sociological Introduction*, 2nd edition (Melbourne, 1970), pp. 437–75.

3. J. Jupp, *Arrivals and Departures* (Melbourne, 1966), pp. 121–41; 182–86.

4. H. Mol, 'Church Schools and Religious Belief' in Davies and Encel, p. 479.

5. Jupp, p. 183. See also the table reporting friendship associations among immigrants in Perth in R. Taft, *From Stranger to Citizen* (Perth, 1965), pp. 40–1.

6. Mol, p. 481.

7. These are discussed in detail in *The Age* (Melbourne, 26 July 1971).

8. See John Goldlust's unpublished M.A. thesis, 'Jewish Adolescents in Melbourne: A Study of their Religious, Social and Political Attitudes' (Melbourne University, 1969) for further evidence on this. In chapter 4 he shows conclusively that even in non-Jewish schools Jewish students had more extensive and intimate friendships with other Jews than with non-Jews (two-thirds had three or all of their four closest friends Jewish, and about 85 per cent had at least half of their four closest friends Jewish). Although predictably they also had more non-Jewish friendships than students at Jewish schools (where about 90

per cent had all of their four closest friends Jewish). Moreover as they got older and presumably as dating became more relevant the proportion of Jewish friendships increased (32 per cent of all thirteen-year-olds had their four closest friends Jewish; by age seventeen this had increased to 62 per cent).

9. Lipset, p. 165.

Appendix I

Interviewing

Advertisements calling for interviewers were placed in the Jewish Press and at the universities.

Interviewers were selected on the basis of: academic qualifications, with a preference for training in the empirical social sciences, and social psychology in particular; interviewing experience; knowledge of relevant languages; personal integrity.

Dr L. Mann trained the interviewers, who conducted 'practice' interviews on each other and a pilot interview before the actual study.

Thirty-eight interviewers altogether participated in the study.

Eleven completed between 1 and 5 interviews, whilst between 50 and 54 interviews were completed by two interviewers, with the rest spread between these points.

The interviewers were supervised by the Research Director, Mrs R. Beebe, until her resignation in February 1967, and by Mrs L. Mann until the completion of the study. Each interviewer was assigned 10 addresses and these were supplemented as it became necessary. Interviewers were matched for language to the respondent where it was known.

The interviewing commenced in the last week of November 1966, and was completed in May 1967. The total completed was 504, of which 140 were before the end of 1966.

Coding

Professor R. Taft trained and supervised four assistants to code the interviews. Each interview was coded initially by the interviewers, examined by the Research Director, and then coded carefully by a specialist coder and checked by a check coder. Disagreements were resolved by discussion.

The sample was chosen from the Australian Jewish Welfare and Relief Society's Communal Register, comprising 11,380 families. A random sample of 525 families was selected. Female and male respondents were designated alternatively excepting where the card specified a widow, widower, spinster or bachelor. Because of the greater numbers of widows and spinsters compared with widowers and bachelors, the sample contained more females than males.

Substitute Respondent: Where the designated respondent could not be interviewed and there was no available substitute, or where the respondent refused, a replacement was made. This was done by selecting the very next card after that of the original respondent in the Register file.

From the total of 648 cards which were drawn in the original sample or as replacements, a sample of 504 families emerged:

235 Male respondents   269 Female respondents.

Of the original 648, 24 (3.7 per cent) were incorrectly drawn (either non-Jewish, moved or deceased), 12 were not visited, 44 (6.8 per cent) were unavailable (untraceable, uncontactable, or overseas) leaving a total possible sample of 559. The rates of refusal and successful interviews are shown below in Tables A.1 and A.2.

Table A.1   Analysis of Refusals

	Total	% of Total Possible Sample (559)
Males	31 out of 266*	11·6
Females	24 out of 293	8·2
Total	55 out of 559	10·2

* A Chi-square test of the difference between male and female refusal rate was not significant.

Table A.2   Analysis of Successful Interviews

	Male	Female	Total	%
Original Respondent	164	202	365	72·4
Substitute Respondent	24	21	45	8·9
Replacement Respondent	47	46	94	18·7
	235	269	504	100·0

The Communal Register

The compilation of the Jewish Communal Register began in 1958, primarily to assist the Australian Jewish Welfare and Relief Society in its fund-raising efforts. It began with the consolidation of records of the formal members of the Society, the Appeal donors for 1957, and guarantors for loans by the Melbourne Jewish Aid Society.

From then on continuous additions were made, using the above sources as well as:

(a) scanning the Jewish press each week;
(b) using membership lists of congregations and other Jewish organisations;

(c) the electoral roll of the Victorian Jewish Board of Deputies;

(d) the Jewish National Fund lists.

Deletions and corrections are also made continuously by using these same sources, as well as Post Office returns of 'incorrect addresses', and the people's own advice of any change.

Error is occasionally made by relying on notices in the Jewish press, or on guarantors for loans as an indication of being Jewish. Different or incorrect spelling of names can lead to duplication in the files, but the occurrence of this is rare. The main reason for 'error' is lack of information on families' movements.

The cards contain family names, first names, private addresses and phone numbers, as well as the same details for the business or profession where applicable.

Finally, it is worthwhile to note that members of the Steering Committee of the Study tested the Communal Register for its comprehensiveness, by checking with it names they felt may not have been included. In almost all cases, however, the family was registered.

Appendix II

Q.1 (a)   To which Jewish organisations do you belong?
          [If a congregation mentioned record under Q.1 (b). If Mizrachi mentioned ask if a member of the congregation or member of organisation.]

Q.1 (b)   Are you a member of a congregation?

Q.2   To which non-Jewish organisations do you belong?
          [For every organisation mentioned ask if committee member or attend regularly and record in appropriate column above.]

Q.3   [To be asked only where there are answers to both Q.1 & Q.2.]
          Could you tell me which of the activities you have listed, either Jewish or non-Jewish, is the most important one to you personally?

Q.4 (a)   What do you know about the work of the Victorian Jewish Board of Deputies?
          [Record verbatim.]

          [If positive answer to Q.4 (a)   Ask:]
Q.4 (b)   Do you think they do a good job? [Respondent to rate.]
            1. Do a very good job.
            2. Do a fairly good job.
            3. Not much good.
            4. Do a poor job.
            5. (Not sure)

Q.5   What do you think is the most important problem facing the Melbourne Jewish Community today?
          [Record answer verbatim.]

Q.6 What kind of Jewish education, if any, should Jewish children be given? May not necessarily be what your children received.

(a) What subjects?

(b) In what type of Institution?
 1. Jewish day schools.
 2. Part-time classes.
 3. Private tutor or parents.
 4. Religious Instruction Classes in ordinary schools.
 5. None at all.
 6. Don't know.
 7. More than one.

(c) To what age should this education be given?

Q.7 (a) Do you think Jewish children in Australia should be taught Hebrew as a living language?
 1. Yes.
 2. No.
 3. Don't know.

(b) Do you think Jewish children in Australia should be taught Yiddish?
 1. Yes.
 2. No.
 3. Don't know.

Q.8 (a) Do you think that there are adequate Jewish Adult Education facilities available in Melbourne?
 1. Yes.
 2. No.
 3. Don't know.
 [If 'No' or 'Don't know' to Q.8 (a) Ask]

(b) Which subjects do you think should be made available?
 [Record verbatim.]

(c) Do you attend any Jewish Adult Education classes at present?
 1. Yes.
 2. No.
 [If 'No' to Q.8 (c) Ask]

(d) Would you attend if adequate facilities were available?
 1. Yes.
 2. No.
 3. Possibly.
 4. Don't know.

Q.9 (a)   What sort of Jewish education did, or do your children receive? (Those educated in Melbourne only)
[Limit to 3 youngest children of primary or secondary school age.]

Q.9 (b)   Are you satisfied or dissatisfied with the (Jewish) education that your children receive or received in Melbourne?
1. Yes.
2. No.
State reasons? [Record verbatim.]

Q.10   Do you read any Melbourne Jewish newspaper? [If yes] English or Yiddish?
1. English only.
2. Yiddish only.
3. Both.

Q.11   Would you describe yourself as: [Respondent to choose.]
1. Very religious.
2. Moderately religious.
3. Somewhat religious.
4. Not religious at all.
5. Opposed to religion.
6. (Not sure.)

Q.12 (a)   How often do you attend religious services? (Not counting weddings, Barmitzvahs, Kaddish or funerals.) [Respondent to choose.]
1. Daily.
2. About weekly.
3. About monthly and most or all festivals.
4. Major festivals and perhaps other odd occasions.
5. High Holydays only.
6. Yom Kippur only.
7. On odd occasions.
8. Never.
(b)   [Do not ask if code 8 above.]   Where?

Q.13   In your household how do you observe the Sabbath? [Record verbatim.]

Q.14   Which of the following do you observe or participate in?
  (a)   Attending Passover Seder?
              1. Every year.
              2. Sometimes.
              3. Never.
          How about last Passover?
              1. Yes.
              2. No.
          Lighting Chanuka Candles?
              1. Every year.
              2. Sometimes.
              3. Never.
          How about last Chanuka?
              1. Yes.
              2. No.
  (c)   Do you buy Kosher meat for your home?
              1. Always.
              2. Sometimes.
              3. Never.
  (d)   Do you keep your milk and meat crockery separate?
              1. Yes.
              2. No.
  (e)   When outside your own home do you:
              1. Eat only Kosher food.
              2. Prefer to eat Kosher food but don't insist.
              3. Don't care.
              4. Prefer non-Kosher food.

Q.15   Did you fast last Yom Kippur?
              1. Yes.
              2. No.
              3. Partly.

Q.16   [Ask males only] Do you lay tephillin daily?
              1. Yes.
              2. No.
              3. Sometimes.

Q.17   Approximately what percentage of your personal friends,
          (excluding business acquaintances) are non-Jewish?

Q.18   Have you entertained a non-Jewish friend in your home
          in the past six months? (Other than a purely business
          acquaintance.)
              1. Yes.
              2. No.

Q.19   Have you been entertained in the home of a non-Jewish friend in the past six months? (Other than a purely business acquaintance.)
1. Yes.
2. No.

Q.20   Do you feel more at ease among Jews or non-Jews? [Respondent to choose.]
1. Jews.
2. Non-Jews.
3. Both the same.
4. Don't know.

Q.21   Do you feel that you are socially accepted by non-Jews as fully as you are by Jews?
[Record answer no probe.]

Q.22   Do you think that it is harmful if Jews stick together?
[Probe to whom if necessary.]

Q.23   Do you think that teenage Jewish children should have:
1. Only Jewish friends.
2. More Jewish friends than non-Jewish.
3. About half and half.
4. More non-Jewish friends than Jewish.
5. Only non-Jewish friends.
6. Be free to choose their own friends either Jewish or non-Jewish as they wish.

Q.24   Would you like (or have liked) your children to bring up their children as Jews? [Respondent to choose.]
1. Desire it strongly.
2. Would prefer it.
3. No feelings in the matter.
4. Prefer them not to bring up their children as Jews.
5. Don't know.

Q.25   How do you feel about a Jew marrying a non-Jew?
[Record verbatim.]
[If conversion mentioned state that conversion does not apply.]
[Respondent to choose.]
1. Favour.
2. It makes no difference.
3. Am opposed.
4. Am opposed strongly.
5. Don't know.

Q.26   [Ask only if answer to Q.25 is 3 or 4]
        Does it make any difference to your attitude if the non-
        Jewish party converts to Judaism?
        [Record verbatim.]

Q.27   How satisfied do you feel with life in Australia?
           1. Completely satisfied.
           2. Very satisfied.
           3. Fairly satisfied.
           4. A little dissatisfied.
           5. Very dissatisfied.

Q.28   Are you interested in politics?
           1. Very interested.
           2. Quite interested.
           3. A little interested.
           4. Not at all.

Q.29   Do you discuss politics with your friends?
           1. Often.
           2. Sometimes.
           3. Not at all.

Q.30   Are you eligible to vote?
           1. Yes.
           2. No.

Q.31   If not born British, when were you naturalised?

Q.32 (a) Are you a member of a political party?
           1. Yes.
           2. No.
          [If yes]
    (b)   Which party?
           1. ALP.
           2. Liberal.
           3. DLP.
           4. Other.

Q.33   For which political party in Australia did you vote in
        the 1963 Federal Election?
           1. ALP.
           2. Liberal.
           3. DLP.
           4. Other.
           5. Not registered to vote.
           6. Did not vote.

Q.34 (a)   Have you always voted for this party?
1. Yes.
2. No.
[If no]
(b)   When did you change?

Q.35 (a)   How are you going to vote (or how did you vote) in the Federal Election in November of this year?
1. ALP.
2. Liberal.
3. DLP.
4. Other.
5. Don't know.
6. Not registered to vote.
(b)   What are your main reasons for voting for the . . . party?
[Record verbatim.]

Q.36   What percentage of Jewish voters do you think are voting (or voted) for the same political party as you in this election?

Q.37 (a)   Do you think that the Jewish Community as such should concern itself with the rights of other minority groups living in Australia?
1. Yes.
2. No.
3. Don't know.
[If yes]
(b)   Which ones?

Q.38   Do you think the Government should allow Asian immigrants into Australia on the same basis as European migrants?
[Record verbatim.]

Q.39   Does being Jewish play an important part in your life?
1. Plays a very important part.
2. Plays an important part.
3. Is of little importance.
4. Plays no part.
5. Don't know.

Q.40   What does your being Jewish mean to you personally?
[Record verbatim.]

Q.41   In the Commonwealth Census which was conducted recently you were asked to state your religion, but you were told that it was not compulsory to answer. We could learn a lot about the Jews of Australia if we know how they answered this question.

(a)   Did you fill in this item about religion?

[If yes]

(b)   What did you put?

Q.42 (a)   How would you describe yourself according to your feelings about being Jewish?

'I am a person with': [Respondent to rate.]
1. A very strong positive feeling about being Jewish.
2. A strong positive feeling about being Jewish.
3. Slightly positive feelings about being Jewish.
4. No feelings one way or another.
5. Slight feelings against my being Jewish.
6. Strong feelings against my being Jewish.
7. Don't know.

Q.43 (a)   How would you describe yourself according to your feelings about being Australian?

'I am a person with': [Respondent to rate.]
1. A very strong positive feeling about being Australian.
2. A strong positive feeling about being Australian.
3. Slightly positive feeling about being Australian.
4. No feelings one way or another.
5. Slight feelings against my being Australian.
6. Strong feelings against my being Australian.
7. Don't know.

Q.44 (a)   Do you think that there is anti-semitism in Australia at present? [Respondent to rate.]
1. None.
2. A little.
3. Some.
4. A fair amount.
5. A great deal.
6. Don't know.

(b)   Have you come across any anti-semitism in Australia that was directed against you personally?
1. Yes.
2. No.

[If yes]

What were the circumstances?

[Record verbatim.]

Q.45   How do you think the average Australian feels toward most Jews?
          [Respondent to rate.]

          1. Very friendly.
          2. Friendly.
          3. In between.
          4. Unfriendly.
          5. Very unfriendly.
          6. Don't know.

Q.46   How much anti-semitism would you say that you have *personally* experienced in the *whole* of your life?
          [Record verbatim.]
          [Respondent to rate.]

          1. None at all.
          2. A slight amount.
          3. A moderate amount.
          4. A great amount.
          5. An extremely great amount.
          6. Don't know.

Q.47   Would you like to spend the rest of your life living in Australia? (Apart from possible holidays.)

          1. Yes.
          2. No.
          3. Don't know.
          4. Qualified yes [Record qualification].
          5. Qualified no [Record qualification].

Q.48   If you did not live in Australia in which country would you most like to live?
          [Record verbatim.]

          [Ask only if Israel not mentioned in Q.48]
Q.49   Would you like to live in Israel?

          1. Yes.
          2. No.
          3. Don't know.

Q.50   What personal obligations, if any, should Jews in Australia feel toward Israel? [Record verbatim.]
          [If answer 'Work for Israel' probe for more details.]

[If children mentioned as possible migrants in Q.50, *do not ask.*]

Q.51   Would you like your children to settle in Israel?

    1. Yes.
    2. No.
    3. Evasive answer (e.g. it depends – must decide themselves).
    4. Don't know.

Q.52   What does the State of Israel mean to you personally? [Record verbatim.]

Q.53   Have you contributed to any Jewish appeals and/or causes in the past two years?

    1. Yes.
    2. No.

[If yes] Which Jewish appeals and/or cause did you support?

Q.54   Have you contributed to any non-Jewish appeals and/or causes other than door-knock appeals during the past two years?

    1. Yes.
    2. No.

[If yes] Which non-Jewish appeals and/or cause did you support?

Q.55   If it were up to you to distribute $100 of Jewish funds between Israel on the one hand and Melbourne Jewish community projects on the other, how would you divide the $100 sum?

    Israel $ . . . . . .   Melbourne $ . . . . . .

Q.56   If you had a limited amount of money and could only give to one charity would you *prefer* to give to a Jewish or non-Jewish one.

    1. Jewish.
    2. Non-Jewish.
    3. Equal or 'It all depends'.
    4. Don't know.

Q.57 (a) Do you think it would be a good idea to reduce the number of Jewish appeals in Melbourne by having 3 separate appeals?
 (i) One appeal for Israel.
 (ii) One for all educational purposes.
 (iii) One for welfare and community purposes.
 1. Yes.
 2. No.
 3. Don't know.

 (b) If this were done which ones would you support?
Israel, Education, Welfare?
 1. Israel only.
 2. Education only.
 3. Welfare and Community only.
 4. All these.
 5. Israel and Education only.
 6. Education and Welfare only.
 7. Israel and Welfare only.
 8. None.
 9. Don't know.
[Do not ask if 8 above]

 (c) Would you give the same or less money to such combined appeals than the total you are now contributing to a number of causes?
 1. More.
 2. Less.
 3. The same.
 4. Don't know.

Q.58 (a) Do you know anything about the work of the Jewish Welfare and Relief Society?
 1. Yes.
 2. No.
 3. Never heard of it.
[If yes]

 (b) What do they do? [Record verbatim.]

Q.59 Do you think that there should be such a society?
 1. Yes.
 2. No.
 3. Maybe.
 4. Don't know.

Q.60   Do you know of anyone who has needed personal help which they were not able to get from the Jewish Community?
         If so, what was their need?
         [Record verbatim.]
         Now I would like to ask you a few questions about yourself.

Q.61   What is the date of your birth?

Q.62   Where were you born?

Q.63   [If migrant] When did you first arrive in this country? [Record year.]

Q.64 (a) [If migrant] Where did you reside immediately before coming to Australia?
     (b) How long did you live there?

Q.65   How long have you resided in Melbourne?

Q.66   How long have you resided at your present address? [Do not ask area of residence code only.]

Q.67   In which suburb did you previously reside?

Q.68   Do you own outright, are you paying off, or do you rent your present home?
         1. Own outright.
         2. Paying off.
         3. Rent.

Q.69 (a) Are your parents living?
     (b) With whom do they live?

Q.70 (a) Are your parents-in-law living?
     (b) With whom do they live?

Q.71   Are there any members of the household that are housebound due to disabilities?

Q.72 (a) Are any members of the household in receipt of an Australian Government Benefit or Pension? [If yes] How many members of the family?
     (b) What type of benefit or pension?

Q.73 (a) What is the usual language spoken in the home?

(b) [If not English] Can you speak, read or understand English?

(c) [If not Yiddish] Can you speak, read or understand Yiddish?

(d) [If not Hebrew] Can you speak, read or understand Hebrew?

Q.74 Could your mother or father speak Yiddish?

Q.75 What education did you receive?
Did you receive any degrees or diplomas?

Q.76 (a) What Jewish education did you receive?

(b) Was it full or part-time?

Q.77 (a) What was the country of birth of your mother?

(b) What was the country of birth of your father?

(c) What was the country of birth of your spouse?

Q.78 (a) Are you a proprietor who employs others, are you self-employed, or are you an employee?
[If employer ask]

(b) How many people do you employ?

Q.79 What is your normal occupation?
[Exact definition.]
[If female respondent ask for husband's or late husband's occupation.]
[If retired or investor ask for prior occupation.]
[If manager or executive probe for exactly what kind and how many subordinates.]

Q.80 Are you working at present?

Q.81 What was your father's occupation?

Q.82 Here are the names people use for social classes.
If you had to say to which of these social classes you belong, what would you say?
[Respondent to rate.]
1. Upper.
2. Upper Middle.
3. Middle.
4. Lower Middle.
5. Working.
6. Lower.
7. Other.

Q.83   Have any immediate relatives of yours ever married non-Jews?

Q.1   Could you give me some information now about the rest of the family starting with your wife/husband? [Ask first name and record but code sex only.]

Q.2   Can you tell me the date of birth of . . . . . . ?

Q.3   Where was . . . . . . born?

Q.4   What education did . . . . . . receive? Did they receive any degrees or diplomas?

Q.5   Can you tell me the occupation of . . . . . . ? [Define as in Q.79.]

Q.6   Can you tell me the marital status of . . . . . . ?

Q.7   What relationship is . . . . to the head of the household?

Q.8 (a) Is . . . . residing at home?
        1. Yes.
        2. No.
        [If no]
    (b) Can you tell me where . . . . is residing [District of Melbourne, Overseas, or other Australian City/Town to be recorded.]

Appendix III

THE CONSTITUENT SCORING OF THE 7 IDENTIFICATION
SCALES, AND THE IDENTIFICATION WITH AUSTRALIA,
AND THE PERCEPTION OF DISCRIMINATION SCALES*

To economise in the handling of the data, and to increase the reliability of the measures, a scale was devised for each area of identification. The appropiate items for each scale were chosen from the questionnaire by a committee of three and were assigned weights in accordance with both their importance to the area and their possible range. In order to increase reliability of scoring there were two coders for the indices; wherever they disagreed, differences were resolved by discussion, and, if necessary, by the arbitration of a third rater. Most of the scores required only the mechanical application of the formulae. Eight of the scores were a matter of judgement, and the percentage of complete agreement between the raters before discussion was 100 per cent on four of these. The scores on which differences occurred were Scale 7g (84 per cent agreement); Scale 3d (90 per cent); Scale 1a (94 per cent). These differences would have had little effect on the reliability of the final scores on the scales. The scales and the scoring are set out below.

Normalisation

The scores on each scale were summed and distributed, and then converted to a seven-point scale (0–6). The distribution sought was a compromise between a rectangular distribution and a normal one; although a normal distribution has certain statistical properties that make for more exact computations, a rectangular distribution provides a better dispersion of the scores. In actual application, the uneven distributions of the raw scores made it impossible to achieve a common mean and standard deviation for all scales, so that any individual's score on a scale is not exactly comparable with his score on another scale. It was possible, however, to achieve a reasonable amount of consistency in the distribution: thus the means of the seven scales ranged between 2.80 and 3.67 and the S.D. between 1.40 and 1.86.

* These scales were devised and developed by Professor Ronald Taft. Thanks are expressed to Dr Leon Mann and Dr Peter Medding for their comments.

The relative standardisation of the distributions of the scales enabled them to be summed to achieve a total Jewish identification score in which each scale makes an approximately equal contribution.

SCALE 1 *Defence of Jewish Identity* (7 items)

The degree to which the respondent is concerned is that Jewish identity be preserved against internal erosion. The items refer to the desirability of preserving Judaism for future generations, the need for the Jewish community to take action such as education in order to combat 'assimilation', and support for voluntary social segregation of Jews. Within this context, the opposition to mixed marriages and conversions to Judaism is seen as a desire to preserve the strength of Judaism rather than as an exaggerated sense of pride or arrogance.

Negative scoring was employed for answers that suggest that the respondent favours the disappearance of Jews as a separate entity.

Defence of Jewish Identity	Score
(a) 'What do you think is the most important problem facing the Melbourne Jewish community today?'	
Any reference to need to combat apathy or assimilation.	2
Any reference to failure of Jews to assimilate enough	−2
(b) 'What kind of Jewish education, if any, should Jewish children be given?'	
'To what age?'	
Jewish day school	2
or Both (i) Part-time classes	
(ii) and beyond thirteen years	1
(c) 'Is it harmful if Jews stick together?'	
No. Not harmful	1
(d) Desirable proportion of Jewish versus non-Jewish friends for teenage Jewish children	
Only Jewish friends	2
More Jewish friends than non-Jewish friends	1
More non-Jewish than Jewish friends	−1
(e) 'Would you like your children to bring up their children as Jews?'	
Desire it strongly	2
Would prefer it	1
Prefer them not to bring up their children as Jews	−1
(f) 'How do you feel about a Jew marrying a non-Jew?'	
Strongly opposed	2
Opposed	1
In favour	−2

(g) 'Does it make any difference to your attitude if the non-Jewish party converts to Judaism?'

(Only if opposed or strongly opposed)

No – it makes no difference   1

Range −7 to 12

SCALE 2 *Social Relations* (3 items)

A preference for engaging in informal social relations with Jews rather than non-Jews. This is based on the actual choice of friends and relative ease in the company of Jews and non-Jews. Negative scores were used where answers indicated a preference for non-Jews over Jews.

Social Relations

(a) 'Approximately what percentage of your personal friends are non-Jewish?'

No non-Jewish	4
1% – 20% non-Jewish	3
21% – 49% non-Jewish	2
50% non-Jewish	1
75% – 99% non-Jewish	−1
100% non-Jewish	−2

(b) 'Are you more at ease among Jews or non-Jews?'

Jews	2
Non-Jews	−2
Both the same	0

(c) 'Do you feel socially accepted by non-Jews as fully as by Jews?'

Accepted by Jews more than by non-Jews	1
Accepted by non-Jews more than by Jews	−1
Both the same	0

Range −5 to 7

SCALE 3 *Jewish Community* (7 items)

Involvement in Jewish organisations that form part of the Melbourne Jewish community structure by way of formal memberships, interest in local organisations, and knowledge of communal activities. There was no negative scoring.

Jewish Community

(a) Financial member of one or more Jewish organisations and/or congregations   1

(b) Respondent is an active member of one Jewish organisation or congregation

(i.e. is a committee member and/or attends regularly)   1

Respondent is an active member of two or more Jewish organisations and/or congregations   2

(c) 'Do you know anything about the work of the Victorian Jewish Board of Deputies?' 'What does the Board do?'

Any knowledge of what the Board does   1

(d) 'What do you think is the most important problem facing the Melbourne Jewish community today?'

Any reference to existing or proposed Jewish communal institutions (e.g. lack of harmony between Orthodox and Liberals; schools; welfare societies)   1

(e) Reads a Melbourne Jewish newspaper   1

(f) Has personally contributed to two or more Jewish appeals and/or causes in the past two years   1

(g) 'Do you know anything about the work of the Jewish Welfare and Relief Society?' 'What do they do?'

Any knowledge of what the Society does   1

Range 0 to 8

SCALE 4 *Positive Emotional Involvement* (6 items)

The degree to which the respondent has positive (or negative) emotional involvement in his identity as a Jew. A high scorer describes Jewishness as important to him; reports positive feelings about being Jewish and gives other answers that indicate that Jews and Jewishness are highly salient to him. Negative scores represent answers that indicate aversion to being Jewish. To cover the case of the respondent who has such an aversion, but is obsessed with his identity as a Jew, the responses to the item on the importance to him of being Jewish were scored negatively where the measures of feelings about being Jewish were also negative on items (c) or (e).

Positive Emotional Involvement

(a) 'What political party in Australia do you prefer?' 'Why?'

Any response involving Jews, Judaism or anti-semitism   1

(b) 'Does being Jewish play an important part in your life?'

Plays a very important part   2

Plays an important part   1

NB When (c) and (e) below, both have negative scores the score on (b) also becomes negative

(c) 'What does your being Jewish mean to you personally?'

Any positive response (positive identification)   2

A tendency towards a positive identification   1

Ambivalence or no form of identification   0

A tendency towards a negative identification   −1

Any negative response (negative identification)   −2

(d) Way in which the item about religion in the Commonwealth Census 1966 was answered

'Jewish' (or equivalent)   1

Any other religion   −1

(e) 'How would you describe yourself according to your feeling about being Jewish?'

A very strong positive feeling about being Jewish	2
A strong positive feeling about being Jewish	1
Slight feelings against being Jewish	−1
Strong feelings against being Jewish	−2

(f) 'If you had a limited amount of money and could only give to one charity would you *prefer* to give to a Jewish or a non-Jewish one?'

Jewish	1
Non-Jewish	−1

Range −6 to 9

SCALE 5 *Religion* (10 items)

Adherence to traditional Jewish religious obligations, observances and customs. Most of the items in this index indicate religiosity of a peculiarly Jewish nature, excepting, possibly, for attendance at religious services and the self-ratings on religiosity which are not prima facie Jewish, but which the respondents probably interpreted in relation to Judaism. A comment should be made about sex differences: according to traditional dictates women do not don phylacteries ('lay tephillin'), nor are they required to attend religious services regularly. For this reason the total scores of men and women have been treated separately, with separate standards. There is no negative scoring.

Religious Involvement and Observance

(a) R. is a member of congregation   2

(b) Self-rating of 'degree of religiousness'

Very religious	3
Moderately religious	2
Somewhat religious	1

(c) 'How often do you attend religious services?' (not counting weddings, Barmitzvahs, Kaddish or funerals)

Daily or about weekly	3
Monthly or on major festivals	2
High Holydays or Yom Kippur only	1

(d) 'How do you personally observe the Sabbath?'

An observance involving at least fairly regular lighting of candles or a more strict form of observance	1

(e) 'Do you attend a Passover Seder?' 'What about last year?'

Every year or last Chanuka	1

(f) 'Do you light Chanuka candles?'

Every year or last Chanuka	1

(g) 'How do you personally observe the Sabbath?'

Completely strict observance	3

Ceremonies and usually desist from work   2
Candles and Kiddush   1
(h) *Kashruth*
   (1) 'Do you buy Kosher meat for your home?'
   (2) 'Do you keep your milk and meat crockery separate?'
   (3) 'Do you prefer to eat Kosher food when eating outside
      of your home?'
   Strictly Kosher (a total score of 3)   3
   Moderately Kosher (a total score of 2)   2
   Somewhat Kosher (a total score of 1)   1
(i) (Males only)
   'Do you lay tephillin daily?'
   Yes   2
   Sometimes   1
(j) 'Did you fast last Yom Kippur?'
   Full fast   1

Range – Females 0 to 18
– Males 0 to 20

SCALE 6 *Yiddish Language* (5 items)

Advocacy of the preservation and use by Jews of the Yiddish language. In this scale a high score requires that the respondent supports the speaking of Yiddish and advocates that Jewish children should learn it. No credit is given for knowing Yiddish, if it is not used. It may be argued that there are other Jewish vernaculars besides' Yiddish, notably Hebrew and Ladino, but Yiddish is the only one that is relevant to the particular Jewish stock that inhabits Melbourne, with few exceptions. There is no negative scoring on this scale.

Yiddish Language

(a) If member of Bund or other 'Yiddish' organisation and/or if
    child attends a Yiddish school   2
(b) Mention of Yiddish culture or equivalent anywhere in the
    interview   1
(c) 'Do you think Jewish children in Australia should be taught
    Yiddish as a living language?'
    Yes   1
(d) Respondent reads the Yiddish section of a Melbourne Jewish
    newspaper   1
(e) Yiddish is the usual language spoken in the home   1

Range 0 to 6

SCALE 7 *Israel* (8 items)

Feelings of personal identification with the State of Israel and belief that Israel is associated with being Jewish. This is measured by items concerning whether the respondent associates himself actively with the support of Israel, considers it a suitable domicile for himself or his children, and feels that Israel has implications for his Jewish identification. A negative score is given for responses implying an unfavourable view of Israel to items (c) or (g).

Identification with Israel

(a) Respondent is an *active* member of Zionist organisation	2
Respondent is just a member of a Zionist organisation	1
(b) Israel as an educational subject	
Any mention of Israel as a subject that should be made available for youth or adult education	1
(c) 'What do you think is the most important problem facing the Melbourne Jewish community today?'	
Mention of Israel in a postive sense	1
Mention of Israel in a negative sense	−1
(d) 'What does your being Jewish mean to you personally?'	
Mention of Israel	2
(e) If R. did not live in Australia, he would like to live in Israel	
If mentioned spontaneously	2
If agreed after prompting	1
(f) 'Would you like your children to settle in Israel?'	
Yes	1
(g) 'What does the State of Israel mean to you personally?'	
Exceptionally strong positive self-identification	3
Positive self-identification with Israel	2
Positive for Jews in general, but no self-identification implied	1
Any unfavourable response	−1
(h) 'If it were up to you to distribute $100 of Jewish funds between Israel on the one hand and Melbourne Jewish community projects on the other, how would you divide the $100 sum?'	
If R. desires to distribute $50 or more to Israel	
and	
If generally would support appeals for Israel	1

Range – 2 to 13

SCALE 8 *Identification with Australia*

An additional scale was constructed to measure aspects of the respondent's relationship to Australia. This *Identification with Australia* scale embodies items that measure *satisfaction* with Australia, *identification* with it and *acculturation* to it. These three aspects measure the degree to which a person feels and behaves like a well-integrated Australian.

Identification with Australia

(a) 'How satisfied are you with life in Australia?'	
Completely satisfied	3
Very satisfied	2
Fairly satisfied	0
A little dissatisfied	−2
Very dissatisfied	−3

(b) Rating of feeling about being Australian
    A very strong positive feeling   3
    A strong positive feeling   2
    Slightly positive feeling   1
    No feelings one way or another   0
    Slight negative feelings   −1
    Strong negative feelings   −2
(c) Speed of naturalisation
    Naturalised within six years of arrival or of British nationality by birth   2
    Not eligible or naturalised after six years of arrival   0
    Not naturalised even after seven years in Australia   −2
(d) 'Would you like to live in Australia for the rest of your life?'
    Yes   2
    No   −2
    Yes with reservations   1
    No with reservations   −1
(e) 'What is the usual language spoken in the home?'
    Only English   2
    Some English   1
(f) Fluency of English
    Understands, speaks and reads English   2
    At least understands English   1

Range −9 to 14

SCALE 9 *Perception of Discrimination*

This scale measures the degree to which subjects believe that Jews in Australia are actively or passively discriminated against, both in terms of the general treatment of, and feeling towards, Jews generally, as well as the personal experience of the subject. It is also a measure of ethnic security or insecurity.

Perception of Discrimination

(a) 'Do you think that there is anti-semitism in Australia at present?'
    A little   1
    Some   1
    A fair amount   2
    A great deal   3
(b) 'Have you come across any anti-semitism in Australia that was directed against you personally?'
    Yes   1
(c) 'How do you think the average Australian feels about most Jews?'
    Very friendly   −2
    Friendly   −1
    In between   0
    Unfriendly   1
    Very unfriendly   2

Range −2 to 6

Index

293

A 3